J. A. HOBSON

CONTEMPORARY ECONOMISTS

General Editor: John Pheby, Professor of Political Economy,
De Montfort University, Leicester, England

The *Contemporary Economists* series is designed to present the key ideas of the most important economists of this century. After an opening biographical chapter, the books in this series focus on the most interesting aspects of their subject's contribution to economics, thus providing original insights into their work. Students and academics alike will be fascinated by the wealth of these economists' contributions and will be able to look with fresh eyes on their discipline.

Published titles

John F. Henry   JOHN BATES CLARK
Steven G. Medema   RONALD H. COASE
Michael Schneider   J. A. HOBSON
James Ronald Stanfield   JOHN KENNETH GALBRAITH

J. A. Hobson

Michael Schneider
Senior Lecturer in Economics
La Trobe University, Melbourne

First published in Great Britain 1996 by
MACMILLAN PRESS LTD
Houndmills, Basingstoke, Hampshire RG21 6XS
and London
Companies and representatives
throughout the world

A catalogue record for this book is available
from the British Library.

ISBN 0–333–58835–5

 First published in the United States of America 1996 by
ST. MARTIN'S PRESS, INC.,
Scholarly and Reference Division,
175 Fifth Avenue,
New York, N.Y. 10010

ISBN 0–312–15981–1

Library of Congress Cataloging-in-Publication Data
Schneider, Michael, 1935–
J. A. Hobson / Michael Schneider.
p.   cm.— (Contemporary economists)
Includes bibliographical references and indexes.
ISBN 0–312–15981–1 (cloth)
1. Hobson, J. A. (John Atkinson), 1858–1940—Contributions in
economics.   2. Economics—History.   I. Title.   II. Series.
HB103.H55S36   1996
330.15'5—dc20   96–2599
                                                                  CIP

10   9   8   7   6   5   4   3   2   1
05   04   03   02   01   00   99   98   97   96

Printed in Great Britain by
Ipswich Book Co Ltd, Ipswich, Suffolk

To my parents, who encouraged me to read books, and to Kirstin and Philip, who I hope will also write them

Contents

List of Tables and Figures

Tables

Figures

Preface

J. A. Hobson thought of himself 'as the champion of a comprehensive study of the conditions of human welfare embracing all the social studies, within which economics and other specialist subjects were really no more than subordinate and closely interrelated branches' (Cole, 1958, p. 12). He would probably have regarded the writing of a book on his contribution to economics, rather than to the social sciences in general, as misguided. But most economists today are too preoccupied with keeping abreast of their own discipline to read books which stray outside it. Thus if John Maynard Keynes' prophecy that Hobson would be 'remembered as a pathbreaker in economic theory' (Keynes Papers, CO/3/276) is ever to be fulfilled, only an account of Hobson's ideas which confines itself to his economic theories is likely to be a contributing factor.

The primary objective of this book is thus to display Hobson the economist. It contains little, for example, on Hobson's liberal version of the idea that human society can best be understood by regarding it as an organism, or on his related seminal contribution to the concept of 'the new liberalism'. Instead, the subject matter comprises Hobson's theories in the areas of welfare economics; income distribution and prices; what is now known as macroeconomics; money and credit; international economics; and territorial expansion, all of which (apart from the last) are generally agreed by orthodox economists to come under the rubric of 'economics'.

In his setting-out of these theories, Hobson made little use of diagrams, and he hardly ever employed equations. This led to some of his expositions being longer, more circuitous, and less intelligible than need have been the case, as a number of his theories lend themselves readily to diagrammatic or algebraic treatment. In the interests of economy and clarity, and therefore ultimately of Hobson himself, we do not eschew the use of diagrammatic or algebraic techniques where they are helpful.

Despite this book's focus on economics, Hobson's view of the nature of his work is not totally ignored. Reference is made to ethical, social and political factors wherever they throw additional light on Hobson's economics, despite the fact that these factors are regarded by most economists as being outside their discipline.

Given the subject matter of this book, what is the best way of dealing with it? Axel Leijonhufvud (Leijonhufvud, 1968, p. 116) argues that 'the usual [and appropriate] approach to the analysis of a man's life work, whether it belongs to the arts or to science, rests on the assumption that his thought will show a consistency and continuity of development which, once grasped, make it possible to view his work as a coherent whole'. This is a laudable aim, which is, however, generally difficult to achieve. Recognising the difficulty, Leijonhufvud advises interpreting 'consistency' and 'continuity' generously. We take the alternative path, hoping none the less that drawing attention to inconsistencies and discontinuities in Hobson's writings will not blur the 'coherent whole' which underlies them.

Some critics emphasise Hobson's inconsistency, others the discontinuities in his thinking. Take, for example, his theory of imperialism. On the one hand, Peter Cain (Cain, 1978, p. 565) argues that Hobson's *Imperialism: A Study* was 'an interim statment of his position which was to be modified drastically thereafter'. In response, Peter Clarke (Clarke, 1981, p. 308) asserts that 'most students of Hobson's work would probably ... consider him not only more consistent over time in general outlook but also less consistent at any one time in all the ramifications of his arguments than he emerges in Cain's article'. Disagreements relating to perceived inconsistencies and discontinuities in Hobson's theories, such as that just cited, are referred to explicitly in this book.

Chapter 1 provides a prelude to the subsequent exposition and critique of Hobson's economic theories by offering an account not only of Hobson's personal and intellectual life, but also of the socio-economic and political context in which his theories were developed. Chapters 2 to 6 concentrate on exposition; though where particular points are clearly open to question, reference is made to both sides of the argument. Chapter 7 presents a critical assessment of Hobson's contributions to each of the areas of economics covered in the earlier chapters.

In one sense, to compartmentalise Hobson's economics is to mislead. There are interconnections between the various economic theories he developed, and these in turn reflect the overall 'vision' that Hobson had of the nature of the human world. This vision, its impact on Hobson's economic theories, and its relevance to the past and future development of economics, are discussed in a brief concluding chapter.

For some decades after Hobson's death, the only full-length books on his ideas were W. T.-C. Liu's *A Study of Hobson's Welfare Economics* (1934) and E. E. Nemmers' *Hobson and Underconsumption* (1956). But the literature on Hobson has grown apace in recent years. Hobson is a key figure in Michael Freeden's *The New Liberalism: An Ideology of Social Reform* (1978). John Allett's *New Liberalism: The Political Economy of J. A. Hobson* (1981) and Jules Townshend's *J. A. Hobson* (1990) have a broader scope than this book, but, given their titles, not surprisingly say less about Hobson's economic theories; for a succinct account of Hobson's economics, see the chapter on Hobson in John King's *Economic Exiles* (1988). Collections of articles about Hobson's ideas were published in 1990 (*Reappraising J. A. Hobson: Humanism and Welfare*, M. Freeden, ed.) and 1994 (*J. A. Hobson after Fifty Years: Freethinker of the Social Sciences*, edited by John Pheby). Collections of excerpts from Hobson's writings now available are *J. A. Hobson: A Reader* (M. Freeden, ed.), *Writings on Distribution and Welfare* (edited by Roger Backhouse), and *Writings on Imperialism and Internationalism* (P. J. Cain, ed.).

MICHAEL SCHNEIDER

Acknowledgements

The writing of this book has put me in the debt of many, and I take this opportunity of thanking them. Roger Backhouse, Peter Cain, Michael Freeden and Geoffrey Harcourt made a major contribution with their criticisms of an early draft. Helpful advice was also given at various stages in the gestation of this book by Kenneth (later Sir Kenneth) Berrill, the supervisor of my Cambridge M.Sc. thesis, and by John Allett, Anthony Brewer, Peter Clarke, Bernard Corry, Peter Groenewegen, Emma Hutchinson, Steven Kates, Ed Nell, Gabriele Pastrello, John Pheby, Sunanda Sen, Emmett Sullivan, John Wells, and participants in the first and seventh conferences of the History of Economic Thought Society of Australia. Access to sources was cheerfully and efficiently provided by staff at the Bodleian Library, the Borchardt Library (La Trobe University), the British Library, the British Library of Political and Economic Science, the University of Cambridge Library, Derby Central Library, Derby Local History Library, Derby Museum, the Archives Department of the Hull University Library, the Modern Archives Department of King's College Library (Cambridge), and the Marshall Library. Keith Povey and Beth Morgan did a superb professional job with the copy editing and indexing respectively. To all these people, who I hope will get sufficient pleasure from recognising their input to excuse me for not providing more details, I say 'thank you'. I wish to thank also La Trobe University for granting me study leave to complete this book, the members of the Faculty of Economics and Politics at the University of Cambridge who made me welcome during my seven months in Cambridge in 1994–5, and Giovanna Davitti of Macmillan for her advice on editorial matters.

Above all, I wish to acknowledge my enormous debt to my colleague John King, who through suggestion and discussion has provided continuous support ever since the writing of this book was begun, and who, going far beyond the bounds of duty or friendship, has exercised his incisive red pen on no less than three drafts of this book.

None of the above acknowledgements should be taken as implicating those named in such shortcomings as the book no doubt possesses; the responsibility for them is mine.

MICHAEL SCHNEIDER

Author's Note

Quotations included in the text are indentified by author, date and page, except in the case of the numerous citations from works by Hobson, where only date and page are indicated. The date of publication of a work is specified on the first occasion on which it is cited, but not thereafter. Where individuals are referred to, the first name, or an alternative where common usage suggests it, is included on the first occasion when the name is used, but in general not thereafter.

1 Hobson's Life and Times

Hobson was 'a major in the brave army of heretics ... who, following their intuitions, have preferred to see the truth obscurely and imperfectly rather than to maintain error' (Keynes, 1936, p. 371). He spent much of his life developing and defending economic theories that challenged the existing paradigm; in the realm of ideas, he was a revolutionary. This was not because he was adversarial by nature. It was rather because he believed that there were important aspects of the workings of an economy which orthodox economic theory either explained incorrectly or did not explain at all.

Hobson's contributions to economics span just on half a century, and over that time economies, the 'truth' he sought to 'see', underwent substantial change. So did social and political forces, which Hobson viewed as interacting with economic ones. In this chapter, therefore, we give an account not only of Hobson's life, but also of the socio-economic and political background to it.

1.1 FORMATIVE YEARS (1858–86)

John Atkinson Hobson was 'born [6 July 1858] and bred in the middle of the middle class of a middle-sized Midland industrial town' (Hobson, 1931c, p. 13), to wit, Derby. He was the second son of William and Josephine (née Atkinson) Hobson. His father was the founder (in 1846), joint proprietor (with his younger brother, Robert) and editor of the *The Derbyshire Advertiser and Journal*, published weekly, and successor to *The Derbyshire Advertizer* co-founded in 1809 by William's father, John.[1]

Hobson's education in economics began early. In the Michaelmas Term of 1874, when Hobson had just turned sixteen and was in only his second last year at Derby School, he completed a Cambridge University Extension course in economics offered in Derby.[2] The economics he was taught in this course was essentially classical political economy as expounded by John Stuart Mill in his *Principles of Political Economy* (1848), though in the lectures reference was made also to some chapters of Adam Smith's *Wealth of Nations* (1776). However, the lecturer, the Revd William Moore Ede, was not uncritical of classical political economy; in particular, he took the view that it should be subjected to the higher authority of moral considerations, and he believed that there were still fresh truths to be discovered (Kadish, 1990, p. 138).[3]

Hobson's preparation for a university scholarship included the study of two other works by John Stuart Mill, namely *On Liberty* (1859) and *Utilitarianism* (1863). By his last year at school Hobson had abandoned the Nonconformist Christianity in which he had been brought up, and these books 'caught my sympathy as a budding rationalist' (Hobson, 1938b, p. 23). He read, too, *Study of Sociology* by Herbert Spencer (also from Derby), in which it is argued that Darwin's theory of evolution opens the way to the application of the methods of biology to the social sciences.[4] Thereafter, Hobson was never to waver from the view that societies and the ideas which go with them need to evolve in a Darwinian way, adapting to survive.

In 1876 Hobson proceeded on an open scholarship to Lincoln College, Oxford, where after four years he had obtained second class honours in Classics and third class honours *In Literis Humanioribus*.[5] While at Oxford, Hobson, like many of his contemporaries, came under the intellectual influence of the idealist philosopher T. H. Green (Hobson, 1938b, p. 26), though it is doubtful 'whether T. H. Green or any of the Neo-Kantians influenced him greatly: the cast of his mind was traditionally English' (Brailsford, 1948, p. 6). As interpreted by Green, liberalism confines the function of the state to the removal of hindrances to the fulfilment of individual character, which in Green's view involves both self-reliance, and spontaneous choice of behaviour which is moral in the sense that it contributes to the common good.

Hobson left Oxford in 1880 to teach classics, for two years in Faversham, and subsequently in Exeter, where he also gave lectures on English literature for the Oxford Extension Delegacy. In 1885 (Tawney, 1949, p. 435) 'he married a rather formidable well-to-do lawyer's daughter from New Jersey, Florence Edgar' (Lee, 1972, p. 176).

1.2 THE INNOVATIVE PERIOD (1887–1902)

Hobson abandoned schoolteaching in 1887 in order to take up journalism, and moved for this reason to West London. On arriving in London Hobson applied for, and received appointment as, lecturer by both the London Society for the Extension of University Teaching and the Oxford Committee for University Extension. In his first year Hobson offered courses in the field of English literature only, but from 1888 he also offered for the Oxford Committee a course in political economy (Kadish, 1990, pp. 140–1).

Among Hobson's journalistic commitments, from 7 October 1887 until 26 February 1897, was a weekly 'London Letter' for *The Derbyshire Advertiser and North Staffordshire Journal,* as his father's paper had by then been retitled. The articles for 1887 and 1888 are of particular interest, as they reveal some of Hobson's thinking on economics before the publication of his first book in 1889.

Hobson reported, for example, that he had read through Karl Marx's *Capital* (Volume I) with a view to writing a critique of it, but that he could not recommend it to readers 'unless they should happen to be thrown on a desolate island with only that book', and that it was 'full of the most appalling Germanity' (18 November 1887, p. 8). He opposed the intro-duction of a shorter working day on the ground that 'even assuming the energy displayed by the workmen were increased by the shorter day this could not compensate for the longer idleness of the machinery which works with him [*sic*] ... It is true that shorter hours will affect profits first; but the speedy result of diminished profit will be diminished investment of capital in manufacture, a diminished demand for labour and a rapid fall of wages' (17 February 1888, p. 8). As economic conditions improved in early 1888, he wrote approvingly: 'Once let us establish general confidence in a coming "boom", and that prophesy is the surest cause of its own fulfilment – it is simply the "faith cure" for industrial disease' (23 March 1888, p. 8).

With his wife, Hobson made his first trip to the United States in 1888, and from 25 May 1888 wrote seventeen articles for *The Derbyshire Advertiser* under the title of 'First Impressions of America'. These articles suggest that Hobson, had he so wished, could have written a book bearing comparison with de Tocqueville's *Democracy in America* (1835 and 1840); though lacking the depth of de Tocqueville's analysis of the American political system, they look at American politics with less rose-tinted spectacles, and are more penetrating on the workings of the American economy. In brief, Hobson found: the United States a land of liberty, equality and fraternity; Americans 'a hard-working and a hard-playing race' (10 August 1888, p. 8), and far from being vulgar, to have good taste imbued in them through the influence of Paris; newspapers, like Americans, 'full of information, void of thought, and sensational' (17 August 1888, p. 8); public 'arrangements' in the towns, notably roads, vastly inferior to private ones; and politicians corrupt, as in the United States 'politics is a game of pillage' (29 June 1888, p. 8). In a glancing blow at prohibition in some states, he lamented that in Maine and Vermont an Englishman is 'unable for love or money to wet his lips even with a glass of lager beer' (24 August 1888, p. 8).

Of relevance to the later development of his economic thought is his
first impression of Wall Street (of which he said he was going to refrain
from consequent moral reflections): 'Here at my feet, lay the greatest
"gambling hell" the world has ever seen, where every minute made and
marred a man in the only sense he could understand, whose gigantic transactions spread comfort or ruin over thousands of families throughout the
land' (1 June 1888, p. 8). In the same article he added that in the United
States 'the science of advertising has reached its zenith, and new wants are
daily discovered and supplied'. In the following week he built on the latter
comment as follows:

> The demand for every recognised form of necessity or luxury is so large
> and constant, that the productive power of the nation is nearly always
> taxed to the utmost. This, I am convinced, will be found, despite the
> teaching of ordinary political economy, an important clue to the mater-
> ial prosperity of the country at large. In other countries the individual's
> thrift heaps up capital beyond the possibility of useful investment; in
> America, where people are less thrifty, every dollar that is saved is sure
> of useful and profitable employment, for the amount of capital and
> labour required to furnish the evergrowing demand for new com-
> modities is enormously greater than in a thrifty country like Germany. I
> throw this out as a small hint which has an even more important bearing
> on the commercial prosperity of the United States than the vast quantity
> of virgin soil, which is generally quoted as the true explanation.   (8
> June 1888, p. 8)

In these words Hobson for the first time implied that prosperity, such as
that to be found in the United States, is to be attributed to a rapid growth
in consumption, and absence of prosperity to the underconsumption
resulting from excessive thrift.

Subsequently Hobson foreshadowed what were to become two other
important lines of argument in his economics, namely those relating to
tariffs and to industrial concentration:

> Knowing how heavily American manufacturers were hampered by their
> tariff in competition in foreign markets, I was at first at a loss to under-
> stand how they could produce goods as cheaply as they do. I can now
> understand it. Though labour is about twice as dear as in European
> countries, the difference is made up by advantages in labour-saving
> machinery, larger scale of production, and the cheapness of most raw
> materials. There is a constant strong tendency to throw production into

the hands of a few large manufacturers – a tendency which exists elsewhere but nowhere so powerfully as in the States ... The formation of "Trusts" or "Pools" is the most important economic fact of the age. A few large manufacturers combine together to get into their hands a monopoly of a certain product. By lowering prices for a season they crush smaller competitors, and obtain control of the market.   (13 July 1888, p. 8)

Hobson returned from the United States in late 1888. In 1889 he published his first book, *The Physiology of Industry*, written jointly with A. F. Mummery, a businessman and mountaineer whom he met in Exeter, and who persuaded him of the truth of the underconsumption theory.[6] The publication of *The Physiology of Industry* had an almost immediate effect on Hobson's life. Its heretical underconsumption theory was badly received by its two reviewers. Francis Ysidro Edgeworth, appointed to the Drummond Professorship of Political Economy at Oxford in the year following that in which his review was published, noted with an air of astonishment that Mummery and Hobson 'attack Mill's position that saving enriches and spending impoverishes the community along with the individual', adding:

The attempt to unsettle consecrated tenets is not very hopeful, unless the public, whose attention is solicited, have some security against waste of their time and trouble. It may fairly be required of very paradoxical writers that they should either evince undoubted speculative genius, or extraordinarily wide learning. We do not feel able in the present instance to offer these guarantees to the reading public.   (Edgeworth, 1890, p. 194)

The other reviewer, the Fabian W. A. S. Hewins, was also highly critical, stating that:

Messrs. Mummery and Hobson appear to have a mistaken idea of the character of economic science. They speak of J. S. Mill's theories as a "creed", of their own divergence from the "orthodox school", and of "currently accepted dogmas", – expressions which are meaningless applied to economics. Their main argument is fallacious, and their conclusions untenable.   (Hewins, 1891, p. 133)[7]

Pace Hewins, there had been 'an orthodoxy' in economics for some time before Sismondi coined the term in 1826, and it was the unfavourable attitude towards *The Physiology of Industry* by the 'orthodox school' which in fact led to the refusal of the London Society for the Extension of University Teaching to include Hobson on its list of lecturers in the field of economics.[8] This refusal was due in particular to the exertions of the Cambridge economist H. S. Foxwell, also Professor of Political Economy at University College, London, who in 1891 in reply to a request on Hobson's behalf from the London Ethical Society added a note to a copy of his letter referring to 'a curious example of the purposes of an Ethical Society, they asked a man only notorious for a very fallacious attempt to prove that thrift is morally & socially a vice' (Kadish, 1990, p. 145).[9] In 1893, however, the London Society for the Extension of University Teaching added Hobson's name to its list of lecturers in economics, after an enquiry which found 'the opinions from Oxford were strongly in favour of recognition, whilst those at Cambridge were more doubtful' (quoted in Burrows, 1978, p. 12).[10] None the less, Hobson was not offered a teaching post when the London School of Economic and Political Science was founded in 1895.[11]

Four decades later, when he was preparing *The General Theory* for publication, John Maynard Keynes evidently wrote to Hobson seeking information about the early development of his underconsumption theory (the letter has not survived). Hobson replied (19 July 1935) by sending Keynes a copy of a 'popular address' he had delivered on the previous Sunday, in which *inter alia* he referred to his being refused permission to lecture on economics for the London Society for the Extension of University Teaching because of the intervention of a Professor of Economics.[12] In his response, Keynes asked if he might include part of this address in his forthcoming book, specifying that 'the bit which I should like to quote begins from the last paragraph of page 2 to the end of the first paragraph on page 5' (Keynes Papers, CO/3/276).[13] Keynes also commented, with reference to the critics of *The Physiology of Industry*:

> What a disgraceful old crew these orthodox gents were. I wish you would tell me the name of the economic [*sic*] professor referred to on page 4.   (Keynes Papers, CO/3/276)[14]

It was immediately following this passage that Keynes made his reference to Hobson being remembered as a pathbreaker in economic theory after even the existence of the professor had been forgotten. Hobson disclosed Foxwell's name in his subsequent letter (2 August 1935) to Keynes (Keynes Papers, CO/3/270).

Two years after the publication of *The Physiology of Industry*, two articles by Hobson appeared in the *Quarterly Journal of Economics*. That entitled 'The Law of the Three Rents', was the first to enunciate one of the basic features of the marginal productivity theory of distribution, namely that the concept of rent can be applied not only to land but also to all other factors of production.[15] The year 1891 also saw the publication of 'Can England Keep her Trade?', which appeared in the *National Review*, and a book entitled *Problems of Poverty*. The latter was followed by *Evolution of Modern Capitalism* (1894), one of Hobson's most widely read books, which combined economic history with analysis of contemporary economies, and *The Problem of the Unemployed* (1896a), the first book in which Hobson linked underconsumption with the unequal distribution of income. Hobson's career as a prolific writer had begun, his life-time publications including innumerable articles and over fifty books; Hobson's practice was to incorporate in many of the latter some of his previously-published articles. At the same time he maintained his activities as a journalist and an Extension lecturer, the resulting three sources of income supplementing the income he received as a result of his father's stake in *The Derbyshire Advertiser*; though after the death of his father in 1897 he was in receipt of a sufficient private income to be able to give up Extension lecturing.

During the 1890s Hobson became a member of a number of organisations, taking part in discussions at their regular meetings and giving the principal address from time to time. In 1890 he joined the London Ethical Society, which 'was an attempt of a few Oxford philosophers, not content with the seclusion of an academic life, to furnish thought and leadership to movements "for the amelioration of the condition of the working classes"' (1938b, pp. 55–6); from 1891 he was for five years a member of its committee. In 1894 he was co-founder, with the Fabian journalist William Clarke and the future Labour Prime Minister Ramsay MacDonald, among others, of the Rainbow Circle, a group whose aim was 'to stimulate informed discussion and to formulate broadly collectivist political principles' (Lee, 1972, p. 176), which it sought to achieve in part through the *Progressive Review*, founded in 1896, of which Hobson was a director. Although the journal lasted only two years, the group continued to meet monthly for some three decades.[16] In 1895 Hobson left the London Ethical Society, which he regarded as having become too closely associated with the individualistic views of the Charity Organisation Society, to join the more radical South Place Ethical Society, where 'he preached the principles of rational democracy every Sunday morning for forty years' (Lee, 1972, p. 177). It was 'in this ethical sub-culture that Hobson first made the acquaintance of labour men, mostly London intellectuals and Fabians' (Lee, 1972, p. 177).

Hobson had been a supporter of the Liberal Party from his early days. During the 1890s, however, both through his writings and through his active participation in the several organisations of which he was a member, he played a major role in developing what came to be known as 'the new liberalism', which sought to give due recognition to the elements of 'Socialism in Liberalism', as the text of the chapter given this title in Hobson's *The Crisis of Liberalism* (1909a) illustrates.[17]

It was during this period of his life that Hobson became familiar with the ideas of Karl Marx, Henry George, and the Fabian Socialists. In 1887, as we have already seen, he read the first volume of *Das Kapital* (1867) in English translation; but he was put off by what he saw as the mysticism of the Hegelian dialectic and the unreality of the labour theory of value. Though receptive to Henry George's emphasis on the importance of rent, he found too limited the central prescription of George's *Progress and Poverty* (1879), namely that either existing taxes should be replaced by a single tax on land (and other natural resources), because unlike existing taxes such a tax would not reduce the supply of factors of production, or land should be nationalised; Hobson believed that George's argument could be applied to many forms of capital and labour, as well as to land. Nor did the *Fabian Essays*, published in 1889 with George Bernard Shaw as editor, with their arguments for gradual movement to a technocratic socialism, convert him to the socialist cause, even though Hobson was to establish a close friendship with three of the leading Fabians, namely William Clarke, Graham Wallas and Sidney Webb.

Hobson was, on the other hand, strongly attracted to the ideas of John Ruskin and Richard Cobden. His sympathy with many of Ruskin's ideas led to his agreeing to write an exposition and appraisal of them in *John Ruskin: Social Reformer* (1898a).[18] Hobson was later to acknowledge that from Ruskin 'I drew the basic thought for my subsequent writings, viz. the necessity of going behind the current monetary estimates of wealth, cost, and utility, to reach the body of human benefits and satisfactions which give them a real meaning' (1938b, p. 42); in *Unto this Last* (1862) and *Munera Pulveris* (1872) in particular, Ruskin took 'there is no wealth but life' as his text, combining this with the argument that political economy cannot be dissociated from ethics. While Hobson wholeheartedly accepted these ideas, he rejected Ruskin's assumptions that values are absolute rather than evolving over time, and that values can be laid down by an elite on behalf of the majority, and regretted the fact that after his exposure of the dehumanising effects of the division of labour on workers Ruskin in his later works failed to pay the same attention to production as he did to consumption.

Hobson's book on Cobden, *Richard Cobden: The International Man* (1919a), took the form of a largely sympathetic commentary linking a selection of Cobden's correspondence and speeches. These supported free trade by arguing that it not only brings material benefit to every nation, but is also a means by which international peace can be achieved, an example of Cobden's general belief that 'the most rational course was also the most moral' (Taylor, 1957, p. 56). Hobson took up this belief and applied it to economic behaviour in general.

In 1898 Hobson published an article entitled 'Free Trade and Foreign Policy' which contained all the essential elements of his theory of imperialism.[19] This article was noticed by Hobson's friend, L. T. Hobhouse, who was at the time chief political leader writer for the *Manchester Guardian*, and Hobhouse persuaded its editor, C. P. Scott, to send Hobson 'out on a voyage of political inquiry to South Africa when the outlook began to be dangerous' (1938b, p. 60). Before the outbreak of the Boer War, Hobson met most of the leaders on both sides, and reported on the political situation in a series of articles for the *Manchester Guardian*, later included in a book entitled *The War in South Africa: Its Causes and Effects* (1900b).[20] Two years later there followed the work for which Hobson is most widely known, namely, *Imperialism: A Study*, with its thesis that the 'taproot of imperialism' is economic.

In 1899 Hobson had moved from West London to 'the important Fabian intellectual community at Limpsfield, Surrey' (Lee, 1972, p. 177), which was to be his home until his final move to 3 Gayton Crescent, Hampstead, shortly before the First World War. The following two years saw the publication of two of Hobson's most important books in the field of economics. *The Economics of Distribution* (1900a), while incorporating material from the two articles by Hobson published in *The Quarterly Journal of Economics* in 1891, attempted to go beyond them by developing a complete theory of income distribution. *The Social Problem: Life and Work* (1901b) was the first, and most innovative, of several books which Hobson devoted to welfare economics.[21]

1.3 A PERIOD OF CONSOLIDATION (1903–18)

In 1904 Hobson became a founder member of the London Sociological Society, serving first on its Council and Editorial Committee, before becoming Chairman (1913–22) and then Vice-President (1922–32).

Having returned to the United States in 1902, he then spent some time in Canada as well as the United States during 1904–5. There his views on economics were already well known through his writings, notably the several articles already published in American journals. While in North America Hobson observed at first hand the workings of protection and of Imperial preference; in *Canada To-day* (1906a) he reluctantly concluded that Canada was unlikely to adopt free trade in the foreseeable future, and he reached a similar conclusion with respect to the United States in *The Fruits of American Protection* (1906b). It was during this period that he became attracted to the sociological and economic theories of Thorstein Veblen, of whose ideas he was later to write a well-organised but relatively uncritical account in *Veblen* (1936).

In response to a plea from Hobhouse in 1905, Hobson cut short his latest stay in North America to write editorials and anonymous articles for the newly-founded liberal daily, *Tribune*, though he did not continue with this for long, possibly because his health was not sufficiently robust to cope with the continuous demands of journalism (Lee, 1970, p. 78).[22] After the success of the Liberal Party in the 1906 election, Hobson's writings were dominated by the objective of ensuring that the new government would pursue a programme of reform; in Lee's words, the 'social reform programme owed much to radicals like Lloyd George and Churchill, and Masterman and Chiozza Money, but the pressure of the type exercised by Hobson and his colleagues may have had some effect, even if it is difficult to document, and they themselves felt somewhat frustrated' (Lee, 1970, p. 81). Hobson's influence on Liberal Party thinking was at least sufficiently appreciated for his name to be included in 1911 on a list of potential peers drawn up by the government to swamp the House of Lords, should that become necessary; in the event it did not, because the House of Lords backed down from its threat to reject a finance bill already passed by the Commons.

In 1907 Hobson became a director of, and regular contributor to, the newly-established liberal weekly, *Nation*, under the distinguished editorship of H. W. Massingham, as a result of which he became a participant in the discussions which took place among leading journalists at the *Nation*'s weekly lunches. He continued his association with the *Nation* until 1923, when he took strong objection to the proprietors' acceptance of Massingham's resignation, though he resumed contributions to the *Nation* in 1925, and continued them when in 1931 it merged with the *New Statesman*.[23]

In 1909 Hobson published *The Industrial System: An Inquiry into Earned and Unearned Income*, designed to reinforce his analysis of the connection between unequal distribution of income and underconsumption. Continually rising prices were the inspiration for *Gold, Prices and Wages* (1913); and his ideas on welfare were further expanded on in *Work and Wealth: A Human Valuation* (1914).

This period saw the emergence of the guild socialism movement, whose members stressed the importance of pluralism, but argued that it was compatible with a socialism based on worker collectives rather than the state. Although some of his friends, notably G. D. H. Cole, were involved in this movement, Hobson was not converted, believing that such collectives would inevitably pursue the interests of their own members, at the expense both of other workers and of consumers as a whole (see *Work and Wealth*, pp. 263–8).

Many of the organisations and movements with which Hobson was associated before the First World War 'were by name or character democratic, pacifist, anti-Imperialist, and the War was an acid test for all such professions' (Hobson, 1938b, p. 93). Some of Hobson's friends became fervent supporters of the war. By contrast, others, like Hobson, signed a letter announcing the formation of the British Neutrality Committee, later known as the Bryce Committee in recognition of the contribution made by its Chairman, Lord Bryce. In 1915 this committee published the *Bryce Report*, advocating a League of Nations Union; Hobson's own somewhat dissenting opinions, based on a more optimistic view of the nature of man, were put forward in *Towards International Government* (1915). Hobson was also present at the inaugural meeting in the early autumn of 1914 which set up the Union of Democratic Control (UDC). The UDC, 'as its name implied, was directed primarily against "secret diplomacy", or perhaps against any diplomacy at all. It echoed Cobden's "no foreign politics"' (Taylor, 1957, p. 136). It was the 'most active of anti-war agencies during the War and for some years after' (1938b, p. 104); Hobson served on its executive committee for a quarter of a century, from the time of its foundation.

In 1917 V. I. Lenin published *Imperialism, the Highest Stage of Capitalism*, acknowledging that he had 'made use of the principal English work on imperialism, J. A. Hobson's book, with all the care that, in my opinion, this work deserves' (Lenin, 1933, p. 7), and adding the comment that Hobson's book 'gives a very good and detailed description of the principal economic and political characteristics of imperialism' (Lenin, 1933, p. 15).[24] In the following year Hobson became a member of the '1917 Club', which, according to Hobson's recollections, was initiated by 'the Kerensky revolution of the spring, not the Lenin revolution of October ... [and] was a free meeting-place for advanced men and women concerned with political and economic reforms, or with new literary or artistic movements' (1938b, p. 115); though Lee (1970, p. 94) argues there is no evidence that its foundation was in any way related to the Kerensky revolution.

In 1915 the Chancellor of the Exchequer, Reginald McKenna, had imposed duties which as part of the war effort 'were intended to reduce "luxury" imports rather than for any Protectionist purpose. All the same, they were a sin against Free Trade' (Taylor, 1965, p. 40). Hobson had had his disagreements with Liberal Party policies over the years, culminating in his opposition to the declaration of war in 1914; by his own admission (1938b, p. 126) McKenna's imposition of duties was the last straw, and in 1916 he finally resigned his membership of the Liberal Party. He then narrowly failed to become an Independent member of the House of Commons in the 1918 election, which was the first based on suffrage extended to all men who had attained the age of twenty-one and women who had attained the age of thirty.

1.4   RESPONSE AND REFLECTION (1919–40)

From the time of his resignation from the Liberal Party, Hobson began to be involved in Labour politics. Shortly after his defeat in the 1918 election he joined the Independent Labour Party, becoming a member of its Advisory Committee on International Relations. He subsequently served on a committee set up by the Labour Party to report on the 'Douglas – "New Age" Credit Scheme', that is to say, the set of proposals based on the social credit theory advanced by Major C. H. Douglas; the committee submitted its report in 1922, recommending against the proposals.[25] In the same year, Hobson revived his underconsumption theory in *The Economics of Unemployment*, which also included a chapter setting out reasons for rejecting Douglas's theory which closely parallel those in the Labour Party committee's report.

In 1924 Hobson was appointed to the Independent Labour Party's Living Wage Committee, set up in the face of widespread calls for a reduction in wages, which was seen both as a remedy for Britain's high unemployment and as a necessary condition for a return to the Gold Standard; the Committee saw its task as attempting to define precisely a minimum wage at which the Labour Party and trade unions could aim. The Committee's Report (see Brailsford *et al.*), delivered in 1926 after the failure of the General Strike in opposition to an attempt by coal owners to reduce the wage rates paid to miners, bears Hobson's imprint. After stating that 'the benefits of mass production cannot be realised to the full, because the power of the masses to consume fails to keep pace with the power of the machines to produce' (p. 8), the Report stipulated that 'the Labour Movement must base itself upon this fact of "underconsumption"' (p. 9), and used this as a reason to advocate a national minimum wage. However, the Report failed to find favour either with leading members of the Labour Party, who believed its adoption would be a threat to the Party because of the unrealistic nature of its proposals, or with the trade unions, who saw it as a challenge to their power (see Allett, 1981, p. 43).

Another critique by Hobson of current thinking in the social sciences in general, and in economics in particular, *Free-thought in the Social Sciences*, also appeared in 1926; this book incorporated his critical article 'Neo-Classical Economics in Britain' (1925). A further work in the area of welfare economics, *Wealth and Life: A Study in Values*, which brought together and sometimes supplemented the ideas advanced in Hobson's earlier writings in this area, was published in 1929. In 1930 Hobson responded to the current clamour for 'rationalisation', which is to say reduction in unit costs by amalgamation or other means even if this means the laying-off of workers; in *Rationalisation and Unemployment: An Economic Dilemma* he argued that the unemployment resulting from rationalisation, which, perhaps surprisingly, he did not oppose, further strengthened the case for an increase in consumption.

Although Hobson wrote two letters to Keynes in 1926, the first interaction between the two on economic issues probably did not occur until the end of 1929, when both took part in the second and third of three luncheon parties hosted by the Prime Minister, Ramsay MacDonald, as a prelude to the setting up of an Economic Advisory Council (Middlemas, 1969, ii, pp. 219–24).[26] Unlike Keynes, Hobson was not invited to become a member of the Economic Advisory Council; nor did he make a submission to the Macmillan Committee on Finance and Industry, of which Keynes was also a member.

Correspondence between Hobson and Keynes involving discussion of economic issues was initiated with a letter by Hobson (24 July 1931) commenting on Keynes' *Treatise on Money*, which was published in 1930. This correspondence was seen by Hobson as a means of bringing his underconsumptionist ideas and the views held by Keynes closer together; by the beginning of November 1931, eight letters had passed between the two.[27] Keynes' subsequent handsome acknowledgement in *The General Theory* of the importance of Hobson's ideas brought more recognition of Hobson's underconsumption theory than it had ever previously had from an economist of Keynes' stature. Ironically, however, the success of

Keynes' demand deficiency explanation of unemployment led to the subsequent eclipse of the rival demand-side theory of underconsumption advanced by Hobson.

Hobson had finally become a member of the Labour Party in 1924. In 1931 he was offered a peerage by Ramsay MacDonald, but refused it because of his bitter disillusionment with the failure of the Labour Government to introduce what he saw as appropriate measures to deal with the country's economic problems.

In 1938 Hobson published *Confessions of an Economic Heretic*, an autobiographical work which had much more to say about his ideas than about his life, and of which Brailsford was to write that it was 'perhaps the most reticent autobiography ever written' (Brailsford, 1948, p. 5).[28] Hobson died on 1 April 1940; his ashes were dispersed in the Garden of Remembrance, Golders Green Crematorium. In an obituary of Hobson, G. D. H. Cole, who was a close friend for the last thirty years of Hobson's life, provided what remains the best thumbnail sketch of Hobson the man:

> Personally, Hobson was a man of great charm, with a strong sense of humour that found all too little expression in most of his writings. He was kindly beyond measure, and a most entertaining talker; but above all else he was a man of inflexible principle, to whose lot it fell, while sustaining one unpopular cause after another, to miss the recognition which he would have valued from his fellow-workers in the fields of economics and the social sciences as a whole. But with all this, no one was ever less like a disappointed man. Hobson went on cheerfully saying what he believed, whether anyone liked it or not, and whether what he said was attended to or simply ignored.   (Cole, 1940, p. 359)[29]

1.5   THE SOCIO-ECONOMIC CONTEXT (1873–1940)

When Hobson left Oxford in 1880 the British economy had enjoyed at least six decade-average annual rates of growth over successive thirty-year periods of between 1.0 and 1.9 per cent per head of the total population (Deane and Cole, 1967, p. 283, table 73; see also Crafts, 1985, p. 45, table 2.11, and p. 103, table 5.5).[30] The economy had been characterised not only by this upward trend, however, but also by a cyclical pattern of behaviour, with the average duration of the cycle being about seven years (Aldcroft and Fearon, 1972, p. 9, table 1). In addition, structural changes over this period had resulted in a fall from about one third to one tenth in the proportion of national income accounted for by agriculture, forestry and fishing (Deane and Cole, 1967, p. 291, table 76).

By the middle of the nineteenth century Britain had become known as 'the workshop of the world'; its economy was the most industrialised. This facilitated Britain's movement towards free trade, marked by the repeal of the Corn Laws (in 1846) and of the Navigation Act (in 1849), and by the abolition of the remaining tariffs by 1860.[31]

The 1880s, at the end of which Hobson published his first book, lay in the middle of a period during which the progress of the British economy seemed to many contemporaries to have faltered. Between 1873 and 1896 there was a continuous fall in prices, accompanied by a falling trend in the rate of interest and the rate of profit. Some observers interpreted these events as indicating a general economic decline, and by 1924 the economic historian L. C. A. Knowles was referring to this period as being characterised by 'a great depression' (Knowles, 1924, p. 141).[32] We now know, however, that in the last two decades of the nineteenth century the British average annual rate of growth of national product per head of total population exceeded, if anything, that over the previous eighty years (Deane and Cole, 1967, p. 283, table 73); Deane and Cole refer to 'the process of acceleration in the United Kingdom rate of growth to its climax in the last quarter of the century' (Deane and Cole, 1967, p. 283). Furthermore, the 'volume of investment was ... sufficiently high over the Great Depression period as a whole to avoid a significantly greater average level of unemployment than in the trend periods which preceded or followed' (Rostow, 1948, pp. 49–50).

The British economy continued in this period to be characterised by cyclical fluctuations in the level of economic activity. From a trough in 1879 the economy revived to reach a peak in 1883 (Aldcroft and Fearon, 1972, p. 9, table 1), followed by a downswing which was seen at the time as being unusually severe.[33] Contemporary perceptions of the state of the British economy became so pessimistic that in 1885 the government set up a Royal Commission to inquire into 'The Depression of Trade and Industry'. Given that 'the holding of an inquiry of this sort was novel and disapproved of by strict adherents to the ideas of economic liberalism, for whom trade prosperity and depression were matters for business, not for government' (Court, 1965, p. 18), it is not surprising that only those actually engaged in trade and industry, not economists, were called by the Commission to give evidence. However, in 1887–8, Alfred Marshall, Professor of Political Economy at the University of Cambridge, appeared before members of the newly-appointed Gold and Silver Commission, and provided the following comment on the Depression of Trade and Industry Commission:

> I have read nearly all the evidence that was given before the Depression of Trade and Industry Commission, and I really could not see that there was any serious attempt to prove anything else than a depression of prices, a depression of interest, and a depression of profits; there is that undoubtedly. I cannot see any reason for believing that there is any considerable depression in any other respect.   (Marshall, 1888, volume II, p. 21)

Although evidence is lacking as to whether the poor were or were not becoming relatively poorer, the end of the nineteenth century saw a marked increase in awareness of the coexistence of comfortable living for many, with great poverty for a substantial part of the population, especially in the towns. Arnold Toynbee's lectures in economic history at Oxford, published posthumously in 1884, drew attention to the continued existence of poverty after the Industrial Revolution. Contemporary poverty was documented in William Booth's *In Darkest England, and the Way Out* (1890), the findings of the Royal Commission on Labour (1891), Charles Booth's nine volumes of empirical evidence on the extent of poverty in *Life and Labour of the People in London* (1892-7), and B. Seebohm Rowntree's York-based investigation, *Poverty: A Study of Town Life* (1901).

One of the contemporary economic facts to which Hobson drew attention in 1902 with the publication of *Imperialism: A Study* was the enormous amount of capital that Britain and other European countries had exported since 1870, by the purchase of foreign bonds and debentures as well as of foreign shares. The export of capital by Britain continued at an ever-increasing pace after the publication of Hobson's book, a trend that was halted only with the outbreak of war in 1914.

The rate of growth of the British economy 'slackened again at the beginning of the twentieth century' (Deane and Cole, 1967, p. 285), and fell close to zero during the First World War. Rostow's view is that '1914 is the first year of what would, almost certainly, have been a more protracted depression' (Rostow, 1948, p. 48, n. 1) had it not been for the outbreak of war, a depression comparable with the downswings of 1904-6 and 1909-10.

Between the First and Second World Wars the rate of growth of income per head in the United Kingdom was positive, but below that prevailing on average during the nineteenth century. This lower rate of growth was accompanied by unemployment rates which were unprecedented. With a work force of twelve million, the number of workers unemployed rose above two million in 1921, and thereafter never fell below one million until the advent of the Second World War (Taylor, 1965, p. 145); in 1932 it rose to almost three million.[34]

After enjoying a boom in 1920, Britain fell rapidly into a trough in 1921, when both prices and money-wage rates fell, though the latter not as far as the former; the next peak in the trade cycle did not occur until 1929 (Aldcroft and Fearon, 1972, p. 9, table 1). The subsequent period is still known as that of 'the Great Depression', with economic conditions incomparably worse than those during 'the Great Depression' of the nineteenth century. The trough occurred in 1932, the economy recovering to a peak in 1937 (Aldcroft and Fearon, 1972, p. 9, table 1) before it suffered another downturn.

1.6   THE POLITICAL CONTEXT (1859–1940)

Minimal government involvement in the domestic economy and free trade internationally were advocated in particular by a coalition of politicians who in 1859 founded the Liberal Party. Support for the new party came from Nonconformists and the working class, as well as from the rising capitalist class. Dominated by William Ewart Gladstone, who was Prime Minister from 1868 to 1874, and again from 1880 to 1885, the Liberal Party was the most powerful force in British politics from the time of its formation until 1874. It was then replaced in government by the newly-named Conservative Party, led by Benjamin Disraeli, who was Prime Minister from 1874 to 1880. The Conservative Party, 'organ of all that was out of sympathy with industrial Britain' (Hobsbawm, 1968, p. 120), was supported by the established Church as well as by the landed interests. One of the areas in which it sought to distinguish itself from the Liberal Party was in its attitude to the British Empire. This objective was heralded by Disraeli in a speech made in 1872, which included the following piece of rhetoric:

> If you look to the history of this country since the advent of Liberalism – forty years ago – you will find that there has been no effort so continuous, so subtle, supported by so much energy, and carried on with so much ability and acumen, as the attempts of Liberalism to effect the disintegration of the Empire of England.   (Monypenny and Buckle, 1929, p. 534)[35]

In the same speech Disraeli went on to state that to 'uphold the Empire' was one of the three great objects of the Conservative Party.

While agreeing on the need for an extension of the electoral franchise, the two parties differed as to how this should be done. It was ultimately the Derby–Disraeli administration which succeeded, in 1867, in pushing through the first Reform Act since 1832. Mainly by lowering the property qualification, the 1867 Act increased the electorate, in a population of roughly thirty million, from about one million to about two million (Deane and Cole, 1967, p. 8, table 3; Halèvy, 1951, p. 443).

Pessimistic views about the future of the British economy may have played some part in the emergence during the early 1880s of a questioning of Britain's traditional policy of free trade, notably by the leader of the Radical faction in Parliament, Joseph Chamberlain, with backing from Birmingham manufacturers.[36] When the Liberal Party split over the issue of Home Rule for Ireland, this Radical faction was one of those which subsequently formed the Liberal–Unionist coalition, which brought down Gladstone's government in 1885 and formed a 'Unionist' Government. Before his loss of office, however, Gladstone had succeeded in pushing through the Reform and Redistribution Acts of 1884, which extended the electoral franchise to all property-owners and resulted in 'something like equal electoral districts' (Halèvy, 1951, p. 466). Another political land-mark during this period was the election to Parliament in 1892 of Keir Hardie, who was to be chosen as leader of the Independent Labour Party when it was founded in the following year.[37]

Such opposition to the policy of imperialism as there was within the Liberal Party had begun to weaken as early as 1882, and was completely submerged during the ascendancy of Lord Rosebery while the Party was in office from 1892 to 1895. In 1900, the year after the Boer War began, the incumbent Unionist Government was returned to office with a large majority, in the so-called 'Khaki' election. The government's war policy was supported by the Liberal Imperialist faction of the Liberal Party under Rosebery, which for a time formed a majority in the party; those Liberals under Lord Morley and Henry Campbell-Bannerman who opposed the government's foreign policy were dubbed 'Little Englanders'. During the four years over which the war dragged on, however, imperialist fervour dwindled. The Unionists lost further favour as a result of speeches made in May 1903 by Joseph Chamberlain, then Colonial Secretary, in favour of the introduction of Imperial preference; though Chamberlain subsequently resigned, the support he had attracted within the party led the Prime Minister, A. J. Balfour, to compromise by endorsing the use of tariffs as a retaliatory measure where necessary. This was never put into effect, because in 1906 it was the Liberal Party, with Campbell-Bannerman at its head, which won a resounding electoral victory. When Parliament resumed sitting, twenty-nine members elected with support from the Labour Representation Committee formed themselves into a group which called itself 'the Labour Party'.[38]

First under Campbell-Bannerman, who resigned in 1908 due to ill-health, and then under H. H. Asquith, the Liberal Government pushed through a series of Acts which met with the approval of new liberals such as Hobson, in that they were designed to improve the conditions under which the majority of the population worked and lived. At the end of 1906 a Trade Disputes Act was passed, making 'peaceful persuasion' during a strike lawful, and 'directly exempting trade unions from all actions for tort' (Ensor, 1936, p. 392). Then

> during the session of 1908 two social reforms of the first magnitude were carried by Asquith's Cabinet – the Act limiting the working day in the mines [to eight hours], which for the first time laid down the principle of a legal limitation of hours for adult male workers, and the Old Age Pensions Act, which affirmed the principle of the right to live by recognizing the right of those too old to work to receive a pension from the community.   (Halèvy, 1952, Book I, p. 285)

In 1909 two further reforming Acts were passed, setting up, respectively, Trade Boards with power to determine minimum wage rates, and eighty Labour Exchanges. But while Lloyd George's 1909 Budget, designed among other things to finance these Acts, passed the House of Commons, it was rejected by the House of Lords. The consequent General Election of 1910 resulted in a Liberal Government, now dependent on support from the Labour Party (with about forty seats) and the Irish Nationalists. The resulting political instability led to a second election in the same year, the Liberal Government being returned with an increased majority. In 1911 the House of Lords finally accepted the principle that it would not reject financial legislation sent to it by the Commons.

Asquith was still Prime Minister when, in 1916, criticism of the way in which the war was being prosecuted resulted in his being replaced by a coalition including members of all four main parties, headed by Lloyd George. This coalition survived the general election of 1918, though Lloyd George's unwillingness or inability to press ahead with a programme of social reform led to a split in the Liberal Party which resulted in many of its members defecting to Labour. These defections occurred despite the fact that in 1918 the Labour Party committed itself to the radical progamme of common ownership of the means of production.[39]

In the general elections of 1922, Lloyd George's coalition government fell, being replaced by a Conservative Government, with the Labour Party for the first time obtaining more seats than the Liberal Party. Following a snap election at the end of 1923, in January 1924 a minority Labour Government was formed, under Ramsay MacDonald. Before the year was out there was a further election, resulting in the Labour minority Government being replaced by a Conservative majority Government. With Winston Churchill as Chancellor of the Exchequer, this government returned Britain to the Gold Standard in April 1925. Surviving the General Strike of 1926, directed against an attempt to support the return to the Gold Standard by reducing the wage rates of miners, the Conservative Government lasted until the general election of 1929.

This election resulted in a second Labour minority Government, of which A. J. P. Taylor states that with 'Labour again in a minority, there could be no question of a socialist programme, even if the leaders had believed in socialism or had known what it meant' (Taylor, 1965, p. 272). With rapidly worsening economic conditions, and defections from within Labour Party ranks over a proposal in 1931 to reduce unemployment relief, Ramsay MacDonald cobbled together a 'National Government' which, although it had representatives from each of the three major parties, was dominated by the Conservative Party. This government marked a major departure from its predecessors over the previous 85 years by completely abandoning the policy of free trade. A continuing capital outflow problem also forced it to take Britain off the Gold Standard in September 1931, notwithstanding which it was re-elected in the following month. The National Government was replaced in 1935 by a Conservative Government with an absolute majority in the House of Commons, a government which was still in power at the time of Hobson's death in April 1940.

This brief account of the political events which occurred during Hobson's life completes our outline of the socio-economic and political context in which Hobson developed his economic theories. An exposition of those theories occupies the next five chapters. We begin with Hobson's contributions to welfare economics.

2 Economic Activity and Welfare

Hobson's first book-length excursion into the field of what is now known as welfare economics was in *The Social Problem: Life and Work*. Such prior contributions by others as there had been in this area sometimes took the form of negative prescriptions, which made the task of future economists dealing with welfare more difficult. William Stanley Jevons, while basing his theory on the Benthamite assumption that individuals attempt to maximise pleasure and minimise pain, explicitly denied that the amount of feeling in one mind could ever be compared with that in another (Jevons, 1871, p. 21); in modern terminology, he denied the possibility of making interpersonal comparisons of utility. Edgeworth, also a follower of Jeremy Bentham, pointed out that the utility a consumer derives from one commodity depends on the quantities of other commodities that the consumer possesses, as a result of which a consumer's total utility cannot be calculated by simply adding up the utility derived from consuming each commodity separately (Edgeworth, 1881, pp. 20 and 104).[1]

On the other hand, Jevons simplified matters for some with his assertion that 'in the science of Economy we treat men not as they ought to be, but as they are' (Jevons, 1871, pp. 45–6), an assertion which, if accepted, absolves the economist from the task of discussing the ends at which economic activity is directed.[2] Marshall, in turn, made a helpful contribution in his *Principles of Economics* (1890) by refining the concepts of consumer's surplus and producer's surplus, though he finessed the question as to how these might be aggregated, stating, for example, with reference to the former that aggregation would be possible 'if we were to neglect for the moment the fact that the same sum of money represents different amounts of pleasure to different people' (Marshall, 1890–1920, vol. I, p. 128).

By the late nineteenth century, normative questions such as those involved in welfare economics were generally regarded as best treated separately from 'positive' economics. For example, implicitly accepting David Hume's distinction between an 'is' and an 'ought', and building on the methodological writings of Nassau Senior and John Stuart Mill, John Neville Keynes in *The Scope and Method of Political Economy* (1891) defined the three distinct elements of economics as it had been practised up to his time as follows:

> a *positive science* may be defined as a body of systematized knowledge concerning what is; a *normative* or *regulative science* as a body of systematized knowledge discussing criteria of what ought to be, and concerned therefore with the ideal as distinguished from the actual; an *art* as a system of rules for the attainment of a given end. The object of a positive science is the establishment of *uniformities*, of a normative science the determination of *ideals*, of an art the formulation of *precepts*. (Keynes, 1891, pp. 34–5, emphasis in original)

Keynes' view was that 'a positive science of political economy should receive distinct and independent recognition' (Keynes, 1891, p. 50), it being better in this instance to do one thing at a time, partly because economists might otherwise confuse empirical and ethical arguments, or be perceived to be confusing them, and partly because agreement on what 'is' in the economic world is certain to be arrived at more quickly than agreement on what 'ought to be'.

As the concept of 'welfare' relates to what 'ought to be', one implication of Keynes' argument is that discussion of the relationship between economic activity and human welfare is best treated separately from positive economics. This is a question of method which Hobson had to consider. As human welfare clearly depends on non-economic as well as economic factors, he also had to consider the question of how much an economist, *qua* economist, could say about human welfare; that is to say, he was confronted as well with the question of the scope of economics.

On the other hand, Hobson was never brought face to face with the basis of modern welfare economics, namely the Pareto criterion. Vilfredo Pareto's enunciation of this basis, namely that the criterion for an increase in welfare is that at least one person is better off without anyone being worse off, did not appear until 1906, and the Pareto criterion had little if any influence on English-speaking economists until the 1930s.[3] As late as the 1940s, Joseph Schumpeter was able to write that:

> the standard work from which the new Anglo-American welfare economics stems, Professor Pigou's *Economics of Welfare* (1920…) … goes much beyond the limits drawn by the Paretian suggestion, especially as regards transfers of wealth from the relatively rich to the relatively poor. But the new Anglo-American welfare economics itself tries

to respect those limits, though trespass on forbidden ground is still frequent. (Schumpeter, 1954, p. 1072)[4]

2.1 METHOD AND SCOPE

Hobson accepted in general John Stuart Mill's view, expressed in Book VI, Chapter ix of his *Logic* (1843), that economics is a 'concrete' (empirical) science which necessarily employs the ('direct') deductive method. In 1899 he noted that the use of 'speculative analysis' in economics had recently been criticised; the critics whom Hobson had in mind would have included members of the Historical School, most numerous in Germany, but increasing in numbers in Britain towards the end of the nineteenth century. Their principal objection to the use of 'speculative analysis' in economics was that generalisation is useless given that economic and social institutions change so much over time and vary so much between countries. Hobson responded by pointing out that the

> conditions of inductive reasoning from experiment which exist in many branches of physical science are here notoriously lacking, and to supply this defect a process of fictitious experiment is substituted, supposititious [*sic*] cases being framed where unessential circumstances are eliminated so as to enable us to see more clearly the working of certain simple forces. (1899, p. 22)

He also argued that:

> The first and simplest step in every 'inductive science' is directed *a priori*; no collection and ordering of crude facts is possible without importing from outside some principles of collection and order which embody the objects or ends of the process of investigation in a hypothetical way. You cannot investigate phenomena effectively without possessing some clear motive for investigation, and this motive will be related to a wider motive, which will eventually relate to some large speculative idea. (1901b, p. 65)[5]

But, contrary to the orthodox view, Hobson went on to assert that in the social sciences, including economics, this 'large speculative idea' must be ethical in character, because all facts of human significance have ethical implications. He added that to analyse such facts without reference to their ethical implications is to ignore their most important aspect.

Thus Hobson contended, in opposition to J. N. Keynes, that in the context of economics 'the "ought" is not something separable and distinct from the "is"; on the contrary, an "ought" is everywhere the highest aspect or relation of an "is"' (1901b, p. 66). Where, then, is the basis for the 'ought' to be found? Hobson's reply was that it lies in the concept of 'social utility'. The nature of this concept could be discerned by taking three separable steps:

> First we must substitute for the objective commercial standard of money the subjective human standard of efforts and satisfactions according to the valuations of present individual feelings; next, we must adjust this imperfect valuation by reference to the real good or worth of the individual life considered as a whole; finally, we must harmonize the good of the individual with the good of society, taking social utility or satisfaction as a final criterion.   (1901b, p. 39)

The first of these steps involves the replacement of 'the objective commercial standard of money' by 'the subjective human standard of efforts and satisfactions'. Hobson's earliest explanation of how the 'subjective human standard' can be derived is to be found in 'The Subjective and the Objective View of Distribution' (1893). The immediate purpose of this article was to disprove Simon N. Patten's argument that, since each extension of the working day by (say) an hour involves a sacrifice in that it reduces the time available to enjoy consumption, a labourer will cease working at the point where for the last hour of work satisfaction exceeds pain by the amount of this sacrifice involved; Patten concluded that the result for the economy as a whole is a surplus available for distribution or taxation.[6] Hobson responded by stating that this was an 'objective' analysis, and that it should be replaced by a 'subjective' one; his use of terms was unfortunate, as his subsequent argument made it clear that what he was advocating was a replacement of Patten's partial equilibrium analysis by a more general approach. A 'subjective' treatment, he argued, bearing in mind the sacrifice of consumption enjoyment resulting from additional work, would make the satisfaction derived from *each* hour of labour vary inversely with the total number of hours worked, satisfaction always being calculated net of sacrifice, including the sacrifice associated with loss of leisure; in this case there would be no difference between the pain and satisfaction derived from the last hour worked, and no consequent surplus.

However, the ultimate purpose of Hobson's article, far from being to deny the possibility of owners of factors of production receiving surpluses, was to argue that such surpluses should first be amalgamated so that they appear as a single sum, and then be converted from an objective surplus into a subjective one; here, as in most of his writings, Hobson used the terms 'objective' and 'subjective' in the conventional way. His 1891 *Quarterly Journal of Economics* articles, which are discussed in Chapter 3, had shown that rents may accrue to owners of capital and labour, as well as to owners of land. Before economics can be practised as an art, he now argued, the objective surplus made up of these rents needs to be translated into a subjective surplus, by taking into account the way in which the costs and utilities associated with it are distributed between individuals. As he put it, in a passage whose conclusion is as relevant to economics now as to economics at the time when it was written:

> A given quantity of objective costs may obviously be related to any number of different quantities of pain according as they are differently distributed among producers, while a given quantity of objective utilities may be similarly related to any number of different quantities of pleasure according as they fall to different consumers in different proportions. Objective costs and utilities must be reduced to terms of subjectivity and the relation between the law of the distribution of the objective surplus and of the subjective surplus clearly formulated before we can have a science of political economy bearing any assignable reference to human happiness. Until this is done we have ideas of wealth and work which have no human significance; we have a study as far removed from any practical interest as geometry of the fourth dimension. Such a political economy can have no art attached to it. The purely objective treatment of political economists has been, in fact, responsible for nearly all the clumsy errors which its exponents have made when invited to display their art in advice or prophecy. Until the science is thus subjectivised it can be brought into no true relations either with ethics or politics and is not properly a branch of sociology at all, but what Ruskin called it, a branch of 'mental gymnastics'.   (1893, pp. 54–5)

The second and third steps listed by Hobson in *The Social Problem* as part of the process of calculating social utility assume that such a thing as 'social utility' exists. While acknowledging that the concept of 'social utility' may mean different things to any two individuals, or to any two societies, or to one society at any two different stages in its history, Hobson argued that there must be some agreement as to its meaning at each given time in every society, because otherwise no social decisions could ever be made.

In the case of the second step, social utility provides the information necessary to adjust each individual's immediate evaluation of his or her utility so as to yield the 'real good or worth' of his or her life.[7] Taking the third step, which involves adjusting 'the real good or worth' of each individual's life so as to yield 'the good of society', depends on accepting the special view which Hobson had of the nature of society. While trying to remain true to his liberal beliefs by emphasising throughout his writings the overwhelming importance of individual self-fulfilment, Hobson at the same time stressed the necessity of recognising that each individual is a member of a society. Further, he took the view that society is not a mere aggregation of the individuals who are members of it. In *The Social Problem*, for example, he drew an analogy between a society made up of individuals and a musical composition made up of notes; he argued that in both cases the whole is more than the sum of its parts. More commonly, he likened society to an organism, the parts of which consciously contribute to the whole. How he saw the role of individuals in a society is indicated by the following passage:

> Social efficiency, for progress, really means the desire of individuals to merge or subordinate their separate ends of individuality, and to act on the supposition that a common social end realized by the individual consciousness, is in itself desirable. Or, adopting another formula which has its uses, it implies a conformity to the 'general will' seeking by rational conscious progress the welfare of society regarded as an organized whole. The individual will subserves this process in so far as it consents to subordinate passing caprices and desires to a fuller sense of the part which it is capable of bearing in the fulfilment of the larger social purpose. Such conduct of the individual in conformity with the general will is in part a matter of knowledge, in part of rational self-control.   (1901b, p. 263)

Hobson was at least partly aware of the problems associated with the concept of 'the general will'; he wrote of Jean Jacques Rousseau and G. W. F. Hegel, for example, that Rousseau 'essayed to lay a democratic basis for the dogma [of State absolutism] by developing the idea of the supremacy of "the general will", an idea which Hegel skillfully perverted to the purpose of autocracy' (1917, p. 116). What he did was attempt to reconcile his use of Rousseau's concept of the 'general will' with his own liberalism by identifying a society's 'general will' with enhancement of its welfare, and enhancement of the welfare of a society with a movement towards greater self-fulfilment on the part of each of its individual members; he justified the latter on the Darwinian ground that the survival of a society requires diversity.[8] By this means he was able to convince himself that the 'real' interest of each individual is identical with that of society as a whole.[9]

Hobson saw his theory of social utility as a form of utilitarianism; he was inclined, he said, 'to identify Welfare and its values with conscious satisfactions, so rescuing ethics from vague conceptions of self-realisation, in order to make of it a New Utilitarianism in which physical, intellectual, and moral satisfactions will rank in their due places' (1929a, p. 16). His method of approach to the problem of the relationship between economic activity and welfare was to judge such activity in the light of its effect on social utility as currently understood in the society under consideration.

In another work dealing with methodological questions, *Free-thought in the Social Sciences*, Hobson provided a further reason for believing that economics cannot be a purely objective science. He argued that in practice 'no study is so abstract or remote from the passions of humanity as to boast complete "disinterestedness"' (1926a, p. 14). More specifically, with respect to the 'sciences of Man', including economics, he took it as 'self-evident that what we would like to believe is liable to interfere at every point in the selection of enquiries and areas of attention, the formation of hypotheses, the observation and assessment of evidence, [and] the reasoning upon the evidence' (1926a, p. 16). Objectivity need not be precluded by the first two of these interferences, but the last two open up possibilities respectively of misread or falsified evidence, and invalid reasoning.

These possibilities are frequently realised, Hobson argued, in economics no less than in the other social sciences. 'Private personal biases', including those associated with private intellectual property, are reinforced by 'collective biases' resulting from social taboos, the dominance of the 'usefulness' ethic, and the influence of economic and intellectual interest groups. There is also the 'bias of metaphor', exemplified in economics since the Industrial Revolution by the use of metaphors taken from the mechanical rather than the organic sciences, thereby giving economics a static and conservative bias. This last idea has recently been revived by critics of neoclassical economics, notably in Mirowski (1989), where it is argued that neoclassical economists took over from mid-nineteenth-century physics a static mode of reasoning appropriate neither to physical nor to economic phenomena, a fact subsequently recognised in the case of physics but not in the case of economics. Given Hobson's beliefs concerning the proper method of economics, it is scarcely surprising that his view of its proper scope was broader than that of the leading economists of his day. In *The Social Problem*, for example, he criticised Marshall for stating in the first edition of his *Principles* that economics inquires how a man 'gets his income and how he uses it' (Marshall, 1890–1920, vol. II, p. 131), on the ground that this excludes a great deal of human activity which influences social utility.[10] He would not have agreed, either, with the substitute for the above statement in the fourth and subsequent editions of Marshall's *Principles*, namely that economics 'examines that part of individual and social action which is most closely connected with the attainment and with the use of the *material* requisites of wellbeing' (Marshall, 1890–1920, vol. I, p. 1, emphasis added); he took the view that Marshall should not have excluded from the definition of wealth 'services and other goods, which pass out of existence in the same instant that they come into it' (Marshall, 1890–1920, vol. I, p. 56), arguing that social utility depends on the services as well as the goods produced and used.

Though hedging his statement about with qualifications, Marshall none the less wrote in his *Principles* that 'it is true that "money" or "general purchasing power" or "command over material wealth", is the centre around which economic science clusters' (Marshall, 1890–1920, vol. I, p. 22).[11] Hobson, in contrast, argued in 'Human Cost and Utility' (1896b, p. 11) that 'assuming that we may have a science of negotiable quantities, the monetary estimate of this "wealth" is very defective'. He pointed out that national income in money terms often fails to measure social utility. For example, both goods formerly produced domestically and some formerly free goods have over time become commercial goods, leading to an increase in national income which does not reflect any change in social utility. A variant of this argument is to be found in *Work and Wealth*, where Hobson pointed out that of two nations (with equal populations), the one with the higher proportion of goods available free of charge, such as air, sunshine and scenery, will, *ceteris paribus*, have the lower national income but the higher social utility.

By the time that Hobson's *Free-thought in the Social Sciences* appeared, two books specifically concerned with welfare economics had been published by Arthur Cecil Pigou, namely *Wealth and Welfare* (1912) and *The Economics of Welfare* (1920). In the second of these, which is essentially a revised and greatly expanded version of the first, Pigou followed J. N. Keynes in contending that economics is 'a positive science of what is and tends to be, not a normative science of what ought to be' (Pigou, 1920, p. 5). And he followed Marshall in stating that economics includes in its subject-matter only 'that part of social welfare that can be brought directly or indirectly into relation with the measuring-rod of money. This part of welfare may be called economic welfare' (Pigou, 1920, p. 11). He added, thirdly, the opinion that 'there is a presumption – what Professor Edgeworth calls an "unverified probability" – that qualitative conclusions about the effect of an economic cause upon economic welfare will hold good also of the effect on total welfare' (Pigou, 1920, p. 20).

We have already seen that Hobson rejected the first two of these propositions. The third proposition, Hobson pointed out in *Free-thought in the Social Sciences* (p. 101), 'means that more wealth per head is presumed to carry more total satisfaction, irrespective of the methods of production or the distribution of its toil, upon the one hand, the nature of the wealth, its distribution and the uses and abuses of its consumption on the other hand'. Such a presumption he found to be almost totally unwarranted, for reasons we now explore.[12] In the next three sections we discuss in some detail Hobson's treatments of production and consumption, and then look at what he had to say on the normative aspects of distribution, before turning to the question of social welfare overall.

2.2 PRODUCTION AND CONSUMPTION

To convert economic cost into human cost, Hobson wrote, we need to know the character and condition of the work, the distribution of the work, and the capacities of the workers (1896b, p. 17). By this he meant, first, that conditions of work vary so widely that the cost to human well-being of any particular line of work may greatly exceed or greatly fall short of the actual wage paid, an example of the former being work which results in death, such as in the white lead or linen industries of Hobson's time, and of the latter being work, such as that of an artist or writer, which is 'in itself a pleasurable and ennobling exercise' (1896b, p. 16). He meant, second, that a quantity of goods produced at a given economic cost may be the product of a few working so long a working day that they are driven to exhaustion, or the work of many, for each of whom the burden of the relatively short working day is light. And third, he meant that a working day which in terms of length or physical exertion is tolerable for (say) an adult man may be intolerable for a woman or a child.[13] In sum, as King (forthcoming) puts it: 'for Hobson, work was always a process of joint production, in which inputs of labour give rise to two distinct types of output: goods and services for sale on the market, and a changed (all too often damaged) worker'.

Hobson cited as a further example of an excess of human over economic cost the specialisation characteristic of modern production methods. He cited Thomas Carlyle, Ralph Waldo Emerson, John Ruskin and Leo

Tolstoy as those he supported in protesting 'against the degradation of
individual life and character by this narrowing and monotonizing of all
labour on the one hand, and the grossly materialistic conception of
civilization involved in measuring prosperity by quantity of mechanically-
wrought goods, upon the other hand' (1901b, p. 227); he could have added
to these names those of Adam Smith and John Stuart Mill.[14] Hobson
attributed such over-specialisation to the subordination of the interests of
the producer to the 'supposed' interests of the consumer as represented by
the 'fluctuating, irrational will ... [the] ill-ordered caprices and desires'
(1901b, p. 229) of the individual consumer. His proposed remedy was
social action representing 'the orderly will and true interest of society'
(1901b, p. 229), which would replace material wealth by social utility as
the goal of society, and thereby remove the pressure to produce which
generates over-specialisation.

However, Hobson recognised that labour would always involve toil for
many workers, leaving leisure as the only time during which they would
be able to express their individuality; leisure provides 'the opportunity of
opportunities' (1914, p. 236). Associating toil with 'mechanically-wrought
goods' in particular, and machine production in turn with monopoly or
wasteful oligopolistic competition, Hobson recommended state control or
ownership of such industries, and the leaving in private hands of those
industries which provide satisfying labour. He set out his vision as
follows:

> As the elements of steady common consumption grow in number, the
> common organisation of activity to supply them will grow and where
> the supply has at first been left to private enterprise, the abuse of power
> and growing inconveniences of competition will drive them into public
> industry. But since the very *raison d'être* of this increased social
> cohesiveness is to economise and enrich the individual life, and to
> enable the play of individual energy to assume higher forms out of
> which more individual satisfaction may accrue, more and more human
> effort will take shape in industries which will be left to individual ini-
> tiative and control, the arts in which the freedom of personal sponta-
> neity will find scope in the expression of physical or moral beauty and
> fitness and the attainment of intellectual truth.   (1894, pp. 382–3)

With respect to consumption, Hobson rejected the idea that individual
tastes and preferences provide a complete guide to the relationship
between consumption expenditure and social utility. He pointed out that
individual tastes and preferences are inevitably influenced by social

factors, notably by the occupation of the consumer. To discover the relationship between consumption expenditure and social utility, Hobson wrote, we need to know what the goods and services are, who will get the use of them, and how far the consumers are capable of getting the highest use out of them (1896b, p. 50).

First, Bentham had declared that 'prejudice apart, the game of push-pin is of equal value with the arts and sciences of music and poetry. If the game of push-pin furnish more pleasure, it is more valuable than either' (Bentham, 1825, p. 206).[15] Hobson rejected Bentham's view outright, arguing that some of the goods and services actually produced fall into Ruskin's category of 'illth', their consumption reducing rather than adding to social welfare; examples were 'adulterated foods, shoddy clothing, bad books, pernicious art, snobbish personal services' (1896b, p. 17). He implicitly admitted, however, that such judgements might change with changes in social opinion, the character of society being evolutionary.

Second, accepting the law of diminishing marginal utility, Hobson argued that the social utility of a given quantity of goods and services will depend on 'the nature and intensity' of the wants they satisfy. Thus if any portion of that quantity 'goes to satisfy the most real and urgent want, then it attains its maximum value in a given condition of society; if it goes otherwise, there is waste' (1896b, p. 19).

Third, it was Hobson's view that not everyone is able to make good use, let alone the highest use, of all the goods and services produced. He took as his example a painting, which should be reckoned as 'illth' if used by a vulgar plutocrat for ostentation, but may yield some small utility if hung 'in the public gallery of a money-ridden people, uneducated in the enjoyment of forms of beauty, their finer feelings blunted by coarse lives' (1896b, p. 19), and could yield utility which is infinitely great if such people were appropriately educated.[16]

2.3 DISTRIBUTION

The Pareto criterion, interpreted as requiring the losers in any redistribution of income to be actually compensated, as opposed to potentially compensatable, by the gainers, precludes the possibility of concluding that any distribution of income is better than the existing one. Given the impotence of modern welfare economics in this area, we may find some guidance from writings preceding those belonging to 'the new Anglo-American welfare economics', writings characterised by the belief that something could be said about the correlation between income distribution and social welfare. Hobson, like Marshall before him and Pigou after him, was one who preceded 'the new Anglo-American welfare economics'.

In Hobson's *Work and Wealth* reference is made to both production and consumption when it comes to the treatment of distribution. On the production side, there is the question of the distribution between individuals of the utility as well as the cost; on the consumption side, there is the question of the distribution between individuals of the cost as well as the utility.

The basis of Hobson's approach to distribution is the socialist prescription, 'from each according to his powers, to each according to his needs' (1893, p. 61); in the form 'from each according to his ability, to each according to his needs', this slogan was originated by Moses Hess in his radical youthful days, and made famous by Marx through the use of it in his *Critique of the Gotha Programme* (1875). As Cohen (1994, p. 11) points out, for Marx and his socialist predecessors 'contribution and benefit are separate matters'. Hobson, on the other hand, believed contribution depends on benefit; each would only contribute according to his powers, or ability, if society adopted as the 'rule of distribution, "Each man according to his needs"' (1901b, p. 161).

The term 'needs' was used by Hobson in a special sense. By a person's 'needs' he means what is required to enable him or her to contribute to production according to his/her powers.[17] Underlying this idea of payment according to 'needs' is Hobson's assumption, encapsulated in his phrase 'the economy of high wages', that up to a certain point labour productivity is positively correlated with the wage rate, an assumption which has recently re-emerged in 'efficiency wage' theories (see Yellen, 1984). These theories explain unemployment by the refusal of profit-maximising firms to lower the wage rate below that which minimises labour cost per unit of 'efficiency'; Hobson, on the other hand, used his assumption to argue that an increase in the wage rate would, up to a point, increase the level of output.

Employing the term 'natural' to mean 'necessary', Hobson drew the conclusion that 'all that portion of a product necessary to evoke the effort of producing it is, then, the natural property of the person who exerts the effort' (1901b, pp. 105–6). For only if each person's 'needs' are met will it be possible for all his or her powers to be utilised, making the maximum contribution to social utility.

Hobson went on to argue that where competition is present, an individual employer has no power to prevent the 'needs' of his/her employees being less than met, for if the employer raises the wages he/she pays above the industry norm he/she is likely to go out of business; 'so long as close competition prevails, the rate of wages and other conditions of labour ... are determined by the operations of economic laws over which the individual employer has no control' (1901b, p. 137).[18] Equally, if a person's 'needs', are more than met, for example because of an inheritance, his or her good fortune will be likely to lead him/her to contribute to production less than he/she is able, if indeed he/she contributes anything at all. Similarly, if people are paid according not to their 'needs' but to the effort they exert, some will be paid less than their 'needs', and some in excess of them.

While this idea of payment according to 'needs' thus has both individualist and socialist elements, Hobson rejected those prescriptions for distribution commonly put forward by individualists and by socialists. With respect to the former, he opposed the idea of payment according to what an individual produces, on the ground that when individuals jointly produce a product the separate productivity of each cannot be measured. He argued that the organism or organisation that is 'society has ... a natural claim upon property, on the ground that it is a maker of values of property' (1901b, p. 148), and for this reason no individual living in a society would have a natural right to the full value of everything he/she produced even if this amount could be calculated. As a first approximation, Hobson suggested, 'if we set Brown, Smith and Jones to work, first separately and then together, the difference in value between their added and their joint product might rank as the quantity of social value' (1901b, p. 147).[19] This grossly underestimates the quantity of social value, however, because the skill and knowledge used by each individual separately is itself a social product, and because the value of what each individual produces depends on demand, which would not exist in the absence of society. In the case of unimproved land, the fact that it has any value at all is entirely due to the existence of a society generating demand for it. Hobson regarded the income resulting from such value generation as the earnings of society, by contrast with those individualists who regard it as 'unearned', in the sense it is not earned by any individual. He further took the view that 'where all economic processes tend to the advantage of the strong and the disadvantage of the weak' (1901b, p. 204), some of the earnings of society should be used to support the weak, even though this raises the possibility that not all the rest will produce according to their powers; for 'the present cannot be wholly sacrificed to the chances of an ideal future' (1901b, p. 204). Nor should the recipients of such support feel degraded, for as members of society they have contributed to the earnings of society.

With respect to socialist prescriptions for distribution, Hobson rejected the idea of equality of income distribution on the ground that implementation of such a rule would result in many producing below their ability. He also rejected the idea that income should be distributed so as to ensure equality of opportunity, on the ground that there will always be some individuals who are less capable of achievement than others.

Hobson admitted that 'assuming that individuals press their selfish claims', one consequence of distributing income according to claimed 'needs' would be to reward the selfish more than the unselfish, but concluded with respect to these claims that 'it will be socially useful to admit them in order to evoke the best social service' (1901b, p. 171). Another consequence would be that those whose work was in itself unrewarding would receive higher incomes than those whose work was rewarding, though 'the greedy artist' would be an exception.

Hobson's contribution to the theory of distribution was not confined to its normative aspects. In the next chapter we look at his analysis of the manner in which output is actually distributed. First, however, we discuss the way in which Hobson made use of the various elements of his welfare economics in his analysis of social welfare.

2.4 SOCIAL WELFARE

In *Work and Wealth*, Hobson represents economic activity diagrammatically as generating human utility and incurring human cost on both the production side and the consumption side. Human utility is generated not only by consumption, which satisfies needs or offers 'abundance', but also by production, when it takes the form either of art and exercise or of 'labour', that is to say of satisfying work, as opposed to 'toil'. Human cost is incurred not only by production which takes the form either of 'toil' or of 'mal-production', the latter referring to work which is degrading, but also by consumption which involves either satiety or 'mal-consumption', the latter referring to such 'base' modes of consumption as the taking of drugs. The aggregate excess of human utility over human cost measures what Hobson in *Work and Wealth* called not 'social utility' (the term 'utility' now being put to another use) but 'organic welfare' or 'social welfare'.

This process of aggregation may alternatively start with the individual. While recognising the 'useful distinction of producer and consumer', Hobson argued that since everyone is both producer and consumer, we are ultimately obliged 'to value every act of production or consumption with regard to its aggregate effect upon the life and character of the agent' (1914, p. 14). The value of (say) a day's work to an individual is thus

equal to the net utility he/she believes him/herself to derive from consumption (including future consumption resulting from saving) minus the
net cost he/she believes him/herself to incur through working. To assess
the amount of 'real' value he/she receives, however, it is necessary to
adjust this amount by the differences between perceived and 'real' utility
and cost respectively, so as to arrive at human utility and human cost.
Before social welfare can be calculated, in turn, this amount must be
adjusted for each individual in such a way that the interests of society as a
whole are taken into account; only then can the aggregation process take
place.

But who is to carry out these calculations? It was perhaps in response
to the fact that he had been asked this question many times that Hobson
in 1926 provided a reply, in 'Economic Art and Human Welfare'. By
then, Hobson had arrived at a view on the method of economics which
was close to that of J. N. Keynes. Rather than following out 'all the
implications and indirect results of economic actions into non-economic
fields', he wrote, 'it may be far better that economists should confine their
explorations to what is recognized as the economic field, dealing with
activities and "goods" on a basis of current money valuation, with
perhaps some purely general speculative reflections bearing on the relations of economic and general welfare to the distribution of these activities and goods' (1926b, p. 472). While he believed this prescription of
separation between 'science' and 'art' to be applicable to the calculation
of what the individual members of a society desire, he saw it as so much
the more applicable to the calculation of what is socially desirable, a
calculation necessary if the concept of 'social welfare' is to have any
ethical significance.

If social welfare is to be calculated, a further problem which has to be
faced is the 'insistence of some economists in confining welfare to the distinctively individual consciousness' (1926b, p. 473). It is not necessary to
believe in the existence of a 'social mind', Hobson argued, to see that this
insistence is misguided, because

   the productive unit is not the individual worker but the factory or workshop, the consumptive unit not the wage-earner, but the family his wage
   supports. The group welfare on both sides of the economic fence is an
   organic complex so indissoluble that it must be studied as a whole, and
   not only through its individual constituents ... what they [individuals]
   think and feel cannot rightly be ascertained unless these group
   interactions in the processes of thinking and feeling are taken into
   consideration.   (1926b, p. 473)

These views on the art, as opposed to the science, of economics led Hobson to state that the problem of the art of economics

> has two related but distinguishable aspects, first, how to get a clear defensible conception of human welfare as "the desirable", secondly, how to make economic activities contribute their maximum to this end. (1926b, p. 474)

Hobson argued that the first task is not as impossible as it may seem, as

> men are much more alike than discrepant in their conception of welfare ... We can, therefore, hope to get a fair amount of common acceptance of the desirable even from people whose momentary desires are often refractory to such a standard.   (1926b, p. 475)

These latter, who recognise that their desires fall short of the desirable, 'in many matters of importance are willing to defer to the judgement of wiser or more expert persons' (1926b, p. 475). Hobson might have added that such deference is the more likely if in their search to define social welfare the 'expert persons' have the backing of a democratic process.

The second task, that of making economic activities contribute their maximum to social welfare, Hobson saw as being carried out by a government which adopted the maxim, 'from each according to his powers: to each according to his needs'. Such a government would have to obtain the consent of the governed, and full consent might be a long time in coming, particularly given what Hobson saw as the current existence of an anti-government bias. But there are situations in which such full consent to government based on this maxim has been demonstrated, for example in the case of a '"raft" economy or other vital emergency when everyone voluntarily does his best for the common salvation, and takes his rationed share of food and water' (1926b, p. 477), or of a national war economy.[20] Hobson concluded on the optimistic note that

> a welfare government which secured substantial fairness in the regulation of industry itself and in the distribution of its product, thus minimizing human costs and maximizing human satisfactions, would, by repressing the fears and anxieties that feed selfishness, and removing the causes of conflict which impede co-operation, liberate a sense of social service which, at any rate within the narrower areas of city or neighbourhood, would humanize the whole industrial movement. (1926b, p. 478)

In place of the 'mixture of greed and fear' (Cohen, 1994, p. 9) which motivates productive activity in a market society, Hobson looked forward to a society dominated by a sense of '"community", the anti-market principle according to which I serve you not because of what I can get out of doing so but because you need my service' (Cohen, 1994, p. 9).

3 Income Distribution and Prices[1]

The main features of Hobson's contributions to the interrelated theories of income distribution and prices are to be found in two articles published in 1891 in the *Quarterly Journal of Economics*, namely 'The Law of the Three Rents' and 'The Element of Monopoly in Prices'. These articles, together with 'The Economics of Bargaining' (1899), provide the basis of *The Economics of Distribution*. Before examining the arguments developed in these works, however, we look briefly at Hobson's explanation of changes in the distribution of income between occupational categories.

In the new and revised edition of *The Evolution of Modern Capitalism* (1906a) Hobson added a chapter entitled 'Occupations of the People', in which he cited figures for England and Wales, the United States, France, Germany, Austria and Sweden showing common increases over the previous two or three decades in the relative importance of 'dealers' compared with 'makers', as measured by the proportion of total employment for which they accounted; 'dealers' are defined as comprising all employees not involved in the physical making of goods. He explained this change as being caused by the fact that when 'the general standard of consumption for the great mass of the people has reached a point where the more urgent needs of food, clothing, housing are satisfied, all further rises in the standard represent a larger proportion of demand for recreation, professional services and other immaterial forms of wealth' (1906a, p. 398). This trend, labelled by Caselli and Pastrello (1987) 'a Hobsonian suggestion', was to continue for the rest of the twentieth century.[2]

3.1 INCOME DISTRIBUTION

In the first edition of his *Principles*, Marshall explained the return to labour in terms of its supply (which he saw as varying directly with the real wage rate) and its marginal net product, and similarly the return to capital in terms of its supply (which he saw as varying directly with the rate of interest) and its marginal net product.[3] The return to land, on the other hand, he believed to be explained by the Ricardian theory of rent.

Hobson and J. B. Clark, in articles published in the April issue of the *Quarterly Journal of Economics* in 1891, each in his own way extended the Ricardian theory of rent so as to make it equally applicable to all three factors of production.[4]

This was Hobson's most original contribution to economics, and it provided the basis for his theory of income distribution.[5] In brief, Hobson's theory divides the income received by the owner of a factor of production into three parts: reward for effort or sacrifice; monopoly rent (renamed in *The Economics of Distribution* 'marginal rent', perhaps to highlight the fact that it is rent paid at the margin); and differential rent. We examine each of these parts in turn.

Where there is free competition, Hobson argued, factors of production are paid according to the quantity of human effort or sacrifice they embody. Applied to labour, this proposition excludes the possibility of payments being made for skill that is unrelated to effort; but such payments are, in fact, made. Hobson's response to this gap between theory and practice was to argue that 'if any society were to establish free education in every grade [of labour], with special bounties for the encouragement of professional training, it might rapidly come to pass, assuming competition in the professions and the right to undersell, that professional wages would fall to the level of common day labor' (1891c, p. 6).[6] Under these circumstances the supply price of all grades of labour would be the minimum wage required to maintain the work force at its existing size. Extending the argument to land and capital, Hobson concluded that the 'effort or sacrifice' incomes of land, capital and labour are respectively a negligible rent (that is to say, a rent close to zero), interest paid at the minimum rate required for the maintenance of the capital stock (say three per cent, to induce sufficient saving out of the gross product), and wages paid at the minimum rate already described (say fifteen shillings per week).[7,8]

Hobson's 'grades' of factors of production correspond to what J. E. Cairnes, in the case of labour, called 'non-competing industrial groups'.[9] The way Hobson put it was that lack of competition between factor grades means that at any one time the relationship between the social demand for a specific grade and its current supply may be such as to cause the factor to receive an income in excess of the minimum required. He referred to this part of income as 'monopoly rent', on the ground that if there were really free competition in factor markets, such payments would not be necessary. Examples provided by Hobson of specific grades which typically receive monopoly rent include the following: land used to grow hops (as opposed, say, to wheat) and city building land; capital enjoying some kind of advantage, such as that used in an increasing returns industry and that receiving government aid; and skilled labour, such as that provided by masons and surgeons. In the case of labour, this argument is deficient in that it assumes zero training costs, making no allowance for the possibility that fifteen shillings per week might be insufficient to ensure the maintenance of *skilled* labour from one generation to the next.

We illustrate Hobson's argument by a simple diagram which can be applied not only to labour, but also to land or capital. In Figure 3.1, while the demand for (say) masons is represented in the conventional way by a demand schedule which slopes downward to the right, the supply is represented by a vertical line which cuts the demand schedule at a point above the minimum wage line; the supply schedule does not extend below the minimum wage line, because masons would then turn to unskilled labouring instead.[10] Masons are paid more than the minimum wage because if they were paid only the minimum wage the demand for them would exceed the supply. The rent element in the wage paid to a mason is represented by w^*w_m, and the total rents paid to masons are $(w^*w_m)(On^*)$.

This diagram can also be used to illustrate a point implicit in the analysis, and made explicit by Hobson in later writings. This is that masons could be taxed up to an amount $(w^*w_m)(On^*)$ without there being any reduction in the supply of masons. Thus rent is not only income unrelated to effort or sacrifice, attributable solely to a shortage of supply; it is also income that can be withdrawn without any effect on the supply of the

Figure 3.1   Wage determination for a grade of labour

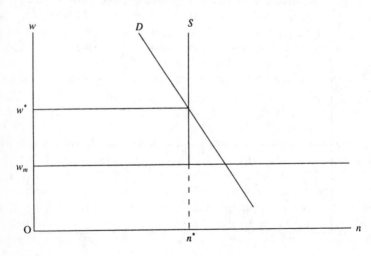

factor of production to whose owner it is paid. In Hobson's words, rental
payments

> are necessary payments, or expenses of production, in so much as the
> owners of factors of production for whose use they are paid can extort
> them from those who need these factors. They are unnecessary pay-
> ments in the sense that if any change in economic circumstances caused
> them to be withheld, this withholding would not cause their owners to
> refuse the use of them.
>   They are also unnecessary in the sense that, after they have been paid,
> they can be taken in taxation without any disturbance of the industrial
> use of the factor of which they rank as surplus payment.   (1909b,
> p. 111)

The size of the monopoly rents paid to each factor grade changes over
time, with changes in the forces of supply and demand. Hobson believed,
however, that in general such rents would continue to be paid to all but
'the roughest, commonest, and most unspecialized forms of land, capital,
and labor' (1891b, p. 275). Figure 3.2 illustrates this. Here the demand
and supply schedules for masons fall within the ranges $D_1 - D_2$ and $S_1 - S_2$
respectively, causing the wage paid to a mason to lie between w_1, when
supply and demand schedules S_1 and D_1 result in equilibrium at point A,
and w_2, when supply and demand schedules S_2 and D_2 result in equilibrium

Figure 3.2   Range of wages for a grade of labour

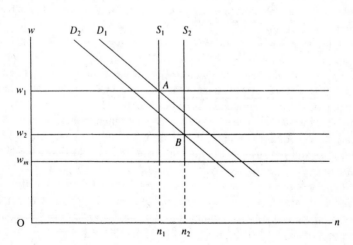

at point *B*. Under these circumstances, no matter where the wage paid to a mason falls, it will continue to incorporate a monopoly element.

The third part of income, according to Hobson's theory, consists of differential rents received by individual elements belonging to a factor grade; Hobson distinguished such differential rents from monopoly rents paid to all owners of a factor grade. Differential rents arise wherever individual elements of a factor grade are heterogeneous with respect to productivity; for example, masons may be good, bad or indifferent. It was in this context that Hobson generalised the Ricardian theory of rent.

David Ricardo is commonly said to have put forward a 'differential' theory of rent. The adjective is, however, ambiguous, in that it has been applied to each of the two fundamentally different, though interconnected, cases of rent generation that Ricardo described.[11] It sometimes refers to the case of extending the 'extensive margin', where land of inferior quality is brought into cultivation, resulting in additional rent on all intra-marginal pieces of land because of their 'different' (higher) quality. Alternatively, it has been used to refer to the case of extending the 'intensive margin', where the application of extra fixed-proportion doses of homogeneous labour and capital to a fixed quantity of land will at some point bring diminishing returns, yielding a 'differential' on the intra-marginal doses due to the law of diminishing returns; in this case no differences of factor quality are involved.

Hobson built on Ricardo's discussion of the interconnection between extending the intensive margin in the cultivation of land and extending the extensive margin.[12] Making explicit reference to 'the law of diminishing returns', he followed Ricardo in arguing that the application of extra doses of homogeneous labour or capital to a fixed quantity of land will at some point result in an additional return that is less than cost.[13] At this point, while it will not be profitable to add an extra dose of labour or capital, it may still be profitable to bring inferior land into cultivation. But Hobson contended also that exactly the same argument applies if the quantity of either capital or labour is held fixed. If the quantity of capital is held fixed, the application of extra doses of homogeneous labour will at some point result in an additional return that is less than cost, at which point, while it will not be profitable to add an extra dose of labour, it may still be profitable to bring inferior capital into use. If the quantity of labour is held fixed, the application of extra doses of homogeneous capital will at some point result in an additional return that is less than cost, at which point, while it will not be profitable to add an extra dose of capital, it may still be profitable to employ inferior labour instead. The argument applies equally to cases in which fixed quantities of capital or labour have extra doses of land applied to them.

According to the Ricardian theory, in the case of land the extensive margin will be extended until wages and profits are just covered by the price received for the product, leaving nothing for rent. Hobson contended that a comparable argument applies in the cases of capital and labour. In the case of capital, the extensive margin will be extended until the price received for the product exceeds rent and wages by some minimum (maintenance) return on capital, say three per cent, necessary to compensate for the sacrifice or effort involved in saving and investing. In the case of labour, the extensive margin will be extended until the price received for the product exceeds rent and profits by some minimum wage, say fifteen shillings per week.

Hobson's generalisation of Ricardo's concept of rent led him to the conclusion that rent is paid not only on intra-marginal land, but also on intra-marginal capital (that is to say, capital on which the return is more than three per cent) and on intra-marginal labour (that is to say, labour that receives a wage of more than fifteen shillings per week). Intra-marginal capital consists of capital which has an advantage because of its large size or which is given superiority by its 'monopolic [*sic*] character of employment, or other advantages natural or conventional' (1891b, p. 267); intra-marginal labour consists of labour that has an advantage because of innate properties such as strength or skill, or 'opportunities partaking of a monopolic character' (1891b, p. 268). An intra-marginal element of a factor other than the roughest, commonest and most unspecialised will thus receive income made up of three components: reward for effort or sacrifice (in the case of labour and capital, the minimum required to maintain the existing stock of the factor), monopoly rent, and differential rent.

His analysis of the role of differential rent in income distribution led Hobson to the conclusion that the degree of heterogeneity of each factor of production relative to the others plays a crucial role in the distribution of income. Hobson took as a simple example the case in which an increase in the product being distributed requires an equi-proportionate addition to the quantities of land, capital and labour employed. If the additional units of land, capital and labour employed are inferior in equal proportion to the last units employed, each factor will receive the same proportionate increase in rent, and the additional product will be distributed in the same proportion as the total product was previously. On the other hand, if the additional units of (say) land and labour employed are very little inferior to the last units employed, but the additional units of capital employed are vastly inferior to the last unit employed, almost all the additional rent will go to capital, which will therefore increase its share of the total product. A comparable argument applies if it is the additional units of land or of labour employed which are vastly inferior to the last unit employed.[14]

Hobson was fully aware that this example has its limitations. He admitted that it needs to be extended to cover the case in which an increase in the product being distributed requires use of factors in different proportions from those which currently exist, because, in this case, even if the additional units of land, labour and capital employed are inferior in equal proportion to the last units employed, there is no presumption that each factor will receive the same proportionate increase in rent. He further noted that these two determinants of the distribution of the additional product may interact with each other, the factor proportions actually used depending on the degree of heterogeneity of each factor relative to the others.[15]

3.2 PRICES

In 1890 the dominant theory of prices was that which had been outlined in 1879 in *The Economics of Industry* (jointly written by Alfred and Mary Paley Marshall) and fleshed out in the first edition of Marshall's *Principles*. This theory states that, in general, the price of a commodity is jointly determined by 'the law of supply' (its supply function) and 'the law of demand' (its demand function). One qualification that Marshall made to this theory, a minor concession to classical thinking, was that in the case of a commodity produced under conditions of constant unit cost, a person 'may be excused for ignoring the influence of demand, and speaking of (normal) price as governed by cost of production – provided only he does not claim scientific accuracy for the wording of his doctrine, and explains the influence of demand in its right place' (Marshall, 1890–1920, vol. I, p. 349). Hobson's theory of prices makes use of both these elements of the Marshallian theory. His theory states that, in general, the price of a commodity exceeds its cost of production to an extent determined by monopoly elements associated with the forces of both supply and demand. Some of these monopoly elements are involved in the process of production, and some in the process of exchange. We begin with the former.

Ricardo drew from his theory of rent the conclusion that, wage and profit rates being uniform, and rent being zero on the marginal piece of land, rent has no influence on the unit price of agricultural produce. Hobson pointed out that once the concept of rent is applied to all factors of production, it appears to follow that neither rent, nor profits (in excess of three per cent), nor wages (in excess of fifteen shillings) has any influence on unit price, a conclusion that is contradicted by commonsense.

Hobson resolved this contradiction between his theory and the facts by pointing out that:

> The simple statement of the law of rent, though equally applicable to all three requisites, only applies to those industries which use the roughest, commonest, and most unspecialized forms of land, capital, and labor. In proportion as specialization of requirements comes in so as to limit competition, the payment at the margin of employment is no longer zero, 3 per cent., and 15s.   (1891b, p. 275)

Thus, if all payments in excess of these basic amounts are included in rent, it follows that wherever there is any 'specialization of requirements' rent does influence price. Hobson's way of putting this was to say that in this case what he called the 'expenses of production', which is the price at which a product will sell when there is perfect competition in the commodity market, will exceed the cost of production.

This is one of the few of his arguments which Hobson himself illustrated diagrammatically.[16] In Figures 3.3 and 3.4, which represent the cases of 'unspecialised' and 'specialised' employment respectively, we use most of the elements of Hobson's two diagrams. In Figure 3.3 the point E on the horizontal axis (OQ) represents the combination of the

Figure 3.3   Price with 'unspecialised' employment

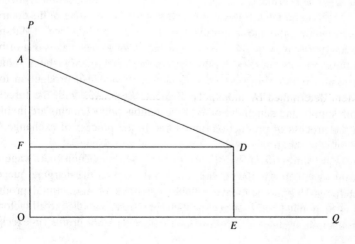

J. A. Hobson

Figure 3.4   Price with 'specialised' employment

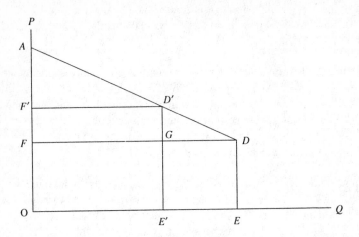

number of units of land (say, *x*), units of capital (say, *y*) and units of labour (say, *z*), each of the roughest, commonest and most unspecialised grade required to produce a commodity. The point *F* on the vertical axis (*OP*) represents the cost of production of the commodity, the factors being assumed to be remunerated at the rate of zero rent on land, 3 per cent interest on capital, and 15 shillings wage per week. *ED*, equal to *OF*, represents both cost of production and price. Intra-marginal units of land, capital and labour, being more productive than marginal units, generate rents which are represented in total by the triangle *ADF*. These rents do not enter into price.

In Figure 3.4 the point *E'* on the horizontal axis represents the same quantities of land, capital and labour as point *E* does, but with each factor belonging to a grade one higher than the lowest, resulting in the production of another commodity; the horizontal axis thus measures the *quality* of the factor combination *x*, *y* and *z*, varying inversely with the distance from the origin. The point *F'* on the vertical axis represents the 'expenses of production' of this second commodity, the factors being assumed to be remunerated, following Hobson, at the rate of 20 shillings per acre rent, 4 per cent interest on capital, and 25 shillings wage per week. *E'D'*, equal to *OF'*, represents price, which in this case is determined not by cost of production but by expenses of production. Rents generated by intra-marginal factor units are represented in total by *AD'F'*.

The quantities of factors of production being the same, the cost of production in this case of 'specialised' employment will be the same as in the case of 'unspecialised' employment, and can be represented by $E'G$, equal to OF. Hobson concluded that '$D'G$ represents the advantage possessed by the owner of the worst forms of specialized land, capital, and labor in full commercial use' (1891b, p. 277), and that the area $D'GFF'$ 'measures the portion [of the product] which falls to classes owning some specialized requisite of production, some special quality of land, some special opportunity of investment of capital, some specific skill in labor-power, as distinct from the individual gain which falls to the superior competitors within these classes' (1891b, pp. 277–8). By contrast with the individual rents received by 'superior competitors', the monopoly rents represented by $D'GFF'$ do influence price.

We turn now from monopoly elements involved in the process of production to those involved in the process of exchange. In his *Principles*, Marshall wrote that 'in a later volume a study will be made of the Protean shapes of modern trade combinations and monopolies, some of the most important of which, as for example "Trusts", are of very recent growth' (Marshall, 1890–1920, vol. I, p. 477). By contrast, having already briefly discussed the growth of trusts in *Problems of Poverty*, Hobson devoted two of the fourteen chapters in the first edition of *Evolution of Modern Capitalism* to an analysis of industries that are imperfectly competitive; he was probably the first to provide such an analysis, at least in Britain. He argued that the origin of such industries lies in the fact that, as capitalism develops, the customs that formerly restrained competition decay, and the intensity of competition increases. As a consequence, firms attempt to mitigate the severity of the struggle facing them by making arrangements which in the 1906 edition of *Evolution of Modern Capitalism* Hobson described as 'primarily directed to restrain underselling by fixing price-lists, and when necessary and feasible, by regulating output: firms do not cease to compete, but endeavour to limit the terms of their competition' (1906a, p. 169). These arrangements will be the more successful the fewer and bigger the number of firms making up the industry, though a necessary condition for success is that the market not be 'overstocked'.

Hobson went on to describe how once it became clear that in spite of the use of various methods of enforcement these arrangements typically did not survive long, cartels and trusts emerged. A cartel reinforces a minimum price agreement by assigning a set proportion of total output to each of its members. A trust involves shareholders in the participating companies handing over their voting rights to a body of trustees, on the understanding that they will pursue an agreed policy, the advantage to shareholders being that, compared with its individual members, the trust will have more power, and in some cases, monopoly power. As Hobson

put it, 'these powers of monopoly may be placed under four heads in relation to the classes upon whose interests they operate – (a) business firms
engaged in an earlier or later process of production; (b) actual and
potential competitors or business rivals; (c) employees of the Trust or
other monopoly; (d) the consuming public' (1894, p. 143).

Subsequent to the publication of the first edition of *Evolution of Modern
Capitalism*, Hobson developed a formal analysis of exchange involving a
relatively small number of buyers as well as sellers; the example he used
was that of a horse market in which there are ten buyers and eight sellers.[17]
Following a line of argument first advanced by Carl Menger, Hobson
assumed that individual buyers and sellers go to the market with price
limits such that there will be excess supply at any price in excess of £21
and 10 shillings and excess demand at any price below £21, these being
the prices above and below which, respectively, the keenest unsuccessful
seller is prepared to sell and the keenest unsuccessful buyer is prepared to
buy.[18] However, within these limits, neither the last successful buyer nor
the last successful seller faces any competition, and the actual price will be
determined by their relative bargaining strengths; as Hobson put it, 'competition stakes out a ring within which bargainers fight it out by force and
craft' (1899, pp. 29–30). Depending on the price agreed upon, either
buyers as a group or sellers as a group, or both, will make what Hobson
labelled a 'forced gain', made possible by the absence of competition
when only a single potentially successful buyer and a single potentially
successful seller remain in the market. Hobson saw this as a further
monopoly element in price determination, applying as much to the case in
which the entire forced gain goes to the buyers as to that in which it goes
to the sellers. He accepted that forced gain virtually disappears when there
are many buyers and sellers, provided that buyers and sellers are well-
informed and that the commodity concerned is minutely divisible, adding,
however, that the restricted locality of the market makes this unlikely
where goods are perishable. But on the ground that most of 'these conditions are notoriously absent in the great majority of cases' (1899, p. 40),
Hobson concluded that his theory of prices was generally applicable, and
that competitively determined prices should be regarded as no more than a
special case, one in which forced gain is reduced almost to zero.

3.3   PRODUCTIVE AND UNPRODUCTIVE SURPLUS

Forced gains received by a seller make up a fourth part of his income, in
addition to maintenance, monopoly rent, and differential rent; when

received by a buyer, they can similarly be regarded as adding to his/her real income. In his 1891 *Quarterly Journal of Economics* articles, Hobson referred to the various payments to factors of production that are un-related to effort or sacrifice, and that can be withdrawn without affecting factor supply, as rent; subsequently, in *The Social Problem* for example, he often used instead the term 'unearned income'. Forced gains resulting from the bargaining process were regarded by Hobson as part of unearned income.[19] Unearned income also includes monopoly rent. With respect to differential rent, Hobson came to admit that 'so far as a differential wage is really a wage of superior skill or productivity, and not a scarcity wage maintained by some artificial ordering of the market, it appears to stand on a different footing from other differential rents with regard to the power to resist taxation' (1900a, pp. 327–8), because unless his/her skill or productivity is rewarded at a rate above subsistence, the labourer may not be willing to supply it. The excess of such a differential wage over a maintenance wage should be seen not as entirely composed of rent, but as including a return on superior skill and productivity resulting from train-ing; as Hobson subsequently stated explicitly, 'to some extent the higher standards of professional incomes may rightly be accounted minimum interest upon capital expended in general and professional education and on the subsidies needed for these non-productive years' (1919b, pp. 38–9). With this proviso, Hobson also included differential rent in unearned income.

Following the example set in Patten's *Annals* article (see Chapter 2), Hobson used the term 'surplus' instead of 'rent' as early as 1893.[20] Given the arguments of Hobson's 1891 *Quarterly Journal of Economics* articles, the conclusions that Patten reached on the opportunity cost, in terms of time to enjoy consumption, of a longer working day must have been music to Hobson's ears; they were that 'if there is a surplus at the margin of pro-duction, a part of the surplus is distributed, not by a law of cost, but by the law of monopoly' (Patten, 1893, p. 427), and that any taxation should in the first instance be directed at such a surplus. Hobson too took the view that taxation should be directed at the surplus.

Initially, Hobson believed that the entire surplus in the economy could be taxed. In *The Industrial System* and in *The Science of Wealth*, however, he modified his earlier analysis to allow for the fact that merely paying maintenance to factors of production does not allow for economic growth. This led him to distinguish between two kinds of income in excess of maintenance, namely what he termed the 'productive surplus', which is that part of the unearned income required to meet the cost of growth, and the 'unproductive surplus', categorised by Hobson as waste.

Of the three kinds of income, *maintenance*, labelled by Hobson category A, includes a minimum wage, whatever is necessary to ensure upkeep of capital and land, and 'a provision for the upkeep of the public services which the State renders to industry' (1911a, p. 86). The *productive surplus*, category B, includes additional payments to labour so that an increased quantity and quality may be evoked, interest payments at a rate sufficient to attract the extra capital which the additional labour requires, and increased payments to the state so as to allow for an increase in the size and efficiency of the services it provides. The *unproductive surplus*, category C, includes all economic rents, interest payments in excess of those which fall within category B, and 'all profits, salaries, or other payments for ability or labour in excess of what is economically necessary to evoke the sufficient use of these factors' (1909b, p. 80). Hobson now believed that it was only category C payments, comprising the unproductive surplus, that should be taxed.

Much of what Hobson had to say about taxation is to be found in *Taxation in the New State* (1919b), where the term 'surplus' is substituted for 'unproductive surplus', Hobson laid it down as a general rule that taxation should not interfere with any 'essential or useful' process of production or element of consumption (1919b, p. 10). With respect to a tax interfering with processes of production, he added that, in time, a tax of this kind would cause such a rise in the price of the factor of production 'as would defeat the attempt to tax it, by enabling it to shift the taxation on to those who bought these productive services, or the products they turned out' (1919b, p. 42). With respect to a tax interfering with elements of consumption, he concluded that 'consumers with "surplus" income alone can pay, and they pay out of this surplus' (1919b, p. 52). He recognised that this created a problem in the case of 'ordinary luxuries', such as alcohol and tobacco bought by the lower-paid grades of workers, who (experience shows) often continue to buy them in the same quantity when the tax on them is increased. His response was to argue that any such 'taxes they pay must normally be held either to encroach on their truly necessary expenditure, or to be shifted on to some other incomes, *e.g.* those of their employers, through their insistence upon money wages high enough to support these "luxuries"' (1919b, p. 60). His general conclusion was that 'all taxation should be directly laid upon surplus, because if any taxation is put on "costs", the process of shifting it on to "surplus", first, involves waste and damage to production and is frequently made a source of extortion from consumers; secondly, deceives the public by concealing the final incidence' (1919b, p. 65). The only exception he allowed was taxation 'allowances or exemptions in respect of such portions of the income of a business as was "put back" into the business' (1919b, p. 74).

From 1907 the British tax system had distinguished between ('earned') income received in return for labour, and other ('unearned') income, imposing a higher tax rate on the latter than on the former. Arguing that surplus income may be received by providers of labour, and that not all 'unearned' income (interest payments, for example) is surplus income, Hobson recommended that this tax system be abolished, and replaced by a single graduated income tax in which allowance is made solely for 'the needs of family efficiency' (1919b, p. 102).[21] As Hobson had maintained since 1901, 'the practical basis of sound taxation is found in the presumption that the proportionate taxable capacity of family incomes varies directly with their size, *i.e.* the larger the income, the larger the proportion of taxable surplus it contains' (1919b, p. 235). Since, in practice, some income would inevitably escape taxation, the income tax should be supplemented by death duties, whose disincentive effects Hobson saw as negligible; death duties would have the additional advantage of decreasing the rate of income tax required to finance government expenditure, thereby reducing any disincentive effects associated with income tax.[22]

Summarising in *The Science of Wealth* the conclusions he had drawn from his categorisation of incomes, Hobson ranked categories of income on a spectrum ranging from 'harmony' to 'discord'. As he put it:

> So far as costs of maintenance for the various factors of production was concerned, we recognized that the industrial system worked almost automatically and accurately. With regard to costs of growth, though there was an ultimate harmony of interests between the factors, present considerations of gain caused discords to arise, a scarcer and therefore stronger factor encroaching upon the fund needed for the growth of some other factor, and taking for itself some surplus gain. The needs and claims of the State, we also saw, were liable to similar depredations on the part of a powerful factor of production. (1911a, p. 252)

Seeing 'the emergence of "unproductive surplus"' (1911a, p. 82) as the source of conflict in an economy, Hobson drew the conclusion that the 'absorption and social utilization of the whole surplus, by converting the unproductive surplus into a productive service for labour and the State, would secure for industry as a whole a harmony resembling that which prevails in a well-ordered business' (1911a, p. 253).[23]

Hobson also believed the unproductive surplus to be the principal cause of underconsumption, as we shall see in the next chapter.[24] First, however, we examine Hobson's criticisms of alternative distribution theories.

3.4   CRITIQUE OF ALTERNATIVE DISTRIBUTION THEORIES

Two kinds of distribution theory alternative to his own were subjected to criticism by Hobson. One was what he called the 'residuary legatee' approach, and the other was the marginal productivity theory exemplified in the writings of J. B. Clark.

Hobson believed that his own analysis of income distribution 'completely destroys what may be termed the "residuary legatee" treatment of distribution ... [which] consists in taking the aggregate product, the object of distribution, showing that two of the three claimants (land, capital and labor) are entitled to a fixed minimum charge upon the product, and thus placing the third claimant in the position of residual claimant to whatever remains' (1891b, p. 279). Marx's theory leads to the conclusion that capital is the residual claimant; Henry George's theory to the conclusion that land is the residual claimant; and Francis Amassa Walker's theory to the conclusion that labour is the residual claimant. Hobson contended that all these theories involve the fallacious method of selecting two of the three claimants, arguing that they impose fixed charges on production, and concluding that the remaining claimant receives the residue.[25] By contrast, the 'law of the three rents' showed 'that three proportionate charges exhaust the whole product' (1891b, p. 280).[26]

Hobson engaged in a more extensive criticism of the marginal productivity theory, according to which the return to each factor is determined by its marginal product. He criticised this theory on five grounds: first, that the marginal product of a particular factor cannot be disentangled from the product as a whole; second, that there is no general tendency to perfect competition; third, that economies are never in a state of general equilibrium; fourth, that to explain distribution, supply as well as demand considerations must be taken into account; and fifth, that the assumption of constant returns to scale which the theory requires does not apply in practice.

A succinct summary of the first three of these objections to the marginal productivity theory is to be found in *Work and Wealth*, where they are set out as follows:

Very few sorts of real capital or labour approach the ideal of infinite divisibility which marginalism requires. An individual worker, sometimes a group, is usually the minimal 'drop' of labour, and capital is only infinitely divisible when it is expressed in terms of money, instead of plants, machines or other concrete terms. Still less is it the case that capital or labour flows or 'tends' to flow with perfect accuracy and liberty of movement into every channel of employment where it is required, so as to afford equality of remuneration at the several margins. Lastly, in most industrial societies the constant changes taking place, in volume and in methods of industry, entail a corresponding diversity in the productivity and the remuneration of the capital and labour employed in the various industries 'at the margin'.   (1914, p. 174)

We shall examine each of these criticisms in turn.

Supplementing the analysis in 'The Law of the Three Rents' and 'The Element of Monopoly in Prices', Hobson argued in *The Economics of Distribution* that withdrawal of a unit of a factor of production reduces the productivity both of the remaining units of that factor of production, and of the other factors of production with which it was combined previously. It follows from this that the separate contribution of the last unit of a factor cannot be calculated, and hence neither can the amount of the residual accruing as rent to the fixed factor(s). Hobson concluded 'that the application of the Law of Rent to the intensive cultivation of a single factor must be rejected as fallacious' (1900a, p. 148), as must the marginal productivity theory.

Hobson made several unsuccessful attempts to illustrate this criticism of the marginal productivity theory by an example; Marshall was correct in stating in the sixth edition of his *Principles* (1910), with reference to a table in *The Industrial System* (1909b, p. 110) used by Hobson for this purpose, that 'the numbers chosen are inappropriate to the hypothesis which he criticises' (Marshall, 1890–1920, vol. I, pp. 516–17, note b; and vol. II, p. 558); this is because, in Hobson's example, where increasing returns occur initially, average and marginal product are equal at a point between the employment of four men and of five.[27] But an appropriate example can be devised, as the following paragraphs show.

We assume throughout a constant returns to scale production function such that 1 unit of labour combined with 1 unit of capital results in 12 units of product. Suppose, in a neoclassical scenario, that the application of labour to 4 units of capital results in an addition to the product given by $(20 - 4x)$, and that the application of capital to 4 units of labour results in an addition to the product given by $(16 - 2x)$; in each case x represents the quantity of the variable factor applied. The resulting marginal products are set out in Table 3.1.

Table 3.1   A neoclassical scenario

Number of labourers	MP_L with 4 units of capital	Number of units of capital	MP_K with 4 labourers
1	16	1	14
2	12	2	12
3	8	3	10
4	4	4	8
5	0	5	6

Suppose also that the wage rate is 4 units of product. Since profit maximisation dictates that the marginal product equals the wage rate, the quantity of labour employed will in this case be 4, and the consequent total product will be 48, of which 16 will be distributed to labour.[28] The total product of 48 will be exhausted if it is also the case that the cost per unit of capital is 8, as profit maximisation dictates that the quantity of capital employed will then be 4, resulting in the distribution to capital of the remaining 32 units of product.[29]

Alternatively, let us suppose, in a classical scenario, that it is possible to increase the product only by increasing labour and capital at unit intervals in the fixed proportions of one to one; given the assumed production function, output will in this case equal min.($12L$, $12K$), where L and K stand for the number of units of labour and capital respectively. Some resulting input–output relationships are set out in Table 3.2.

Suppose, as before, that 4 units of labour and 4 units of capital are used to produce an output of 48. In this case withdrawal of 1 of 4 units of labour by itself will reduce the total product by 12 units, as will with-

Table 3.2   A classical scenario

Labourers	Units of capital	Output
1	1	12
2	2	24
3	3	36
4	3	36
3	4	36
4	4	48

drawal of 1 of 4 units of capital by itself; but simultaneous withdrawal of 1 of 4 units of labour and 1 of 4 units of capital will reduce the total product not by 24 units, but only by 12. Note also that if 3 units of labour and 3 units of capital are employed it would not be profitable to increase the employment of either factor of production by itself, even if the factor were available free of charge, since output would not increase as a result.

The marginal productivity theory is clearly inapplicable to this case. When a factor is increased by 1 unit, its marginal product is zero, and the marginal productivity theory thus requires that none of the total product of 48 is distributed. When it is reduced by 1 unit, its marginal product is 12, and the marginal productivity theory thus requires a total payment to factors of 96 out of a total product of 48.

Hobson was concerned with a third case, lying in between continuously variable factor proportions and perfectly fixed proportions, namely that of factors with limited divisibility. Table 3.3 illustrates a Hobsonian scenario. Suppose that withdrawal of 1 of 4 units of labour by itself reduces the total product by more than 4 but less than 12, say by 8; and that withdrawal of 1 of 4 units of capital by itself reduces the total product by more than 8 but less than 12, say by 10. The withdrawal of these 2 units simultaneously, however, would reduce the total product not by 18 units but only by 12.[30,31] Note also that, in this case, if 3 units of labour and 3 units of capital are employed, it would be profitable to increase the employment of labour by itself by 1 unit only if the cost were less than 2 units of product, and to increase the employment of capital by itself by 1 unit only if the cost were less than 4 units of product. The marginal productivity theory is inapplicable to this case also; for example, withdrawal of 1 of 4 units of labour yields a marginal product of labour of 8, and withdrawal of 1 of 4 units of capital yields a marginal product of capital of 10, so the

Table 3.3   A Hobsonian scenario

Labourers	Units of capital	Output
1	1	12
2	2	24
3	3	36
3	4	40
4	3	38
4	4	48

marginal productivity theory would require a total payment to factors of $[(4 \times 8) + (4 \times 10)]$, that is, 72, out of a total output of 48.

Hobson's way of putting the argument was that assigning a separate productivity to individual factors 'confuses mechanical composition with organic coöperation' (1900a, p. 147), and that the 'root-fallacy of the "dose" illustration consists, then, in a false separation which ignores the organic nature of production' (1900a, pp. 147–8).[32] In modern terms, Hobson was rejecting the assumption of the possibility of continuous variátion in the proportions in which factors of production are employed. As the 'Hobsonian scenario' example illustrates, if output is distributed according to marginal product, the total product will be exactly exhausted only in those cases where factor proportions are continuously variable. Hobson's denial that such cases are common in real life thus gave him a powerful weapon with which to attack the marginal productivity theory.

Hobson reserved some of his most scathing criticisms of neoclassical economics for those, notably J. B. Clark and Philip Wicksteed, who interpreted their conclusion that what each factor receives is determined by its marginal product as implying that in a capitalist economy everyone gets what he creates, or gets what he is worth.[33] He characterised such writers as defending the *status quo* by using an indefensible argument. He claimed that the argument was indefensible because of the impossibility of attributing any particular part of a product to any particular factor of production.[34]

The second and third criticisms of the marginal productivity theory listed in the passage from *Work and Wealth* quoted above, though no less important, are more straightforward. As Wicksell (1902) demonstrated, perfect competition and a state of general equilibrium are necessary assumptions of the marginal productivity theory of product exhaustion. Hobson was among those who pointed out that actual economies are neither perfectly competitive nor in a perpetual state of general equilibrium. The implications for the marginal productivity theory are serious, since, if these conditions are not satisfied, the proof that distribution according to marginal product exactly exhausts the total product falls to the ground.

A fourth criticism of marginal productivity theory is voiced in *The Industrial System*. Here Hobson argued that:

The price per unit of each sort of industrial power is 'caused' or 'brought about' by a variety of forces of demand and of supply, in which the marginal factors play no appreciable part. How can they? How is it possible to say that the five-unit acres, men and machines, 'determine' in the way of *causing* the price of a unit to be so much, when we perceive that the price of the unit has directly caused these five-unit factors, and not four-unit or six-unit factors, to be marginal? It is far more accurate to say that the price per unit causes the margin to be where it is, than to attribute any causative power to the margin, as margin, in relation to the price per unit. (1909b, p. 102, emphasis in the original)

In other words, like Marshall in his *Principles*, Hobson saw the marginal productivity theory as explaining not distribution, but factor employment once distribution has been otherwise determined. To explain distribution in the first place, supply as well as demand considerations had to be taken into account.[35]

Hobson's fifth criticism of the marginal productivity theory turns on its requirement, acknowledged by Wicksteed (1894) and demonstrated by Flux (1894), that there be constant returns to scale.[36] This criticism was set out by Hobson as follows:

Professor Pigou (*Wealth and Welfare*, p. 176), though adopting the general position of marginalism, makes a concession, as to its applicability, which is a virtual admission of its futility. For by showing that only in 'industries of constant returns' are 'supply price' and 'marginal supply price' equal, and that in industries of 'decreasing' or of 'increasing' returns there exists a tendency to exceed or fall short of 'the marginal net product yielded in industries in general', he virtually endorses the criticism that 'marginalism' assumes a statical condition of industry. For only in a statical condition would all industries be found conforming to constant returns: the operation of increasing or diminishing returns means nothing else than that changes in volume or methods of production are raising or lowering productivity and remuneration above or below the equal level which 'marginalism' desiderates. (1914, p. 174, n. 1)

This passage enticed Marshall to write on the front end-paper of his own copy of Pigou's *Wealth and Welfare* that he thought Pigou 'overrates the possibilities of the statical method, and so far I agree with Hobson's criticism of marginalism, *Work and Wealth* p. 174, though most of what J. A. H[obson] says on the subject seems to me invalid' (Bharadwaj, 1972, p. 33).[37] Thus both the fourth and the fifth of Hobson's criticisms of the marginal productivity theory received some support from the leading economist of the time.

4 Underconsumption[1]

Hobson is best known among economists for his exposition and advocacy of the underconsumption theory. He was preceded as an underconsumptionist by James Maitland, Eighth Earl of Lauderdale, Thomas Robert Malthus, J.-C.-L. Simonde de Sismondi and Johann Karl Rodbertus, among others. These predecessors, however, were practitioners of what J. A. Schumpeter termed 'advance economics', by contrast with 'synchronisation economics':

> that is, all analytic patterns that do not in a stationary process assign any fundamental role to the fact that what society lives on at any given moment is the result of past production, on the ground that, once a stationary process has been established, the flow of consumers' goods and the flow of productive service [*sic*] are synchronised so that the process works *as if* society did live on current production. (1954, p. 565, emphasis in original)[2]

In *The Physiology of Industry*, Hobson, jointly with Mummery, was the first to develop an underconsumption theory within the modern framework of synchronisation economics.[3]

Though they were preceded in this respect by 'public speakers and newspapers' (see below), Mummery and Hobson were also the first of the leading exponents of the underconsumption theory actually to use the term 'under-consumption'. The probable reason for the late emergence of this term is the fact that the classical political economists typically used the word 'spending' to refer to what is now known as 'consumption'. When they used the word 'consumption' they were usually referring, in the context of a closed economy, to what we now call consumption plus investment plus government expenditure, and in the context of an open economy, to this amount plus imports minus exports.[4]

The word 'underconsumption' may in fact be of American origin.[5] The earliest use of the term cited by the *Oxford English Dictionary* (2nd edn, vol. XVIII, pp. 958–9) is 1895, which, of course, overlooks Mummery's and Hobson's use of it in 1889. But as early as 1879 the American economist Walker wrote of economic depression as follows:

> How can this be? In the absence of any attempt by professional economists to account for the phenomenon, public speakers and the news-

papers are driven to answer for themselves the question with which we started. This they generally do by the use of one of two phrases, which seem to be regarded as mutually exclusive. 'Over-production' says one party, 'under-consumption' retorts the other; and those who say over-production ridicule those who allege under-consumption, while the latter retort with equal scorn.   (Walker, 1879, p. 118)

Walker's mode of expression implies that in 1879 the word 'under-consumption' was already in common use, at least in North America.

The intuition of 'public speakers and the newspapers' in distinguishing between overproduction and underconsumption was well-founded. Literally interpreted, 'overproduction' involves an excess of aggregate supply over aggregate demand. The underconsumption theory, on the other hand, 'attribute[s] the failure of the total output of an economy to be sold at its cost of production (including normal profit) to too low a ratio of consumption to output' (Schneider, 1987, p. 741). Thus underconsumption is one of the possible explanations of overproduction; an alternative explanation would be 'under-investment'. According to underconsumptionists, however, 'over-production (as distinguished from misproduction, which is a regular necessary waste) *only* arises from under-consumption' (Hobson, 1904, pp. 148–9, emphasis added).

In the underconsumption theory, a deficiency of consumption, and hence excessive saving, is seen as being accompanied by excessive investment. It is thus not surprising that the explanation of depression in terms of underconsumption has sometimes been viewed as no more than a disproportionality theory, that is to say, a theory which explains depression in terms of the disruption caused by the emergence of excess supply in at least one market, accompanied by excess demand in at least one other market.[6] According to this view, underconsumption is simply a case of excess supply in the consumption goods market and excess demand in the investment goods market, from which it may be inferred that a remedy is to be found in a decrease in the price of consumption goods relative to that of investment goods. But, if underconsumption occurred it could not be resolved so simply. To see why, it is helpful to make a distinction between horizontal and vertical disproportionality, the latter involving two or more industries not equidistant in the production process from consumption goods industries (see Haberler, 1937, p. 28). Underconsumption can be seen as an extreme form of vertical disproportionality, in which, at the very beginning of the production process, investment goods are supplied at a level which satisfies a demand for them that is excessive with respect to the demand for their products; this will result in an excessive stock of investment goods, a disequilibrium situation which a change in relative prices can only remove when sufficient investment goods have worn out.[7] To avoid the mistake of seeing underconsumption as being no more than a problem of price inflexibility, it is preferable to think of underconsumption as *sui generis*, rather than a special case of vertical disproportionality.

The underconsumption theory has never become part of orthodox economic doctrine. When Malthus argued the case for the underconsumption theory, both before and during the recessions following the ending of the Napoleonic Wars, Ricardo rejected the theory on the ground that any fall in spending would be accompanied by an offsetting rise in saving and investment, so that there could never be a deficiency of demand.[8] Ricardo was, in fact, not particularly interested in explaining the recessions that followed the Napoleonic Wars. This was due to a combination of his preoccupation with long-run or permanent economic situations, his adoption of Adam Smith's argument that what is important in political economy can be explained without reference to monetary factors, his belief that recessions are always temporary, and his view that they have monetary rather than real causes. In the last two respects he was followed by orthodox economists up to the time of J. M. Keynes. An exception was William Stanley Jevons, who attempted to explain cyclical fluctuations in terms of sunspot activity.

Ricardo's legacy, so far as policy towards recession or depression is concerned, was anti-activism with respect to fiscal policy, combined with attempts to make the monetary system work better, in the hope that this would reduce the amplitude of economic fluctuations. For Ricardo, discretionary fiscal policy was both impotent and unnecessary. First, it was impotent because any change in public sector spending was offset automatically by an opposite change in private-sector spending, an idea which, following a Treasury submission to the Macmillan Committee in 1929, became known as 'the Treasury view'. The contention that this proposition applies even if the change in public sector spending is accompanied by an equal change in borrowing, has become known as the 'Ricardian equivalence theorem', though it should be added that Ricardo himself acknowledged that financing government expenses by borrowing might make the population less thrifty (Ricardo, 1951–73, vol. I, p. 247).[9,10] Second, it was unnecessary because economic fluctuations were both short-lived and largely inevitable. With the exception of debates over the (microeconomic) question of the Corn Laws, the great economic policy disputes of the nineteenth century were over monetary policy: between those favouring and those against a return to the Gold Standard in the period following the Napoleonic Wars, between the members of the

Currency School and those of the Banking School in the 1840s, and between the Bimetallists and the others in the 1880s. Here, the exception was Marx, who would have regarded both fiscal and monetary policy as being impotent; cyclical fluctuations would recur in a society characterised by the capitalist mode of production until revolution gave birth to a more advanced mode of production. This, in brief, was the state of affairs when Mummery and Hobson attempted to revive the underconsumption theory in 1889.

In the subsequent four decades, while Hobson remained an advocate of the underconsumption theory, the attention of those economists interested in what, if anything, should be done about economic fluctuations, continued to be directed towards monetary policy. Wicksell (and subsequently members of the Swedish School), Irving Fisher, Ralph Hawtrey, D. H. Robertson, Friedrich von Hayek, and Keynes himself up to at least 1930, are examples from the ranks of orthodox economists; Silvio Gesell, with his idea of stamped money, and Major C. H. Douglas (whose ideas are discussed in Chapter 6), are examples from the ranks of unorthodox economists. Exceptions are to be found in Schumpeter who, in his explanation of business cycles, combined monetary factors with the uneven introduction of innovations by entrepreneurs, and in the overinvestment theories of Arthur Spiethoff and Gustav Cassel.[11]

4.1 MUMMERY'S AND HOBSON'S UNDERCONSUMPTION THEORY

In *The Physiology of Industry*, Mummery and Hobson assumed not only a given technology at any one time, but also fixed coefficients of production, with no possibility therefore of substitution between capital and other factors of production. On this basis they argued that there must be a fixed relationship between the output of consumable articles and the quantity of capital (circulating as well as fixed) required for their production, terming this 'the law of quantitative relation'. It follows that, although an increase in consumption immediately reduces the level of circulating capital through its effect on stocks of consumable articles, an expectation on the part of capitalists that the increased level of consumption would be sustained would induce them both to replace this circulating capital and to produce the additional fixed capital rendered necessary by the increased level of consumption. A decrease in consumption, on the other hand, would reduce the quantity of capital that could be usefully employed.

Mummery and Hobson termed any capital in excess of the quantity that could be usefully employed 'nominal' rather than 'real', and saving in excess of that required for investment in real capital 'nominal saving'. They concluded that, while an increase in saving entails a decrease in present consumption, additional saving can only be converted into real capital by an increase in future consumption. Since such an increase in future consumption may not take place, however, Mummery and Hobson considered themselves 'entitled to affirm the theoretic possibility of general over-supply' (1889, p. 54).

The essence of this argument was captured subsequently by D. J. Coppock, in the following rudimentary model:

If real capital is denoted by K and real consumption by C, Hobson postulated a ratio of the following type: $K = \beta (1 + e) C$, where eC is the value of distant future consumption. From this ratio the permissable maximum amount of 'socially useful' investment in a period may be derived, *viz.*, $I = \beta (1 + e) \Delta C$.   (Coppock, 1953, p. 9)

Mummery and Hobson went on to relate their theory to periods of depression in trade by tracing a causal relationship between consumption and national income. Their contention was that since 'the profits which form the money incomes of all capitalists concerned in production, the wages of all the labourers concerned, and the rent of all the natural agents required, are, in a regular condition of commerce, paid out of the prices paid by consumers' (1889, p. 71), a decrease in consumption would lead to a 'general reduction in the rate of incomes' (1889, p. 96) or, in other words, to 'a depression in trade', with 'requisites of production', including labour, consequently becoming unemployed or only partially employed.

A counter-argument, put forward by 'most modern economists', was that general oversupply would be checked automatically through a consequent 'fall in general prices, which, by causing an increased demand for Commodities, is alleged to provide an economic use for what would otherwise have been Over-Supply' (1889, p. 117). Mummery and Hobson responded by pointing out that a fall in the general price level entails a fall in money incomes, adding that 'before a person makes a purchase he looks at two things: the price of the article and the condition of his purse' (1889, p. 120). Suppose, however, that in the face of a fall in their money incomes, a considerable number of persons 'thoughtlessly and blindly increase their demand for commodities ... They will find their apparent recklessness to have the force of a well-founded faith' (1889, pp. 124–5), as their increased demand raises their money incomes. This in turn will enable them to save more. As Mummery and Hobson put it:

> it is precisely because they are consuming more that they can save more. This is a paradox, but unlike most paradoxes which gain credence for a falsehood by tickling the ear with a pointed antithesis, it contains a truth which will bear the closest scrutiny. (1889, p. 126)

Here Mummery and Hobson anticipated Keynes' argument (Keynes, 1936, p. 84), that every

> attempt to save more by reducing consumption will so affect incomes that the attempt necessarily defeats itself. It is, of course, just as impossible for the community as a whole to save *less* than the amount of current investment. (emphasis in original)

They saw the orthodox view of saving as involving what is generally known as the fallacy of composition. Hobson later called this (misleadingly) 'the distributive fallacy', which 'consists in arguing that what is true of each must be true of all' (1916, p. 9), a variant of which is 'the separatist fallacy, the belief that what may be good for any must be good for all' (1931b, p. 78); Mummery's and Hobson's view was that, on the contrary, 'though [by saving] any individual may anticipate all future labour, every individual cannot' (1889, p. 111).[12] The orthodox view of saving is one example of what Hobson was to call the 'protean fallacy of individualism, which feigns the existence of separate individuals by abstracting and neglecting the social relations which belong to them and make them what they are' (1901b, p. 67).

What causes underconsumption? The answer that Mummery and Hobson supplied to this question was that in a society in which every individual competes against every other, the fact that the community's saving is already sufficient to satisfy the future demand for consumable articles will in no way deter an individual from increasing his or her saving, and setting the consequent additional capital to work with the object of ousting competitors; this he/she might succeed in doing by using more efficient machines, or cheaper materials, or by paying lower wages. Unless an increase in future consumption takes place, the result in each case will be to render some existing capital idle, thereby turning 'real' capital into 'nominal' capital. As Hobson was to state more explicitly in *The Evolution of Modern Capitalism*, such courses of action 'imply a conflict between the interests of individuals and those of the community' (1894, p. 204).

The practical conclusion that Mummery and Hobson drew from their analysis was that 'where Under-consumption exists, Savings should be taxed' (1889, p. 205), so as to bring demand into line with supply. Underconsumption could, alternatively, be offset by going to war, or:

> if the community, instead of expending its surplus accumulations in the endeavour to cut its members' throats, consented to increase its consumption of luxuries, or applied the surplus funds to the improvement of the condition of the working classes or the sanitation of its great towns, all the contingent advantages of a war would be reaped. (1889, p. 163)

4.2   UNEMPLOYMENT, REDISTRIBUTION AND PUBLIC WORKS

After the publication of *The Physiology of Industry*, Hobson was to restate the underconsumption theory many times, often with significant additions or modifications. For example, in *The Evolution of Modern Capitalism* he was more explicit than before in distinguishing between the early and the later 'stages' of a trade depression. Making reference to the 'depression beginning in 1873 and culminating in 1878' (1894, p. 174), Hobson argued that while in the early stages of a depression underconsumption results in a general glut of goods, it 'shows a deep misunderstanding of the malady' (1894, p. 176) to assume that such a situation can continue. Unable to sell their goods, firms cut back on their production, and the glut of goods is replaced in the later stages of a depression by idle capital and unemployed labour. As he acknowledged that 'the worst features' of a depression do not appear in the early stages, Hobson might more usefully have referred to the early and later stages of an underconsumption cycle.

Following up this theme in 'The Economic Cause of Unemployment' (1895b, p. 746), Hobson gave as examples of the later stages of a depression the ten years 1875–85, and the period which had begun in 1890. In the latter case he estimated that in manufacturing some 8 to 10 per cent of the workforce was unemployed, and that in the distributive trades the proportion of unemployed or underemployed labour and capital was far larger than the unemployment figures suggested, since lack of competition in those trades meant that the depression made itself felt there not in unemployment of resources but in wasteful utilisation of them.[13]

'The Economic Cause of Unemployment' was the second of two articles published by Hobson in 1895 on the subject of unemployed labour; these articles were prompted by the then recent release of a Labour

Department *Report on the Unemployed*.[14] Both articles included in their title the recently-coined term 'unemployment'. While the *Oxford English Dictionary* gives an unambiguous example of the use of the term 'unemployed' in its modern sense as early as 1677, the first case it cites of the use of the term 'unemployment' dates back only to 1888.[15] In 'The Meaning and Measurement of "Unemployment"', however, Hobson went a step further. As Corry (1992) points out, after using the term 'involuntary leisure' (1895a, p. 419), Hobson proceeded to coin the term 'involuntarily unemployed' (1895a, p. 420), and contrasted the 'involuntarily unemployed' with those who are unemployed for voluntary, 'leakage' (Hobson's term for 'frictional') or seasonal reasons. He noted that the percentage of the workforce 'involuntarily unemployed' varies with 'the great tidal movements of trade' (1895a, p. 431), not with such factors as laziness, lack of skill, or introduction of machinery; to this latter list he could have added the average wage rate.

In the second of his two 1895 articles on unemployed labour, Hobson for the first time attributed underconsumption to the way in which income was currently distributed.[16] The classical political economists had generally assumed that wages are too low to allow workers to save, and that all saving consequently comes out of profits and rent. Hobson too reached the conclusion that saving varies with the distribution of income, but by a different route. His argument was that the 'reason why attempts are made by individuals to establish more forms of capital than are socially required, is that they possess certain elements of income which are not earned by effort, and which are therefore not required to satisfy any present legitimate wants' (1895b, p. 756). Hobson gave this idea the status of a 'natural law', according to which 'an attempt to be a very large consumer and a very small producer in the long run defeats itself' (1895b, p. 756), the necessary long-run outcome being a drop in consumption.

Although Hobson referred to the 'brilliant analysis of Malthus', of trade depression, as being in close accord with his own, he went on to reject the remedy of luxurious expenditure recommended by Malthus as being wholly impracticable, even if it were otherwise desirable.[17] Reasons were given in the fifth edition of *Problems of Poverty* (1905), where Hobson argued that since the

> demand for luxuries is essentially capricious and irregular ... the only effective remedy for unemployment lies in a general policy of social and economic reform, which aims at placing a larger and larger proportion of the 'consuming power' of the community in the hands of those who, having received it as the earnings of their effort, will learn to use it

in building up a higher standard of wholesome consumption.   (1905, p. 148)

The various ideas put forward in earlier works were summed up in *The Social Problem* (1901b) as follows:

> where incomes are 'unearned', and come to a man in ways which we have recognized as 'unnatural' or 'miraculous', acquired by luck, craft, force, gift, or other ways that imply no corresponding personal effort, no ... guarantee of natural use or consumption exists. On the contrary, it appears natural that part, at any rate, of the power of consumption should be withheld ... common sense, or a certain nausea and sense of satiety which nature provides as a check upon excess, sets some restrictions even upon luxurious expenditure, and impels the wealthy classes to an amount of 'saving', or withholding of the power of consumption, which grows with every increase in the elements of 'unearned incomes' and in the number of their recipients. It is this withholding of power of consumption by certain classes of individuals that constitutes the maladjustment, from the social standpoint, between power of production and current rate of consumption, and which brings about a larger aggregate of saving than is economically needed to maintain capital which assists in supplying goods for current consumption.   (1901b, pp. 250–1)

In modern terms, the core of Hobson's argument is that the propensity to consume out of earned income is substantially greater than that out of unearned income.

Subsequently, in *The Industrial System*, Hobson made explicit reference to the cyclical character of the unemployment caused by underconsumption. He argued that when, in the 'later stages' of a depression, income falls to a sufficiently low level, 'the proportion of saving to spending is cut below the normal rate, and a process of recuperation begins, no large further increase of capital taking place while the consumption of a growing population increases, though at a slower pace than usual' (1909b, p. 296). Then:

> the cancelment [*sic*] of large quantities of existing capital, representing over-saving, and the retardation of new saving for investment, restore for a time the right adjustment between real capital and [the] rate of consumption, and a spell of good trade with full employment for capital and labour ensues. This continues until the chronic impulse towards over-saving due to surplus income again becomes fully operative,

preparing for a new period of depression... If there exists a normal tendency towards over-saving or under-consumption, such as appears to be involved in the existence of an unproductive surplus of unearned income, the regular pressure of that excess will express itself in some such rhythmic order as that of the booms and depressions which actually occur.   (1909b, pp. 296–7)

That is to say, *chronic* underconsumption causes *cyclical* fluctuations in aggregate output.[18]

Hobson believed that such fluctuations would not be prevented by offsetting changes in the interest rate. With respect to saving out of unearned income, he argued in *The Industrial System* that a 'falling rate of interest, though not wholly inoperative, will be less effective in its action upon this sort of saving than upon any other' (1909b, p. 286), because of the relatively automatic nature of such saving. This led him to the conclusion that, while excessive saving might cause the interest rate to fall, such a fall in the interest rate could not be relied upon to eliminate the excessive saving. In a later work, taking into account the existence of 'target saving', where a rise in the interest rate enables a target level of income to be achieved with a lower level of saving, Hobson went so far as to claim that 'there is no ascertainable relation between the price of saving and the supply' (1932a, p. 30).[19]

The combination of boom economic conditions after 1909 and Hobson's preoccupation after 1914 with bringing an end to the war no doubt account for the absence of any further development in his underconsumption theory until 1922, when *The Economics of Unemployment* was published. Here, Hobson added a further reason for underconsumption, namely 'the conservative character of the arts of consumption', as the following passage indicates:

Why does consumption fail to keep pace with increased powers of production? Or, conversely, why do the powers of production increase faster than the rate of consumption?

The answer is found in two related phenomena: first, the conservative character of the arts of consumption, or standards of living, as compared with the modern arts of production; second, the ways in which the current distribution of income confirms this conservatism of consumption.

In primitive societies the standards or methods of work are almost as conservative as those of consumption. Of civilised societies, and especially of modern industrial nations, this is no longer true. Invention and business initiative, enlisted in the cause of quick profiteering,

transforms [*sic*] with great rapidity the arts of industry, raising this productivity by leaps and bounds. Though modern man, in his capacity of
consumer, is far more progressive than his ancestors, his power of
taking on new economic needs and of raising rapidly the quantity,
variety and quality of his consumption, is limited by a narrowness of
imagination and a servitude to habit which are far less dominant in
production.   (1922a, pp. 32–3)

Such reference to the 'conservatism of consumers', which crops up from
time to time in Hobson's writings, is important because it suggests that a
lasting solution to underconsumption would require a continuous redistribution of income in the direction of greater equality.[20]

Like Malthus before him, Hobson admitted the possibility of periods
during which the ratio of consumption to output is too high. He wrote in
1919, for example, that he believed that 'at the present economic juncture
it will be necessary to take what measures are necessary to evoke a higher
proportion of saving [and investment] to spending than prevailed before
the war' (1919b, p. 112); this belief was no doubt based on the low rate of
capital replacement during the war, and the excess demand in many
sectors of the United Kingdom economy almost immediately after the war
ended. That Hobson took this view helps to explain why at that time it was
possible for him to adopt a position with respect to the national debt,
swollen by borrowing to pay for the war, diametrically opposed to that
taken by the early underconsumptionist Lauderdale when looking ahead to
the conclusion of the Napoleonic wars; Lauderdale opposed the establishment of a sinking fund to repay the debt on the ground that it would trans-
fer income from consuming taxpayers to bondholders, who would use it
for capital accumulation, the outcome being underconsumption. Hobson,
by contrast, advocated paying off the national debt at the fastest practic-
able rate, so as to encourage saving and investment. He also favoured this
course of action because he was concerned to prevent a continuing redistribution of income from taxpayers to relatively wealthy bondholders.

Hobson argued, too, that the national debt should be paid off quickly
because this would bring down the rate of interest. It was in this context
that Hobson made one of his rare admissions that investment may depend
on the rate of interest as well as on consumption. If the national debt were
not paid off quickly, he wrote, 'the present rate [of interest] would be so
high as to depress the effective demand for capital (at any rate for home
uses) more than to stimulate the supply of capital' (1919b, p. 198).

In *The Problem of the Unemployed* Hobson advocated three remedies
for underconsumption, all designed to reduce unearned income. The first

of these was the taxation of unearned income; the second was a rise in wages through trade union action; and the third was an increase in the leisure enjoyed by the working classes through legislation setting a maximum working day or week.

When he came to look at the first of these remedies in more detail, Hobson recognised the difficulty in practice of distinguishing between income that is earned and income that is unearned. Thus in *The Social Problem* he recommended that underconsumption should be remedied by 'a general income tax, graduated upon the supposition that the proportion of unearned and therefore economically taxable income varies directly with the absolute size of incomes' (1901b, p. 332). The appropriateness of this policy was reasserted in *The Industrial System*, where Hobson stated that 'though we fear inductive evidence upon such a point is not available, it will hardly be disputed that the proportion of saving is generally in direct ratio to the size of incomes, the richest saving the largest percentage of their income, the poorest the smallest' (1909b, p. 285). By the time Hobson wrote *The Economics of Unemployment*, some 'inductive evidence' had become available. Estimates made in Ireson (1910) were presented by Hobson in the form of a table showing the average ratio of family spending to income increasing from approximately 0.6 for families with annual incomes of over £5000, to 1 for families with annual incomes of under £52.

The 1926 Report to the Independent Labour Party entitled *The Living Wage*, of which, as noted in Chapter 1, Hobson was probably the principal author, states that a minimum wage for all workers should be set not only for ethical reasons, but also as a remedy for underconsumption. It rejects the counter-argument that firms should not be expected to pay a higher wage than the existing one, on the Hobsonian ground that values are created not by individuals but by society as a whole. Noting the restrictive money and credit policy adopted by the Bank of England after 1920, it recommended that the Bank of England should be nationalised so as to ensure support for the increase in output necessary to enable the introduction of a minimum wage.[21]

In the first edition of *The Economics of Unemployment*, Hobson argued, with respect to those who are unemployed as a result of a 'general trade depression', that 'either they must be set on public works that could not otherwise be undertaken then, or in default of these, they must be provided with food, clothes, etc., or the means to buy them' (1922a, p. 134). In the second edition (1931a), however, he acknowledged that in the case of so deep and protracted a depression as that currently being experienced, the argument for taking the latter course, keeping the unemployed where they are in expectation of an early economic revival, was no longer applicable. Under these circumstances, the state should borrow the unused funds lying in the banks to finance, not payments to the unemployed, but the carrying out of public works. Given the duration of the depression,

> the policy of public works, soundly conceived and well administered, is ... not to be condemned because its direct and immediate value, in the strictly economic sense, may be considered to be less than would accrue if the same amount of expenditure were laid out by private capitalism in normal times. For these times are not normal, as is shown by the very fact that these productive powers of capital and labour lie idle. The direct value, therefore, of publicly employing them is measured not by comparison with their ordinary productivity in private enterprise, but by the surplus gain of whatever they produce over the non-productivity of idleness. The indirect value consists in the stimulus given to general consumption during a period now recognised as suffering from underconsumption. (1931a, pp. 125–6)

However, Hobson warned against excessive expenditure on public works, on the ground that the 'policy of public works is designed to stimulate a general trade recovery, and it must therefore not directly encroach upon the capital and labour needed for normal trade expansion' (1931a, p. 124).[22]

With this qualification, Hobson thus ultimately came to recommend public works rather than payments to the unemployed as the appropriate policy in the case of a sustained depression. By contrast, his view of monetary policy was that:

> though cheap investment money and cheap bank credits are helpful when for other causes recovery begins, experience shows that until definite signs of recovery have appeared in the shape of rising prices and increased orders, cheap money has very little influence in promoting recovery. So likewise when trade is good and prices are rising, dear money has little influence in checking production. (1933a, p. 411)

4.3 HOBSONIAN AND KEYNESIAN THEORY

Hobson's explanation of depression in terms of underconsumption differs fundamentally from Keynes' demand-deficiency theory in two interrelated respects. First, on the theoretical level, Keynes, in *The General Theory*, attributed demand-deficiency unemployment to a level of investment that falls short of full employment saving; Hobson, by contrast, asserted that depression occurs because underconsumption leads to the accumulation of excessive capital equipment, which lies idle, and according to Hobson's later writings, may also be unpurchased. Second, on the policy level, Keynes saw an increase in investment as always being a stimulant to the economy, while Hobson believed that an increase in investment may depress it. We examine these two differences in succession.

From the time of Adam Smith's reaction against the preoccupation with money that characterised what he termed 'the mercantile system', the accumulation of money and other financial assets ceased to play a substantial part in economic writings. Even Malthus, whom Keynes was to praise as a predecessor, wrote that 'no political economist of the present day can by saving mean mere hoarding' (Malthus, 1820, p. 32).[23] The leading role assigned to the propensity to accumulate financial assets was thus one of the revolutionary features of *The General Theory*. Keynes' view was that an increase (say) in the propensity to accumulate financial assets on the part of individuals reflects a level of planned investment that falls short of planned saving, and will necessarily result in a fall in the level of income until equality between planned investment and planned saving is restored. An increase in the propensity to accumulate financial assets in the form of money (that is, to hoard) is likely to cause an even greater fall in the level of income, because it will push up the interest rate and this may further reduce investment. This view led Keynes to speculate as follows:

> The only radical cure for the crises of confidence which afflict the economic life of the modern world would be to allow the individual no choice between consuming his income and ordering the production of the specific capital-asset which, even though it be on precarious evidence, impresses him as the most promising investment available to him. It might be that, at times when he was more than usually assailed by doubts concerning the future, he would turn in his perplexity towards more consumption and less new investment. But that would avoid the disastrous, cumulative and far-reaching repercussions of its being open to him, when thus assailed by doubts, to spend his income neither on the one nor on the other. (Keynes, 1936, p. 161)

By contrast, Mummery and Hobson ruled out the possibility of not spending income either on consumption goods or on investment goods, stating explicitly that saving 'signifies not only abstention from consumption, but [also] application as a further means of production' (1889, p. 47).[24] In *The Industrial System* Hobson even went so far as to identify saving with investment, asserting that 'saving means paying ... capital and labour to produce additional productive goods' (1909b, p. 51). He went on to contradict himself, however, by writing in the same work that, in commercial depressions, 'abnormal hoarding may sometimes play a critical part' (1909b, p. 50, n. 1). He subsequently defined hoarding as 'some lingering of loanable funds in hands of financiers, from slowness in finding any sort of investment' (1909b, p. 292), and played down the importance of hoarding only to the extent of adding that to suppose hoarding might account for as much as one third of an increase in saving would be 'an excessive estimate' (1909b, p. 292). From then on, Hobson ceased to deny the possibility of hoarding. Indeed, as King (1994) points out, in proposition 3 in 'The World's Economic Crisis' (1932b, p. 53) Hobson moved explicitly to the position to be adopted by Keynes in *The General Theory*, namely that income may fail to be spent either on consumption goods or on investment goods. Hobson expressed it as follows: if 'there is insufficient purchase of consumption goods, this must be due either to an excessive purchase of new producers' goods (through saving and investment) *or else to withholding of some purchasing power from purchase either of consumption goods or producers' goods (capital goods)*' (emphasis added by King). Thus, from 1909 onwards, the difference between Hobson's analysis and that to be developed by Keynes lay not in a denial by Hobson of the possibility of hoarding, but in Keynes' denial of the possibility of unpurchased capital equipment, a possibility which Hobson undoubtedly had in mind in the passage just quoted.[25]

Although Hobson hardly ever used the term 'hoarding' after 1909, in the late 1920s and the 1930s he frequently referred to savings which are not invested. In 1929, for example, in a passage whose first two sentences bear some resemblance to the paragraph from *The General Theory* last quoted, he wrote:

> When a general trade depression sets in, the would-be investors refrain from buying and operating the increased plant, &c., available, *i.e.*, they refuse to invest. This refusal is justified by business calculations which indicate that, if bought, the new plant could not be operated so as to sell its product for a profit. Thus the direct effect of 'freezing savings' is to freeze productive capital, and so lower the productivity and income of the whole economic system.   (1929b, p. 903)

This passage, together with similar ones written in the 1930s, suggests that what Hobson intended to convey was the following. Saving is always accompanied by the production of capital goods of an equal value, but, if the saving ratio is too high, in the later 'stages' of an underconsumption cycle some savings will be hoarded and capital goods of an equal value will remain unpurchased and hence unutilised; idle or 'frozen' savings are matched by idle or 'frozen' productive capital. As Nell (1992, p. 497) points out, while money claims are identical to the value of output, money payments made during any period may or may not equal the value of output. What Hobson seems to have had in mind is the case in which money payments fall short of the value of output, money claims which are not exercised being matched by unpurchased capital goods.

With one possible exception, Keynes persistently rejected this argument. Following the publication of his *Treatise on Money* (1930), in responding (24 July 1931) to a letter from Hobson (1 July 1931) which has not survived, Keynes stated bluntly:

> you say that 'there must be a body of real capital corresponding to the uninvestable savings'. I do not accept this as being true in fact or in theory.   (Keynes, 1973, vol. XIII, p. 330)

Keynes went on to refer Hobson to the 'Banana Parable' in the *Treatise on Money* (1930, pp. 158–60), pointing out that 'in this case there is no real capital corresponding to the surplus savings' (Keynes, 1973, vol. XIII, p. 330).[26]

There followed an intriguing correspondence between Hobson and Keynes. Hobson sent Keynes (on 18 August 1931) 'a series of propositions which may go some way to reconcile our respective treatments' (Keynes, 1973, vol. XIII, p. 331). In the sixth of these propositions, labelled overall 'Notes on Oversaving', Hobson argued that following an increase in the saving ratio from 20 per cent to 30 per cent, 'there would exist large quantities of unused excessive plant and other capital goods representing past real savings, but the increase of savings due to a refusal to buy the increased output of consumption goods would not 'invest' itself in the purchase of this excessive and immutable capital' (Keynes, 1973, vol. XIII, p. 332); one may infer, given the existence of 'excessive and immutable capital', that the increased saving would not 'invest' itself in the purchase of new capital, either. Surprisingly, given his opposition elsewhere to the idea expressed in this component of Hobson's 'Notes', Keynes' immediate response (28 August 1931) was, 'I do not think there is anything with which I disagree in your "Notes on Over Saving [*sic*]", and I think that this exposition of your point of view does bring us much nearer together' (Keynes, 1973, vol. XIII, p. 332).

That there remained a difference between Hobson and Keynes was attested to by Keynes in the penultimate chapter of *The General Theory*. There Keynes commented favourably on the criticism in *The Physiology of Industry* of the unlimited support of saving by the classical economists, stating that in that work Hobson had put 'one half of the matter [that saving may be excessive] ... with absolute precision' (Keynes, 1936, p. 368). Keynes contended none the less that the argument was deficient in 'supposing that it is a case of the excessive saving causing the *actual* accumulation of capital, which is, in fact, a secondary evil which only occurs through mistakes of foresight' (Keynes, 1936, p. 367, emphasis in original). Unlike Hobson, Keynes did not believe that the forces of competition would drive capitalists as a class to invest excessively. Keynes' own view was that 'the primary evil is a propensity to save in conditions of full employment more than the equivalent of the capital which is required, thus preventing full employment except when there is a mistake of foresight' (Keynes, 1936, pp. 367–8). By 'mistake of foresight' Keynes here meant an excessive optimism that causes investment to match full employment saving; what precisely he meant by 'the capital which is required' he never explained, though one interpretation was subsequently to be provided by Roy Harrod and Evsey Domar.

After the publication of *The General Theory*, Hobson wrote to Keynes as follows:

> Perhaps you will allow me to explain the difficulty which arises on p. 63 when you deal with Income and identify Saving as to Investment [in the sense that they are always equal]. While the real income of any period must = consumption + more capital (i.e. investment in the shape of plant, materials, etc.), it still seems possible that some remaining income should be withheld alike from buying consumables and buying new capital goods. The crudest example is 'putting into a stocking' or other private hoard which still happens in many countries in periods of crisis. Here it means a slowing down or temporary withholding from production or ordering of more capital goods (investment). (Keynes Papers, GTE/2/2/352)[27]

But Keynes' response (14 February 1936) was to deny the possibility of any such increase in hoarding. He wrote:

> There is, according to my view, no place in which redundant saving, so to speak, can be held in suspense. If some individuals are saving in

excess of the flow of new investment, this means that there must be corresponding losses and dis-saving by others who have to live on their capital. (Keynes, 1979, p. 210)

It is surprising that Keynes was so insistent that there cannot be any 'redundant saving'. In *The General Theory* he explicitly allowed for unplanned changes in stocks (see Keynes, 1936, p. 288), and 'redundant saving' would seem to be an appropriate term to describe the saving which is the counterpart of unplanned increases in stocks. What Hobson essentially did was to extend this argument to apply also to unplanned increases in capital equipment; it was perhaps this extension that produced so dogmatic a response from Keynes.

It seems clear that ultimately Hobson and Keynes were arguing at cross purposes. Keynes was rejecting the possibility of changes in the propensity to accumulate financial assets when the economy is in equilibrium because, when planned investment equals planned saving, an increase in the propensity to accumulate financial assets on the part of one individual implies a decrease in the propensity to accumulate financial assets on the part of another.[28] Hobson, on the other hand, was referring to the possibility of an increase in hoarding 'in periods of crisis', which it seems reasonable to identify with the Keynesian situation of a fall in aggregate demand below the level required to sustain full employment, a disequilibrium position in which a drop in the level of planned investment below full employment saving implies a simultaneous increase in planned accumulation of financial assets. Since an increase in planned accumulation of financial assets in this context is central to the argument of *The General Theory*, and since Hobson had since 1889 anticipated Keynes in stressing changes in the level of income as the principal equilibrating force when demand in an economy falls short of supply, Hobson must be seen as eventually going a considerable way towards both anticipating and accepting the analysis of *The General Theory*.

We turn now to the difference between Hobson and Keynes as to the use of an increase in investment as a means of expanding an economy. In the *Treatise on Money*, where saving is defined as the gap between consumption and 'income excluding windfall profits', Keynes wrote with reference to Hobson and other underconsumptionists:

They are concerned, not with the equilibrium of saving and investment, but with the equilibrium of the production of instrumental capital goods and the demand for the use of such goods ... In so far ... as these theories maintain that the existing distribution of wealth tends to a large volume of saving, which leads in turn to over-investment, which leads to too large a production of consumption goods, they are occupying an entirely different *terrain* from my theory: inasmuch as, on my theory, it is a large volume of saving which does *not* lead to a correspondingly large volume of investment (not one which *does*) which is the root of the trouble.   (Keynes, 1930, pp. 160–1, emphasis in original)

This passage summarises neatly the key features of both the under-consumption theory and Keynes' theory. Hobson believed that in the early 'stages' of a depression there is a glut of consumption goods, caused by the high level of production resulting from prior excessive saving accompanied by excessive investment. Keynes' view was that it is not excessive saving by itself which causes a depression, but the failure of a 'large volume' of saving to be accompanied by an equal amount of investment.

Subsequently, in his reply (28 August 1931) to Hobson's 'Notes on Oversaving' letter, Keynes added that in his view Hobson was canvassing only one of two possible remedies for economic depression:

You are pointing to the exit of diminished savings as a remedy for the situation you are contemplating. But I suggest to you that there is also another way out besides the way of increased consumption, namely, through a fall in the rate of interest – a point which I have mentioned in previous letters. For, if the rate of interest were to fall, consumption goods, the production of which uses much capital, would be cheapened relatively to other consumption goods, with the result that consumption would change over to such goods, thus creating an increased demand for capital, and so absorbing the extra savings.   (Keynes, 1973, vol. XIII, p. 333)

This was a clever line of argument to address to Hobson, as it does not depend on saving being interest-elastic; as already noted, Hobson always denied that the interest elasticity of saving is substantial. Hobson's response to Keynes' letter has unfortunately not survived, but in reply (14 October 1931) to a subsequent letter (2 October 1931) from Keynes he questioned whether the extra supply of consumption goods resulting from a rapid expansion in capital accumulation and consequently in production would find a market, since 'a "conservatism" of the consumer may influence him to save more of his income instead of raising his standard of consumption' (Keynes, 1973, vol. XIII, p. 335).

This correspondence reflects the basic difference between the policy implications of the Hobsonian and Keynesian theories, a difference which was neatly summarised by Lionel Robbins as follows:

In Mr. Keynes' view the difficulty arises when the monetary savings are not turned into real investment, whereas in Mr. Hobson's view it arises because that real investment is excessive in relation to real consumption. For Mr. Keynes, one way out of the slump would be a revival of investment; for Mr. Hobson, this would simply make matters worse. (Robbins, 1932b, p. 420)[29]

Thus, when Hobson wrote to Keynes (10 February 1936), saying, with reference to 'your great book', that he hoped and expected that 'its shattering exposure of the neo-classical theory and policy will have its due effect on those younger economists who are not too deeply committed to the teaching of their textbooks' (Keynes, 1979, p. 209), he should not be interpreted as endorsing *The General Theory* without reservation. In the same letter he reiterated his view that 'the order of events, as I have seen it, is underconsumption or oversaving, [actual] overinvestment, stoppage of new investment, check on saving and upon all production processes with simultaneous and proportionate unemployment of all factors of production' (Keynes, 1979, p. 209). Keynes never accepted the existence of the second of these links in the Hobsonian chain leading to economic depression. In this respect, the Harrod and Domar growth models, which in Harrod's terminology allow for the actual rate of growth of an economy not to be equal to the rate of growth which is 'warranted' in the sense that existing capital stock is fully utilised, are more Hobsonian than Keynesian in character, as we shall see in more detail in the next section of this chapter.

4.4 HOBSON, HARROD, DOMAR AND GROWTH

A resemblance between Hobson's underconsumption theory and the Harrod and Domar growth models was first noted by Domar himself, and then by Joan Robinson in a review of Harrod's *Towards a Dynamic Economics* (1948). Domar saw Hobson, rather than Keynes, as a predecessor who recognised the significance of investment's capacity-creating effect (labelled by Domar the 'σ' effect), as the following passage shows:

Keynes analyzed what happens when savings (of the previous period) are not invested. The answer was unemployment, but the statement of the problem in this form might easily give the erroneous impression that if savings were invested, full employment would be assured. Hobson, on the other hand, went a step further and stated the problem in this form; suppose savings are invested. Will the new plants be able to dispose of all their products? Such a statement of the problem was not at all, as Keynes thought, a mistake. It was a statement of a different, *and possibly also a deeper problem.* Hobson was fully armed with the σ effect of investment, and he saw that it could be answered only by growth [in investment at a particular rate].   (Domar, 1947, p. 52, emphasis added)

No doubt similar considerations led Joan Robinson to comment that 'Mr. Harrod's analysis provides the missing link between Keynes and Hobson' (Robinson, 1949, p. 79). We next look at the relationship between Hobson's underconsumption theory on the one hand and the Harrod and Domar growth models on the other, taking the Harrod model first purely for ease of exposition.

Harrod summarised his growth model in terms of what he called 'fundamental equations'. The first of these is the *ex post* identity:

$$GC \equiv s \tag{4.1}$$

In this identity, G can be interpreted as the rate of growth of output and income between (say) period 1 and period 2; we follow the convention adopted by Keynes in *The General Theory*, as opposed to that adopted in his *Treatise on Money*, in identifying output with income. C is then the *actual* addition to the stock of fixed and circulating capital between the beginning of period 1 and the beginning of period 2, divided by the increase in the flow of goods produced between those two periods; and s is the ratio of saving to income in period 1. The second 'fundamental equation' is the identity that defines Harrod's 'warranted rate of growth' concept, namely:

$$G_w C_r \equiv s \tag{4.2}$$

where C_r is the *desired* marginal capital–output ratio, and G_w is the warranted rate of growth, 'warranted' in the sense that it will result in the full employment of capital.

From identities (4.1) and (4.2) Harrod drew the conclusion that for any given s, if $G = G_w$ then $C = C_r$, and the economy will be characterised by steady-state growth. By contrast, if $G < G_w$ then $C > C_r$; that is to say, there will be idle capacity, which in the next period will drive down investment, and hence reduce the actual rate of growth of output, causing it to be lower than G, which by assumption is itself lower than G_w.

The basic Harrod growth model assumes s to be constant. It follows that if we abstract from the government and foreign sectors of the economy, in Harrod's model the sole source of growth in demand is an increase in investment demand. In this respect the Harrod growth model is the polar opposite of Hobson's underconsumption theory, and in so far as it is used to explain low rates of growth, it might by analogy be labelled an 'underinvestment' theory.

This contrast between the Harrodian and Hobsonian theories notwithstanding, by substituting consumption for output we can derive a pair of equations comparable with equations (4.1) and (4.2) representing Hobson's underconsumption theory, though not incorporating its income distribution elements.[30] First, we have:

$$gc \equiv h \qquad\qquad (4.3)$$

where g is the rate of growth of consumption between period 1 and period 2; c is the actual addition to the stock of fixed and circulating capital between the beginning of period 1 and the beginning of period 2, divided by the increase in the flow of goods consumed as between those two periods; and h is the ratio of saving to consumption in period 1, that is, S_1/C_1. Note that h differs from s in the Harrod model, which is S_1/Y_1.

Second, we have:

$$gc_r \equiv h_w \qquad\qquad (4.4)$$

where c_r is the desired marginal capital–consumption ratio, and h_w is what we shall call the warranted saving–consumption ratio. The concept of a warranted saving–consumption ratio is thus based on the idea that, except in the 'early stages' of an underconsumption cycle, net investment will occur only to the extent required by the rate of growth of consumption and the marginal output–investment ratio.[31] Hobson's argument was that the 'great bulk of capital fructifies in an early increase in commodities, and so the saving embodied in it is only socially useful on condition that an early increase of consumption proportionate to the increased saving takes place ... this implies the maintenance of a definite proportion between the aggregate of saving and of spending over a term of years' (1909b, p. 53); the word 'spending' is here used by Hobson in the classical sense to refer to consumption only, and our 'h_w' can be taken as giving expression to this 'definite proportion'.

From equations (4.3) and (4.4) we can draw the Hobsonian conclusion that the condition for steady-state growth is that, given the rate of growth of consumption, the actual saving–consumption ratio equal the warranted ratio, that is, that h equal h_w. By contrast, if $h > h_w$ then $c > c_r$. That is to say, if the actual saving–consumption ratio is greater than the warranted ratio, there will be idle capacity. This will lead capitalists to reduce their investment in the next period, and the rate of growth of output will consequently decline. In this model underconsumption is represented by an actual saving–consumption ratio which is greater than the warranted ratio.

Like the Harrod model, the Domar growth model rules out underconsumption. It does so by assuming that the marginal propensity to save is constant, and that the marginal and average propensities to save are equal. In the Domar model, first set out in Domar (1946), the condition for sustained full utilisation of capital is derived from the following equation, the left-hand side representing the increase in total demand for output (net of depreciation) between period 1 and period 2, and the right-hand side representing the increase in potential output between the two periods:

$$(I_2 - I_1)/\alpha = \sigma I_1 \qquad (4.5)$$

where I is net investment, α is the marginal propensity to save, so that the multiplier is represented by $1/\sigma$, and σ is the desired marginal output–investment ratio. By rearranging terms we can derive the rate of growth of net investment required for sustained full utilisation of capital, namely:

$$(I_2 - I_1)/I_1 = \sigma \alpha \qquad (4.6)$$

The condition for sustained full utilisation of capital is thus that investment grow at the rate $\sigma \alpha$.

A comparable formula can be derived to represent Hobson's underconsumption theory. In Hobson's analysis there is no autonomous investment, and additional demand can therefore be initiated only by an increase in consumption; an increase in consumption which is expected to persist in turn generates net investment sufficient to produce the greater capital stock it necessitates. Suppose consumption has in the past grown at the rate g, period after period. Then, if this growth rate is expected to continue, the demand for capital stock will as a result also grow at the rate g, and consequently so too will net investment demand.[32] Thus the increase in total demand for net output in period 2, compared with period 1, will be $(gC_1 + gI_1)$, so that the condition for sustained full utilisation of capital is:

$$gC_1 + gI_1 = \sigma I_1 \qquad (4.7)$$

Rearranging terms, we get:

$$(I_1 / C_1)^* = g / (\sigma - g) \tag{4.8}$$

where $(I_1/C_1)^*$ represents the ratio between net investment and consumption required if full employment of capital is to be sustained.

Except in the 'later stages' of an underconsumption cycle, $I_1 = S_1$, and equation (4.8) can thus be rewritten as follows:

$$(S_1 / C_1)^* = g / (\sigma - g) \tag{4.9}$$

where $(S_1/C_1)^*$ represents the ratio between saving and consumption required if full employment of capital is to be sustained; $g/(\sigma - g)$ is thus the precise formulation of the warranted saving–consumption ratio (h_w) to which reference has already been made. The extent to which the warranted saving–consumption ratio exceeds zero thus depends both on the extent to which the rate of growth of consumption (g) exceeds zero and on the size of the marginal output/capital ratio (σ).

Assuming that the current rate of growth of consumption is expected to continue, for every level of income there will be a level of consumption such that the ratio of saving to consumption is the warranted ratio. We shall refer to this level of consumption as lying on the optimal consumption path, designating the latter by C^*; C^* is optimal not in the Ramsay or neoclassical sense, but in the sense that it generates an output path, designated here by Y^*, which sustains full utilisation of capital.

We now illustrate the argument diagrammatically. In Figure 4.1 income is plotted on the horizontal axis, and consumption and investment on the vertical axis.[33] Stemming from the origin is a line representing the optimal consumption path, with a slope of $(\sigma - g)/\sigma$; because, if (S/C) equals $g/(\sigma - g)$, $S = gC/(\sigma - g)$, and given that $Y \equiv C + S$, (C/Y) must equal $(\sigma - g)/\sigma$. Also stemming from the origin is a line which is steeper by a factor of $\sigma/(\sigma - g)$; given that (C/Y) equals $(\sigma - g)/\sigma$, this will be a $45°$ line. It represents the optimal output path, labelled $Y^* = kC^*$, where $k = \sigma/(\sigma - g)$.

Suppose that, up to and including period 1, consumption has followed the optimal path, with consumption, and hence capital stock and income, growing at the rate g. Given that Y_1 is the level of income in period 1, both optimal and actual consumption are represented in Figure 4.1 by the point Q. Then the vertical distance between Q and the 45° line will represent that part of income not accounted for by consumption, namely saving (S_1), which in turn, except in the 'later stages' of an underconsumption

Figure 4.1   Hobsonian steady-state growth

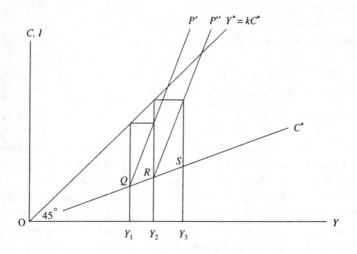

cycle', is equal to investment (I_1). Given that this vertical distance measures I_1, if we draw from Q upwards to the right a linear P' function with a slope $1/\sigma$, showing horizontally the additional potential output resulting from any given investment measured vertically, we can find from the P' line the *potential* level of income in period 2, namely Y_2; since the capital stock is growing at the rate g, $Y_2 = (1 + g)Y_1$. The only level of consumption that will generate just sufficient investment for the actual level of income in period 2 also to be Y_2 is the level represented by the point R, where the C^* line cuts the line running vertically above Y_2. The analysis can be repeated by drawing from the point R a P'' line, parallel with P', generating an optimal level of consumption for period 3 represented by the point S, and so on.

    Suppose, on the other hand, that between period 1 and period 2 consumption grows at a rate less than g. Then the shortfall of consumption compared with the optimal level, together with the consequent shortfall of investment, will cause the actual level of income in period 2 to be less than Y_2. Suppose, for example, that $g = 1/20$ and $\sigma = 1/3$; then $g/(\sigma - g)$, the warranted consumption–saving ratio, will equal 17/20. Suppose, further, that the full capacity level of output in period 2 is 20. Then, while consumption equal to 17 will allow the full capacity level of output to be achieved, consumption equal to 16 will not, except in the 'early stages' of an underconsumption cycle. Our diagram thus illustrates what Hobson was saying in the following passage:

Take the case of an economic community of a progressive type with an income of twenty units, spending seventeen, and saving three for regular investment in new productive capital, which finds full, regular employment in meeting the growing demand for commodities. Now suppose, owing to some change in distribution of incomes, some return to simplicity of living or some increased appreciation of future as compared with present satisfactions, spending is reduced to sixteen, saving raised to four, what must happen? The increased savings cannot take shape in productive capital, for, as the increase of current and prospective consumption of commodities is reduced, a smaller amount of new productive capital can be put into operation, and any attempt to put into operation as much as before must speedily be checked by the obvious glut.

Directly a shrinkage in demand for commodities and new productive capital occurs, the lessened rate of production begins to reduce all incomes, including those of the saving class. Aggregate income no longer stands at twenty, but falls to eighteen, or even seventeen. The saving class who were trying to save four out of a total twenty, leaving sixteen for spending, are not willing to save four or even three out of an aggregate income reduced to eighteen or seventeen. Their permanent standard of comfort stands in the way.   (1909b, pp. 292–3)

To formalise Hobson's example, we could adopt a consumption function of the form $C = a + bY$, with 'some change in distribution of incomes, some return to simplicity of living or some increased appreciation of future as compared with present satisfactions' being represented by a decrease in a. Then the consumption functions respectively before and after (say) a redistribution of income in the direction of greater inequality could for example be $C = 7 + 0.5Y$, and $C = 6 + 0.5Y$. In the 'early stages' of the consequent underconsumption cycle saving and investment would increase to 4, but the lower consumption demand would make this higher level of investment unsustainable, and in the 'later stages' income might fall to 17, and saving and investment to 2.5 (the saving class not being willing to save 'even three' out of an aggregate income reduced to seventeen). Following Hobson in abstracting from the effect of net investment on potential income, we illustrate this example in Table 4.1, where Y^* again represents the optimal level of income in the sense that full utilisation of capacity is sustained, and periods 2 and 3 portray the 'early' and 'later' stages of a depression respectively.

It is notable that the final two sentences in the passage by Hobson most recently quoted imply a Keynesian-type consumption function, with

Table 4.1   Hobson's underconsumption example

Period	Y^*	C	I	Y
1	20	17	3	20
2	20	16	4	20
3	20	14.5	2.5	17

saving, and therefore consumption, varying with the level of income. Indeed, the example as a whole goes a considerable way to anticipating by twenty years the 'Banana Parable' in Keynes' *Treatise on Money*, to which reference has already been made, and to which Joan Robinson was the first to attach special signficance as a precursor of the central argument in *The General Theory*.[34,35]

Let us next illustrate Hobson's distinction between the 'early stages' and the 'later stages' of an underconsumption cycle by means of a period-by-period numerical example based on our algebraic representation of Hobson's theory, with a period representing the time it takes for excess capacity both to emerge and to be recognised by capitalists, say one to two years. Remembering that $(C/Y)^*$ equals $(\sigma - g)/\sigma$, we can derive an expression for the 'warranted' capital–consumption ratio as follows:

$$(K/C)^* = (K/Y)/(C/Y)^*$$
$$= (1/\sigma)/\left[(\sigma - g)/\sigma\right]$$
$$= 1/(\sigma - g)$$

where $(K/C)^*$ is the ratio between capital and consumption required for the full employment of capital to be sustained; $1/(\sigma - g)$ is thus the warranted capital–consumption ratio.

Now consider an economy in which capital stock at the beginning of period 1 is 880, the marginal and average output–capital ratio is 3/4, and full-utilisation-of-capacity output in period 1 is hence 660. Assume that initially the economy is characterised by full capacity utilisation, so that in period 1 income too is 660. The economy is also assumed to be characterised initially by a steady-state growth rate of 0.25, generated by a consumption growth rate of 0.25.[36] The warranted saving–consumption ratio, $g/(\sigma - g)$, is hence 1/2. From this information we can deduce that, in period 1, consumption will be 440, and saving and net investment 220. The steady-state growth path for this economy, a benchmark which is set

out in Table 4.2, yields for period 2 an initial capital stock of 1100, and
values for capacity output, consumption, net investment and income of
825, 550, 275 and 825 respectively; the discrepancy of 1 between potential
output and actual output in period 3 is a result of rounding.

As an introduction to the underconsumption case, let us illustrate this
steady-state growth example, by means of Figure 4.2.[37] In this diagram
the vertical axis is used to measure potential income. On the left-hand side
of the diagram the horizontal axis measures capital stock at the beginning
of the period concerned, generating a potential income determined by the
output–capital ratio; and on the right-hand side the horizontal axis
measures consumption and investment, the sum of which represents actual
income. The 0.25 consumption growth rate represented by the OC line
generates a 0.25 income growth rate represented by the 45° line.

Table 4.2   Example of Hobsonian steady-state growth

Period	K	Y*	C	g	I	Y
1	880	660	440	0.25	220	660
2	1100	825	550	0.25	275	825
3	1375	1031	688	0.25	344	1032

Figure 4.2   Example of Hobsonian steady-state growth

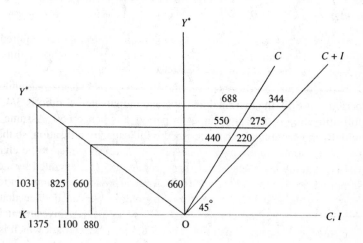

Assume now instead that the rate of growth of consumption between period 1 and period 2 drops from the previous level of 0.25 to 0.22, yielding a level of consumption in period 2 of 537. If we assume that period 2 represents the 'early stages' of an underconsumption cycle, we can conclude that net investment makes up for the 'shortfall' in consumption, and hence equals 288, resulting both in full utilisation of capacity in period 2, and in a capital stock at the beginning of period 3 of 1388.

If capitalists expect the rate of growth of consumption to remain at 0.22 from period 2 onwards, the consequences will be as set out in Table 4.3. With the slower rate of growth of consumption, the warranted capital–consumption ratio $[1/(\sigma - g)]$ will fall from 2 to 100/53, so given that consumption in period 3 will be 655, the warranted level of capital stock at the beginning of period 3 will be only 1236, by contrast with the actual level of 1388. Similarly, given that consumption in period 4 will be 799, the warranted level of capital stock at the beginning of period 4 will be 1508. Net investment in period 3 will thus be 120, and the actual level of income 775, 266 less than the full-utilisation-of-capacity level of 1041. Period 3 clearly corresponds to what Hobson called the 'later stages' of a depression.

Given consumption in period 5 of 975, and the warranted capital–consumption ratio of 100/53, warranted capital stock at the beginning of period 5 will be 1840, and investment in period 4 will be 332. Further, given that consumption in period 4 is 799, actual income in that period will be 1131, equal to potential income. Although period 4 represents recovery from the depression in the sense that there is full utilisation of capacity, the lower rate of consumption that caused the depression has left a permanent mark, in that full-utilisation-of-capacity output (1131) is below that which would have occurred (1258) if consumption had continued to grow at 25 per cent.

Table 4.3   Example of Hobsonian depression and aftermath

Period	K	Y*	C	g	I	Y
1	880	660	440	0.25	220	660
2	1100	825	537	0.22	288	825
3	1388	1041	655	0.22	120	775
4	1508	1131	799	0.22	332	1131
5	1840	1380	975			

Figure 4.2 can be adapted to illustrate this underconsumption case, as Figure 4.3 shows. In this diagram the 'early stages' of an underconsumption cycle are illustrated by net investment in period 2 (288), which exceeds that in the 25 per cent steady-state growth case (275); and the 'later stages' are illustrated by the occurrence in period 3 of net investment (120) which is lower than that in the 25 per cent steady-state growth case (344), and of a level of income (775) well below that involving full capacity utilisation (1041).

The above examples of an economy suffering from underconsumption *inter alia* bring out clearly the point that in the 'early stages' of an underconsumption cycle there is an excess supply of capital in the sense that its use generates a level of output that is not matched by demand. In a closed economy, the only way in which this can be prevented is to reduce the high level of saving that is responsible for the excess supply of capital. As Hobson noted, however, in an open economy there is the alternative remedy of exporting either the surplus capital or the surplus goods. This is the basis of his theory of imperialism, which occupies much of the next chapter.

Before turning to the question of the link between Hobson's theories of underconsumption and imperialism, however, we note a by-product of the underconsumption theory as set out in *The Physiology of Industry*.

Figure 4.3 Hobsonian depression and aftermath

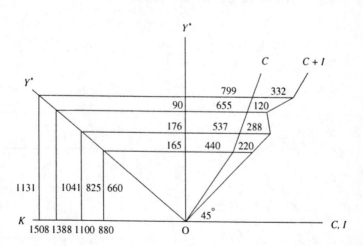

Mummery and Hobson substantially anticipated the acceleration principle. A rearrangement of equation (4.8) yields:

$$I_1 = gC_1 / (\sigma - g)$$
$$I_1 = (C_1 - C_2) / (\sigma - g)$$

where $1/(\sigma - g)$ is a dynamic counterpart of the static 'acceleration coefficient'. Curiously enough, when J. M. Clark first put forward the acceleration principle (see Clark, 1917) he too expressed it in terms of changes in consumption, and not in terms of changes in net output as is the case with most modern versions.[38] Clark's formula for the demand for new construction was $I(\Delta C/C)$, where I is the 'investment necessary to produce output at rate C', C is the 'rate of consumption at time t_1', and $(C + \Delta C)$ is the 'rate of consumption at time of [*sic*] t_2, the increase being distributed evenly through time t' (p. 222, n. 1). I/C thus represents the marginal ratio of capital to annual consumption; Clark assumes it to be substantially greater than unity. In *The Physiology of Industry* Hobson and Mummery argued that 'the plant required to produce any individual commodity by modern methods vastly exceeds in value the individual commodity itself, and we certainly do not over-estimate this difference if we assume that an increase of ten per cent in the annual consumption of any commodity would require an increase of fifty per cent in the production of that community during the year of increase' (1889, p. 85). It seems clear that Mummery and Hobson deserve some recognition for their anticipation of the basic principle of the accelerator theory.

5 Trade, Capital Flows and Imperialism

Hobson was the first to explain policies of territorial annexation in terms of economic factors.[1] The best known version of this explanation is that in *Imperialism: A Study*, which includes an investigation of the potential roles of international trade and international capital flows respectively in prompting such policies, concluding that it is not the former but the latter that is responsible. As a prelude to the exposition of this theory of imperialism we look at Hobson's analyses of these two aspects of economic activity.

5.1 INTERNATIONAL TRADE AND CAPITAL FLOWS

Ricardo's theory of comparative advantage, which is based on the assumption of immobility of capital between nations, states that it is to each nation's interest to specialise in the production of those commodities in which it has a comparative advantage, even in the case where a nation has an absolute advantage in the production of all commodities.[2] Such specialisation results in the maximisation of world output valued at cost of production, and thereby allows for the possibility that every nation will gain through trade.

In his first publication in the field of international economics, 'Can England Keep her Trade?' (*The National Review*, 1891d), Hobson replaced Ricardo's assumption of capital immobility with the assumption that there is international mobility of both labour and capital, on the ground that he regarded this as more realistic. Under these circumstances, he concluded, if England wished to maintain both its standard of living and the number of its inhabitants, it would eventually not only have to follow the example of countries such as the United States and Australia in limiting or prohibiting the importation of cheap foreign labour, but also have to impose restrictions on the export of capital. His argument was that, since labourers from undeveloped countries are able to subsist at a standard of living lower than that required by English labourers, their presence in England would force down the average wage rate. If such immigration were prohibited, but the export of capital permitted, capital would continue to flow out of England, caused by the fact that the lower labour productivity in undeveloped countries such as India was outweighed by the much lower wage rate, causing the labour cost per unit of output to be lower, and accordingly, profitability to be higher. This continuing loss of capital would be followed initially by a consequent continuing decline in labour productivity, and hence the wage rate; eventually, labour productivity and the wage rate in England would fall to a level below that in undeveloped countries such as India, and then emigration would occur. If this were allowed to happen, 'the capacity for the production of material forms of wealth would ride roughshod over all the higher purposes of life, distributing mankind not according to the requirements of moral and intellectual advance, or even of aggregate physical well-being, but according to that method of division which was conducive to the largest nett aggregate of wealth' (1891d, p. 8). His analysis led Hobson to conclude that, if the depopulation of England was to be avoided, it would be necessary to place 'a prohibitive tariff on the migration of English capital' (1891d, p. 10). As Hobson himself noted, there is nothing in this argument which conflicts with the case for freedom of international trade; over his lifetime, Hobson was in fact about as consistent a supporter of free trade as it is possible to be.[3] He was rather arguing that England should ensure by policy measures the capital immobility assumed by Ricardo.

Evidence that Hobson continued to be concerned about the problem dealt with in 'Can England Keep her Trade?' is to be found in *Imperialism: A Study*, where he stated that 'there is no consideration, theoretic or practical ... to prevent Chinese capital with Chinese labour from ousting British produce in neutral markets of the world' (1902, p. 329). However, in its conclusion that England should prohibit the export of capital, the early article differs from Hobson's later writings in the same area. One example of such later work is Hobson's article on 'The Inner Meaning of Protectionism' (*The Contemporary Review*, 1903), a response to Chamberlain's revival of the protectionist movement, which included among its aims the preservation in Britain of a large volume and variety of industry and industrial population. This piece reads as if, twelve years on, Hobson had revisited his earlier article and found its argument incomplete. The later article repeats the analysis of the earlier one, but in addition makes explicit reference to the fact that depopulation could only be prevented if prohibition of the export of capital were accompanied by prohibition of emigration by labourers. This addition assisted Hobson in stressing the isolationist character of a policy designed to maintain the standard of living and number of inhabitants in Britain; it 'would injure our national life by narrowing the stream of intercourse with other nations, upon which in the future, as in the past, the growth and enrichment of our nationality depend' (1903, p. 370). Hobson concluded that, rather than follow such a policy, even 'if it were a case of making immediate economic sacrifices, it would pay us better as a nation in the long run to maintain a free expansive intercourse with foreign civilised nations' (1903, p. 370).

Hobson's *International Trade: An Application of Economic Theory* (1904) dealt more specifically with international movements of commodities, as opposed to factors of production. In this book, Hobson objected to Ricardo's exposition of the theory of comparative advantage on the ground not that it is invalid, but that it is less necessary to the explanation of international trade than to that of internal trade. Taking the British economy at that time as an example, Hobson argued that, in it, trade unions and professional associations greatly limited mobility of labour between occupations, and agreements between large companies restricted substantially the mobility of capital between industries; on balance it was easier for both labour and capital to move between Great Britain and other nations than between occupations and industries within Great Britain. Indeed, Hobson believed the commodities involved in trade between nations to be produced and exchanged under conditions so closely approximating those of free competition that no separate theory was required to explain international trade. This allowed him to move directly to the conclusion that any act of interference with trade between nations would be to the detriment of most, if not all, the nations affected by it, including the nation responsible for the interference. With respect to international trade, he thus endorsed Cobden's policy of non-intervention.[4]

Hobson used this line of attack to reject arguments advanced in favour of the following: import duties, for reasons of either revenue or protection; duties giving preference to certain countries, notably colonial territories; and anti-dumping measures, that is to say measures designed to prevent foreign goods being sold at below their cost of production. He added that to view such measures as favouring producers at the expense of consumers is a mistake; since all consumers are also producers, the consequence is that some producers are favoured at the expense of others, as well as at the expense of the nation as a whole.

Hobson admitted two possible exceptions to the general argument for freedom of international trade. The first was the case of dumping intended to destroy local industry, so that the dumper can charge higher prices permanently in the future. Hobson concluded that in practice, however, it would be impossible to distinguish such cases of dumping from other cases, so that making this an exception would leave the way open for special interests to obtain protection in inappropriate circumstances.

The second exception was the case of a nation experiencing unemployment. Given the importance Hobson attached to the reduction of unemployment, one might have expected him to support the use of protection as a means to this end. In *The Physiology of Industry*, however, Mummery and Hobson cautiously concluded only that 'in a condition of depressed trade, Protective measures do not inflict the damage which the orthodox Freetraders assign to them' (1889, p. 209), drawing attention to the fact that the higher cost of production in a protected industry is to a greater or lesser degree offset by the accompanying employment of previously idle resources. In *International Trade*, Hobson looked at the practical aspects of such a policy, concluding that 'between this theoretic service of protection [reduction of unemployment] and a practically serviceable tariff there is a great gulf fixed' (1904, p. 157). In practice, it would be necessary first to estimate how much unemployment of resources would be required before protection would increase employment instead of diverting resources from other industries where they were more efficiently employed. Second, it would be necessary to ensure that the industries protected were not 'decaying' industries which should be allowed to run down. Even if these requirements were met, imposition of such a tariff would come up against what Hobson saw as an insuperable obstacle, namely that governments in practice impose tariffs not on economic grounds but for political reasons, at the behest of special interests.

In any case, 'protection, regarded as a remedy for unemployment, is the substitution of a bad palliative for a cure' (1904, p. 163). Believing the true cure to lie in an increase in consumption, Hobson saw protection as a bad palliative because it was likely to reduce consumption rather than to increase it. Given the absence of trade unions in agriculture, the gains from agricultural protection were likely to go almost entirely to landlords, while the gains from protection in manufacturing were likely to go mostly to profits in the industries protected, even in unionised industries. This redistribution of income, from wages to rent and profit, far from increasing consumption, would reduce it.

In 'Can Protection Cure Unemployment?' (1909) Hobson attempted to cap his earlier arguments by producing a purely economic case for free trade even in times of depression. He argued that even if there is zero elasticity of demand for the protected commodity, the additional employment created in the protected industry with the introduction of protection during a period of unemployment would initially be offset by an exactly equal reduction in employment in unsheltered industries.[5] His argument in support of this conclusion was that those who spent more on the now-protected 'luxury' would either spend the same amount less on other luxuries, or save less; in the former case, employment would fall in industries producing unprotected luxury consumption goods, and in the latter case employment would fall in the investment-goods industries. If pressed, Hobson would at the very least have been forced to confine the applicability of the latter case to the short run, as his underconsumptionist explanation of unemployment demanded precisely that in the long run there *should* be a reallocation of resources from the investment-goods to the consumption-goods sector.

Regardless of whether there is free trade or protection, if there are no international capital flows, then exports must always tend to equality with imports. As Hobson put it in *International Trade*, under a fixed exchange rate regime such as the Gold Standard system which prevailed in his time, an excess of exports over imports, which drives the exchange rate to the upper limit of the narrow bounds allowed by that system, has to be paid for in gold by foreign countries. The inflow of gold will in turn cause the central bank to lower its discount rate, with a consequent rise first in borrowing from banks and then in the price level, which itself will discourage exports and encourage imports.[6] Hobson accepted this idea of an indirect mechanism, working through interest rate changes, by which current account imbalances are automatically removed.[7]

When there is international mobility of capital, on the other hand, one country's excess of exports over imports can alternatively be paid for by borrowing on the part of other countries. Even if the rest of the world possessed no gold, Great Britain (say) could export more commodities than it imported by lending to the rest of the world, that is to say, by exporting capital. As Hobson put it, 'every ... loan when it takes place represents a quantity of exports for which no corresponding imports are required in the ordinary balance of trade' (1904, p. 107).

A country that has previously lent to other countries will receive a flow of interest payments, dividend payments, or both, except to the extent that such payments are not repatriated. As a result, the surplus of exports over imports which a given amount of current lending will finance will be reduced; in this case, 'the creditor nation is sending out exports which exceed her imports by the amount of the loans, less the interest from the sums previously loaned' (1904, p. 107). And if a country should lend to other countries the same amount year after year, in time the interest payments it receives annually will exceed the amount it is currently lending, and it will no longer be possible for that country to export more than it imports; for example, if the interest rate were 5 per cent, this would happen in the twenty-first year of lending. These non-controversial

connections between trade imbalances and international capital movements are central to Hobson's theory of imperialism.

5.2   IMPERIALISM AND UNDERCONSUMPTION

When Hobson put forward his theory of imperialism the word
'imperialism' was:

> altogether of recent origin. It started its career when Europe, and
> especially England, pondered over the destinies of the the second
> French Empire [founded in 1852]. Twenty years later it was called in to
> denote the contemporary ways of English foreign politics, the politics of
> Disraeli.   (Koebner, 1949, p. 2)

Even then:

> the word 'imperialism' itself, in those days of Disraeli's Premiership
> (1874–80) always appeared in self-conscious quotation marks,
> even in Conservative newspapers and quarterlies ... imperialism was
> still equated with Caesarism, arbitrary power.   (Thornton, 1959,
> p. 30)

Following Robert Lowe's use of 'Imperialism' as the title of his 1878
Fortnightly Review article attacking Disraeli's foreign policy, the meaning
of the term became established by usage; imperialism in Hobson's time
meant 'a policy aiming at the formation and maintenance of empires'
(Kohn, 1951, p. 122).

Hobson's attempt to explain imperialism, so defined, was significantly
influenced by the ideas of Cobden. In particular, one of the letters written
by Cobden which Hobson included in *Richard Cobden: The International
Man* includes the following pregnant passage:

> I often wish I had the leisure to do justice to the argument which is
> always uppermost in my mind, that the modern application of the
> principles of political economy has destroyed the motive of self-interest
> which formerly tempted us to wars of conquest. I *could* turn the batter-
> ies against the L.s.d. argument most successfully. (quoted in Hobson,
> 1919a, p. 89, emphasis in the original; 'L.s.d.' stands for pounds,
> shillings and pence)

Cobden was referring here to the use of political economy to rebut the idea that territorial annexation brings economic benefit. But Cobden's belief in the beneficence of *laissez-faire* would have precluded him from developing an explanation of imperialism in economic terms. It was Hobson's underconsumption theory that made it possible for him to succeed where Cobden would have failed. As Koebner (1949, p. 27) noted, it was:

> difficult for a liberal to weld all the indictments against imperialist state-craft and imperialist society into a coherent system of interpretation. To attain such a high goal and to form a real theory of imperialism was possible only to a mind which was prepared to combine the Cobdenite motives with unorthodox views concerning the mechanism of society. This it is that J. A. Hobson did.

Hobson first linked underconsumption with imperialism not in *Imperialism: A Study*, but in an article published in 1898 in the *Contemporary Review*, under the title of 'Free Trade and Foreign Policy'. His theory of imperialism, far from arising out of his experiences as a correspondent in South Africa during the Boer War, as has sometimes been supposed, led (as noted in Chapter 1) to his being sent to South Africa.[8]

In 'Free Trade and Foreign Policy', which was a response to British government attempts to gain exclusive economic rights in parts of China under the ambiguously-named 'Open Door' policy, Hobson made a rudimentary attempt to draw up a 'dry debtor and creditor account' of the kind referred to by Cobden. He noted that between 1873 and 1897 British expenditure on armaments had increased from £24 065 876 to £41 238 802 (Deane and Cole, 1967, p. 332, estimate that gross national product at market prices rose from £1357m in 1873 to £1696m in 1897). Noting that 'the taxation imposed upon the British nation in order to support the cost of our increasing army and navy is defended chiefly on the ground that it is necessary in order to safeguard our colonial possessions and to enable us to secure new markets by increasing the area of the Empire' (1898b, p. 175), Hobson then showed from figures for the period 1855–97 that, in spite of the large increase in British possessions, the sum of imports from and exports to British possessions as a proportion of total British imports and exports had, in fact, declined. Thus it was *not* true that 'our colonial trade has justified the conviction that "trade follows the flag", and that it is therefore a profitable policy for England to plant her flag upon new tracts of territory throughout the world' (1898b, p. 173). The conclusion he drew was that 'so far as trade statistics have any value, they convict us of conducting our national trade with a reckless folly which would quickly bring any individual merchant into the Bankruptcy Court' (1898b, p. 176).

Still seeking a rational explanation for Great Britain's continuing expansion of its Empire, Hobson found it in the existence of underconsumption. Drawing on his underconsumption theory, Hobson argued that 'our surplus products, which the working classes cannot buy and the wealthier classes do not wish to buy, must find customers among foreign nations, and, since those who sell them do not even wish to consume their equivalent in existing foreign goods, they must lie in foreign countries as loans or other permanent investments' (1898, p. 178); the terms 'investment(s)' and 'capital' here, and subsequently in this chapter, refer to the purchase or ownership of financial as well as physical assets. This was the explanation of Great Britain's massive export of capital. Referring to underconsumption, Hobson wrote:

> If direct testimony to this fact and its consequences is desired, it is found in the large surplus of our national income which, being needed neither for home consumption nor for capital in home industries, seeks foreign investments, – a sum which, though it admits of no precise computation, must far exceed a total of two thousand million pounds sterling. It is possible, indeed, that the growing pressure of the need for foreign investments must be regarded as the most potent and direct influence in our foreign policy. (1898b, p. 178; note that Hobson's figure for overseas assets owned by British residents is of the same order of magnitude as Great Britain's annual gross domestic product at the end of the nineteenth century)

Hobson then converted this possibility into a certainty. As Great Britain had 'lost all belief' in its capacity to find, under conditions of free trade, the required new overseas outlets for its surplus products, it had been led to acquire new territories, where necessary by force.

At this time in the development of his thought Hobson had no doubts about the capacity of consumption to keep pace with production, provided that income was distributed to those who worked for it. He wrote:

> Among our people there lies an immense potential market for the conveniences and comforts of life. A progessive nation, with an infinite capacity of developing new tastes and new needs, should harbour no fear of failing markets.[9]   (1898b, p. 177)

Measures which redistributed income from property-owners to workers would thus be followed by an increase in consumption, and this in turn would relieve the pressure for the pursuit of imperialist policies overseas. As Hobson put it, 'the issue, in a word, is between external expansion of markets and territory on the one hand, and internal social and industrial reforms upon the other' (1898b, p. 179). Or as Brewer (1990) expresses it:

> First, there is an economic theory intended to explain high levels of foreign investment, and to show that it would be unnecessary if income were redistributed. Second, there is a political theory linking foreign investment to imperialist policies.   (Brewer, 1990, p. 75)

In an attempt to reinforce the idea that a nation need not depend on 'the external expansion of markets and territory', Hobson asserted that the increase in consumption that would follow a redistribution of income to workers would mostly be on basic domestically-produced goods, as opposed to foreign luxuries, as a result of which the ratio of imports and exports to national output would fall. Indeed, 'during the period 1898 to 1905, Hobson was several times at pains to prove that there was a tendency, amounting to a law, for the percentage of national income accounted for by foreign trade to decline naturally' (Cain, 1978, p. 572). And, in the 1906 edition of *The Evolution of Modern Capitalism*, he argued that the increase in the size of the 'dealing' relative to the that of the 'making' trades as a nation becomes more wealthy will in time cause the ratio of its foreign trade to its output to decline, a point he believed Great Britain had reached in 1885 (1906a, pp. 399–400). As Cain (1978, pp. 571, 577) points out, belief in the existence of such a 'tendency, amounting to a law', runs counter to Cobden's vision of a world in which increasing trade between nations was to be a force for peace, and Hobson subsequently abandoned this belief, notably in *An Economic Interpretation of Investment* (1911b).

To sum up, the theory of imperialism set out in 'Free Trade and Foreign Policy' runs as follows. Territorial annexation is costly. This expenditure cannot be explained by trade, as empirical evidence shows trade does not 'follow the flag'. But it can be explained by a need for an outlet for capital, a need caused by underconsumption.

This argument, while logically consistent as far as it goes, is incomplete. In order to support the idea of a connection between the need to export capital and territorial annexation, Hobson had to show that capital 'follows the flag'. Moreover, to forestall an obvious potential criticism, it would also have been prudent of him to have made it clear that capital can 'follow the flag', even if trade does not; he could have pointed out, for example, that British capital sent to Canada might be used to finance imports from the United States, which then used the receipts to finance imports from Britain. Did Hobson take up these matters in *Imperialism: A Study*? To answer this question, we look next at the way in which Hobson expounded and extended his theory of imperialism in that book.

5.3   IMPERIALISM AND ECONOMIC PRESSURE GROUPS

In *Imperialism: A Study* Hobson examined the three decades of European territorial expansion that followed the Franco-Prussian War of 1870, noting that by far the greater part of this expansion took place from about 1884. Taking Great Britain first, he calculated that at the end of this period, in 1901, the proportion of its exports going to British possessions was only 36.5 per cent, and the proportion of its imports coming from British possessions was only 20 per cent. Moreover, of Great Britain's imperial exports and imports, the greater part was with self-governing colonies, all of which had been acquired before 1870. In addition, recent years had seen increased military and naval expenditure. Echoing the argument of 'Free Trade and Foreign Policy', Hobson wrote:

> this new expenditure is nothing else than a huge business blunder. An individual doing business in this fashion could not avoid bankruptcy, and a nation, however rich, pursuing such a policy is loaded down with a millstone which must eventually drag her down.   (1902, p. 70)[10]

He concluded that it seems 'unintelligible that the enormous costs and risks of the new Imperialism should be undertaken for such small results in the shape of increase to external trade, especially when the size and character of the new markets acquired were taken into consideration' (1902, p. 60).

A solution to this puzzle had already been proposed in 'Free Trade and Foreign Policy'. In *Imperialism: A Study*, Hobson provided evidence to support his earlier argument, pointing out that 'while our foreign and colonial trade, and presumably the income from it, are growing but slowly, the share of our import values representing income from foreign investments is growing very rapidly' (1902, p. 60). He cited tax assessments on income derived from foreign and colonial stocks of a public or semi-public character, which showed such income to have increased from £33 829 124 in 1884 to £60 266 886 in 1900 (Deane and Cole, 1967,

p. 332, calculated gross national product at market prices to be £1401m in 1884, and £2040m in 1900). Hobson noted, further, that Robert Giffen had estimated from tax returns that the total income derived by Great Britain from foreign investment had grown by 1899 to £90 million; taking account of such income as was not included in tax returns, he concluded that the total amount must have been of the order of £120 million.[11] This was the basis for his pronouncement that 'by far the most important economic factor in Imperialism is the influence relating to investments' (1902, p. 56); that is to say, of all those who had an economic interest in territorial annexation, owners of assets held overseas were far and away the most effective in putting pressure on the government to expand the British Empire.

As we have already seen, in 'Free Trade and Foreign Policy' foreign investment is treated as a national need for a nation both suffering from underconsumption and unwilling to remedy it through internal measures. But Hobson did refer once in that article to an explanation of imperialism which can be seen as either complementary or alternative to the one already outlined, namely that it arises out of the use of 'the public purse for the purposes of private profit-making' (1898b, p. 178) entailed by protection of foreign investment, which generates income only for a few. In *Imperialism: A Study*, by contrast, this became the dominant explanation; the pressure for imperialist policies is there seen as coming principally from those who, in the absence of profitable domestic opportunities, send their funds overseas, and even more from the financiers, international rather than domesic, who arrange these investments. In Hobson's view:

> to a larger extent every year Great Britain has been becoming a nation living on tribute from abroad, and the classes who enjoy this tribute have an ever-increasing incentive to employ the public policy, the public purse, and the public force to extend the field of their private investments, and to safeguard and improve their existing investments. (1902, p. 60)

The 'tribute' is shared by investors and financiers, in the form of abnormally high profits on risky overseas investments protected by the imperial power; Hobson implies that the policy brings little benefit to manufacturers and traders, and only costs to the average citizen.

Hobson argued that the relevance of this analysis was by no means confined to Great Britain; 'what is true of Great Britain is true likewise of France, Germany, the United States, and of all countries in which modern capitalism had placed large surplus savings in the hands of a plutocracy or

of a thrifty middle class' (1902, pp. 60–1). In the case of the United
States there was an additional factor making for an imperialist policy.
Towards the end of the nineteenth century the United States' economy
had become characterised by a 'concentration of industry in "trusts",
"combines", &c., [which] at once limits the quantity of capital which can
be effectively employed and increases the share of profits out of which
fresh savings and fresh capital will spring' (1902, p. 81). Hobson's
argument was that concentration of industry restricts the quantity of
capital that can effectively be employed because large firms possess the
power to shut down unprofitable plants. Concentration increases the
share of profits in national income because large firms are in a position to
raise prices or cut costs, or both, as Hobson had already explained in
Evolution of Modern Capitalism.

What happened to Hobson's earlier idea that imperialism is among the
remedies for underconsumption? The answer is that in *Imperialism: A
Study*, Hobson concentrated almost exclusively on the alternative ways of
remedying underconsumption. Thus he wrote that:

> there is no necessity to open up new foreign markets; the home markets
> are capable of indefinite expansion. Whatever is produced in England
> can be consumed in England, provided that the 'income', or power to
> demand commodities, is properly distributed ... Social reform bifur-
> cates, according as reformers seek to achieve this end by raising wages
> or by increasing public taxation and expenditure.   (1902, pp. 94–5)

Hobson regarded these means of social reform as complementary. Trade
unions seek to increase the share of national income going to wages,
through either private co-operation or political activity. Alternatively:

> State Socialism aims at getting for the direct use of the whole society an
> increased share of the 'social values' which arise from the closely and
> essentially co-operative work of an industrial society, taxing property
> and incomes so as to draw into the public exchequer for public expen-
> diture the 'unearned elements' of income, leaving to individual produc-
> ers those incomes which are necessary to induce them to apply in the
> best way their economic energies, and to private enterprises those busi-
> nesses which do not breed monopoly, and which the public need not or
> cannot undertake ... Trade unionism and Socialism are thus the natural
> enemies of Imperialism, for they take away from the 'imperialist'
> classes the surplus incomes which form the economic stimulus of
> Imperialism.   (1902, p. 90)

The nature and cause of Hobson's change of tack between 'Free Trade and Foreign Policy' and *Imperialism: A Study* is neatly encapsulated in Cain (1978, p. 582), where it is stated, with reference to Hobson being sent to South Africa, that 'in some ways this was unfortunate for him ... turning what was to be a "systemic" theory into a conspiratorial one'; though a conspiratorial theory may be systematic, it is unquestionably true that the theory of imperialism to be found in *Imperialism: A Study* is less systematic than that in 'Free Trade and Foreign Policy'.

Hobson was fully aware 'of the part which the non-economic factors of patriotism, adventure, military enterprise, political ambition, and philanthropy play in imperial expansion' (1902, p. 66), and discussed these non-economic factors at length, not only in *Imperialism: A Study* but also in particular in *The Psychology of Jingoism* (1901a).[12] But, in his view, although these factors provide the driving power, finance is 'the governor of the imperial engine, directing the energy and determining its work' (1902, p. 66).

The last four chapters of *Imperialism: A Study* deal mainly with the impact of policies of territorial annexation on those who lose the ownership of their land. Hobson believed it to be inevitable that imperial possessions would be governed in the interests of imperialist industrialists and financiers, who would take advantage of local cheap labour and state protection to reap high profits by establishing and expanding those industries that were most profitable. Where local laws or customs were in the way, they would be overridden, and the pace and direction of investment would take no account of the needs of the local population. This is not to say, however, that Hobson opposed economic development in undeveloped areas of the world, which in any case he thought to be both desirable as far as the human race was concerned, and inevitable. Rather, he was one of the very few at that time who advocated economic development at a pace determined by the local people, protected by an international overseeing body.[13] In this respect he anticipated a view that was to attract substantial support only with the much later publication of Paul Baran's *The Political Economy of Growth* (1957) and of the works in the field of economic development that emerged subsequently; though few of these later writers shared Hobson's belief in the possibility of a benevolent international overseeing body.

Imperialism; A Study did not complete Hobson's earlier argument by showing either that capital 'follows the flag', or that this is compatible with trade not 'following the flag'. With respect to the former, in 1902 the relevant figures were in any case still not available. But nine years later George Paish published estimates of annual British investment overseas, classified according to destination; the figures for the year 1910 were included by Hobson in *An Economic Interpretation of Investment* (1911b, p. 71). It can be deduced from these figures that in 1910 British investment in Asia and Africa, the only two continents in which Britain had recently pursued or was still pursuing a policy of territorial annexation, accounted for merely 20 per cent of Britain's total foreign investment. Of the eleven countries receiving the most British capital, apart from the self-governing Dominions of Canada and New Zealand, only three were part of the British Empire, and they accounted for only 21 per cent of British investment in the eleven countries.[14]

It seems surprising that Hobson appears not to have recognised the similarity between these facts and those that had led him to reject the thesis that imperialism is explained by the needs of foreign trade. A possible explanation of this oversight is to be found in the fact that, by 1911, influenced no doubt by a relatively peaceful and prosperous decade, Hobson was inclined to emphasise the benefits rather than the disadvantages of the export of capital by advanced countries (1911b, pp. 112–24).[15] His new view was that:

> though Cobden was too optimistic in attributing to the growth of foreign trade so early and so complete an efficacy as peacemaker, he was correct in his judgement of the tendency ... But the cross ownership of capital involved in international investment is a far stronger and steadier pledge of peace ... Where the international character of an investment has been further marked by the substantial participation of investors of several nationalities, there will not be either the same temptation or the same ability to induce a government to bring pressure on a foreign state in the interest of financiers, many of whom are not its own subjects. (1911b, pp. 112–13)

Hobson now thought that capital-exporting countries would be dissuaded from going to war by the enormous prospective losses of capital they had exported to foreign countries, developed as well as undeveloped.

This optimism was short-lived, being shattered by the outbreak of war in 1914, although, as Cain (1990) points out, elements of it are still to be found in *Towards International Government* (1915). Reverting to his earlier view, Hobson reaffirmed in *The New Protectionism* (1916) that 'it is the competition between groups of business men, financiers, and traders, in the several nations, using the offices of their respective Governments to assist them in promoting ... profitable business enterprises, that has underlain most of the friction in modern diplomacy and foreign policy, and has brought powerful nations so often into dangerous conflict' (1916, pp. 118–19). In *Democracy After the War* (1917) Hobson added that although within each nation the interests of these groups were opposed to 'the welfare of the nation as a whole' (1917, p. 76), the groups had the ability 'to impose their class interests upon the statecraft of their country' (1917, p. 76). And the experience of the First World War led him finally to recognise that 'a fundamental assumption of Cobdenism, and of the liberalism to which it appertained, that war and militarism were doomed to disappear with the advance of industry and commerce, is definitely false' (1917, p. 27).

It was also in *Democracy After the War*, however, that Hobson for the first time admitted that the imperialist engine may not always be governed by financial interests. He now thought it was true 'that in some instances political motives have an independent origin' (1917, p. 89), stating with respect to financial arrangements made over the previous two decades in China that Russia and Japan 'were motivated primarily by considerations of territorial and political aggrandisement' (1917, p. 95), and with respect to British involvement in the Boer War that 'the chief agents of this policy, Chamberlain, Rhodes and Lord Milner, were, so far as history shows, actuated by political motives in which the idea of imperial expansion doubtless coalesced with the sense of personal ambition, but in which distinctively economic gains either for themselves or for others played no determinant part' (1917, p. 84).[16] He went even further in this direction in *Free-thought in the Social Sciences*, where he claimed not only that imperialism is 'mainly the expression of two dominant human instincts, self-assertion and acquisitiveness' (p. 192), but also that 'to the former the primacy may be accorded, in the sense that individual or collective self-assertion, or lust for power, which inspires men to take or enforce rule over others, uses the arts of acquisition both as means to furtherance of this end, and as instruments for the direct satisfaction of positive self-feeling' (pp. 192–3). This reversed his previous view, namely that national 'self-assertion' is the means to an acquisitive end.

While the importance of self-assertion or power as a motive of human action continued to be emphasised in Hobson's subsequent writings, there are some indications that, on balance, he finally came to the conclusion that acquisitiveness, as well as self-assertion, is an independent cause of imperialism.[17] In 1936, for example, Hobson criticised Thorstein Veblen for explaining economic nationalism in purely sociological terms, thereby ignoring its explanation in economic terms, which he modestly attributed to Marx (1936, p. 139). Further, in his introduction to the third edition of *Imperialism: A Study* (1938a), Hobson repeated the view expressed in the first edition that, though 'patriotism has its own basic and instinctive origins, it is fed and directed in its activities by economic motives' (1938a, p. xii).[18]

Hobson's theory of imperialism, by contrast with his underconsumption theory, attaches considerable importance to the role of the financial sector of an economy. His writings on the economic roles of money and credit are examined in the next chapter. First, however, we look at the question of whether Hobson's writings on imperialism are compatible with empirical evidence.[19]

5.4   TESTING HOBSON'S THEORY OF IMPERIALISM

In subjecting Hobson's theory of imperialism to empirical test, let us take first the 'Free Trade and Foreign Policy' version of the theory, namely, that although territorial expansion is not driven by trade, it *is* driven by the need to export capital to prevent depressions caused by underconsumption. In the case of Britain, did underconsumption cause the export of capital? Further, did the export of capital cause imperialism?

The first of these two questions is particularly difficult to answer. The most thorough attempt to answer it is that to be found in Michael Edelstein's *Overseas Investment in the Age of High Imperialism: The United Kingdom, 1850–1914* (1982). On the basis of the empirical work reported in 'Realized Rates of Return on U.K. Home and Overseas Portfolio Investment in the Age of High Imperialism' (Edelstein, 1977), Edelstein concluded that 'a crude model investigating the relationship between realized returns and anticipated risks suggests that the overseas portfolio had a slightly lower level of *ex ante* risk associated with it than the home portfolio but, relative to these *ex ante* risk measures, the overseas portfolio generated higher *ex post* returns' (Edelstein, 1982, pp. 157–8).[20] This conclusion is at the very least not incompatible with Hobson's theory; the reason for the lower returns on the home portfolio, after discounting for risk, could have been excessive saving in relation to domestic investment outlets.

Using empirical evidence provided by Deane (1968) and Feinstein (1972) to test the applicability of Hobson's 'classical' saving model to the years 1870–1913, Edelstein went on to conclude that 'neither the share of nonwage income or its velocity, nor the volatility of the U.K. business cycle supports the hypothesis that there was a rise in the trend of oversaving' (Edelstein, 1982, p. 182). However, after finding that savings for the period as a whole were quite well explained by the Friedman–Ando–

Modigliani (permanent income/life cycle) savings model, Edelstein went on to point out that for the years 1877–9 and 1903–5 there are substantial discrepancies between the savings predicted by this model and actual savings. This led Edelstein to the following conclusion:

> At the major turning points for the Hobson oversaving hypothesis, 1877–79 and 1903–5, the years when the rate of net foreign lending moves off its lowest cyclical values into its major surges of the 1870–1913 period, 1887–90 and 1903–13, the best models of gross private savings rates make their worst overestimating errors; that is, predicted desired savings exceed actual savings rates. Some evidence seems to suggest that these errors may be interpreted as the *ex poste* [*sic*] resolution of an *ex ante* disequilibrium between desired savings and desired domestic investment spending, part of the resolution taking the form of savings, unwanted by domestic investment decision makers, spilling over into foreign investment. (Edelstein, 1982, pp. 194–5)

What we can add to Edelstein's analysis is the fact that A. H. Imlah's estimates of the annual export of capital show that all except one of the depth of depression years from 1862 to 1908 were immediately followed by an extended period of increasing overseas investment; the exception, 1894, was followed by two years of increasing capital export, though in this case the expansion failed to continue.[21] A. K. Cairncross (Cairncross, 1953, p. 197) reaches a similar conclusion as to the facts, and adds a causal relationship, asserting that 'in the short period an increase in activity abroad, generally associated with an increase in foreign investment in Britain, pulled the country out of pre-1914 slumps by improving the prospects of the export industries'.[22] This evidence tends to support Hobson's case.

On the second question, empirical evidence referred to by Hobson himself (both in *Imperialism: A Study*, citing the entry of M. G. Mulhall in Palgrave's *Dictionary of Political Economy*, and in *An Economic Interpretation of Investment*, citing the work of George Paish), and confirmed in Jenks (1927), shows that the capital exported by Britain between 1870 and 1914 went mainly to areas over which Britain either had no political control or was relinquishing control. In 1913 some £2870m out of £3710m of capital invested overseas was placed in countries that were independent of the British Government (see Paish, 1914). There is no reason to think that evidence relating to other periods or to other imperial countries points in any other direction.

Hobson might have responded to this counter-evidence by arguing that capital export was so important to Britain that the need for increases at the margin was sufficient to generate a policy of imperialism. As Cain (1978, p. 570, n. 7) points out, Hobson used an argument of this kind with respect to emigration, making reference to 'that disproportionate interest which always attaches to the margin of employment' (1902, p. 56). But, to be consistent in extending this argument to the export of capital, Hobson would have had to apply it to trade as well, and making his theory turn purely on reactions at the margin would have rendered it less powerful.

The alternative version of Hobson's theory of imperialism, propounded in *Imperialism: A Study*, states that territorial expansion is driven principally by financiers whose political influence induces governments to acquire territory, resulting in additional financial gain to them, but loss to the nation as a whole. This is a theory of which it is easy to provide examples, notably in the case of the Boer War, but difficult to test overall.[23] And Hobson himself implicitly threw doubt on it by his argument in 'Free Trade and Foreign Policy' that, in so far as imperialism is a remedy for underconsumption, the nation as a whole stands to benefit.

6 Money and Credit

Underconsumption theories belong to the pre-Keynesian tradition in that they can be applied to a non-monetary economy. Mummery and Hobson, in rejecting scarcity of gold as a cause of depression in trade, even went so far as to claim that 'money, while it obscures, in no wise changes the facts of barter' (1889, p. 189). Hobson's first and sole comprehensive work in the field of money and credit, *Gold, Prices and Wages, with an Examination of the Quantity Theory*, did not appear until twenty-four years after the publication of *The Physiology of Industry*, though a few of the ideas in it had already been put forward in the 'Money and Finance' chapter of *The Industrial System*. As noted in Chapter 1, the writing of *Gold, Prices and Wages* was prompted by the rise in prices experienced in industrialised countries from 1896 onwards, which Hobson regretted, mainly because he saw it as leading to greater inequality in the distribution of income.

Nine years later Hobson responded to the new credit theories advanced by Major C. H. Douglas, devoting a chapter of *The Economics of Unemployment* to a critique of Douglas's ideas.[1] In both cases Hobson incorporated the substance of previously-published articles; 'The Causes of the Rise of Prices' was published in the *Contemporary Review* in 1912 (and was reprinted as a pamphlet in the same year in Washington, DC), and 'The Douglas Theory' was published in the *Socialist Review* in February 1922, drawing a response from Douglas in March, followed by Hobson's 'A Rejoinder to Major Douglas' in April (the preface to *The Economics of Unemployment* is dated July 1922).

6.1 MONEY, CREDIT AND PRICES

Two years prior to 1913 the quantity theory of money had been reaffirmed in Irving Fisher's *The Purchasing Power of Money*, with Fisher encapsulating it in the equation $MV = PT$: the quantity of money multiplied by the velocity of circulation equals the price level multiplied by the number of transactions.

The centuries-old quantity theory had first been thought to work through what has become known as the 'direct mechanism' (an increase in the money supply being spent necessarily driving up the price level when the number of transactions is constant). By 1913, however, it was accepted by some that the quantity theory worked alternatively through the effect of a change in the money supply on bank credit. First outlined by Henry Thornton (1802), what has become known as the 'indirect mechanism' was clearly described by Marshall in his evidence to the Royal Commission on Gold and Silver in 1887, when in reply to a question he said, with respect to the effects of an influx of bullion into London's financial centre:

> Having this extra supply, lenders lower ... the rate which they charge for loans, and they keep on lowering it till a point is reached at which the demand will carry off the larger supply. When this has been done there is more capital in the hands of speculative investors, who come on to the markets for goods as buyers, and so raise prices.   (Marshall, 1888, vol. II, p. 7)

Marshall had previously been asked by the Commission to reconcile the idea that a low interest rate is accompanied by a rise in prices with recent experience of a low interest rate and a falling price level. He responded with the argument that the combination of these phenomena could be explained by the current limited availability of profitable investment opportunities:

> The amount of capital has been increasing so fast that, in spite of a great widening of the field of investment, it has forced down the rate of discount. The fall in the rate of discount so caused failed to stimulate speculation, because it was itself caused by the difficulty of finding good openings for speculative investment ... .(Marshall, 1888, volume II, p. 7)

This was a precursor of the theory to be developed by Knut Wicksell in *Geldzins und Güterpreisen* (1898). Wicksell distinguished between a natural rate of interest determined by the interaction between real saving and real investment, and a money rate of interest, fluctuations in which are largely due to changes in the money supply resulting from decisions by banks. He concluded that whenever the natural rate of interest (say) falls short of the money rate, the price level will fall, because of the contraction in investment that such a relationship between the two rates of interest brings about.

Hobson's approach to the interaction between the monetary and the real sectors of an economy was characteristically unorthodox. Interpreting the term 'quantity of money' as referring to a flow, he defined it as 'currency and deposits multiplied by their respective velocity, *i.e.* the number of times they change hands in one year [in exchange for goods]' (1913, p. 9).[2] He thus identified the quantity of money not with Fisher's M but with his MV. He argued that the rise in prices experienced since 1896 must have been due either to an increase in the 'quantity of money', that is to say in the flow of money supplied in exchange for marketable goods, or to a decrease in the flow of marketable goods exchanged for money, or both.

Logically, there is nothing wrong with this approach; in fact, the argument is tautological, although this is not to say that it is without interest. A similar flow approach was to form the basis of Oskar Lange's influential article, 'Say's Law: A Criticism and Restatement' (1942). Moreover, as Lange was to do, Hobson incorporated a stock element in his analysis, allowing for the flow of money supplied in exchange for marketable goods to increase or decrease as a consequence of increases or decreases either in the stock of minted gold, or in the stock of 'credit'; the latter he defined in his own peculiar way to mean the 'form of money manufactured by bankers with the assistance of bill-brokers and other finance agencies' (1913, p. 77), that is to say, bank notes and bank deposits.[3] However, he made no reference to the possibility that the flow of money supplied in exchange for marketable goods might also change as a result of hoarding or dishoarding, possibly because of his belief that hoarding occurs only in times of crisis.

Hobson's subsequent line of argument follows step by step from this foundation. He rejects increases in the stock of gold as a significant direct cause of the observed price increases, on factual grounds; the ratio of gold mined and minted over the period 1895–1910, both to the annual flow of 'credit' and to national income, had been too small for gold production to be able to exert any substantial influence on prices. Hobson took pains here to counter the argument that if there is an increase in gold to the amount of (say) one million pounds, 'the gross purchasing power of the community will ultimately be increased by the million pounds multiplied by the number of times it changes hands during the year' (Layton, 1912, p. 34). His counter-argument was that the initial expenditure of the one million pounds will push up prices just to the extent required to equate the value of the marketable goods exchanged for money with the increased flow of money supplied.

Hobson also rejected the idea that the price increases had been brought about by increases in the stock of gold, working indirectly through their effect on 'credit'; his argument here was that the basis of 'credit' is not gold, but marketable goods. We return to this argument shortly.

Hobson turned next to 'credit' itself. He rejected the indirect mechanism version of the quantity theory as an explanation of price level determination, on the ground that in the case of the United Kingdom the facts, set
out by Hobson in tabular form for the period 1870 to 1911, contradicted it.
In particular,

> the only period in which [a] low discount [rate] is associated with a
> large increase of gold output is 1895–99. For the rest, we are confronted
> by the fact that in the period of small gold output and rapid fall of
> prices, 1875–1894, the average rate of discount is considerably lower
> than in the last decade 1900–11, when the rapid rise of prices has been
> accompanied by a great increase of gold.   (1913, p. 43)

Citing the second of the two passages from Marshall's evidence to the
Royal Commission on Gold and Silver quoted earlier in this chapter,
Hobson not only agreed that the coexistence of falling prices and low
interest rates could be explained by a lack of profitable investment opportunities, but also contended that an equivalent argument could explain the
coexistence of rising prices and high interest rates recently experienced.[4]
'May we not say', he asked rhetorically, that 'the field of investment has
been widening so fast that, in spite of an increasing amount of capital, it
has forced up the rate of interest and, by a necessary consequence, the rate
of discount?' (1913, p. 65).[5] He found a basis for the rapid 'widening of
the field of investment' in the economic development that had taken place
over that period, for various reasons, in South America, Canada, South
Africa and Asia.

As noted above, it was Hobson's belief that 'credit is based on goods
and expands with the quantity of goods available as security' (1913,
p. 88). His sympathies clearly lay with the Banking School, rather than the
Currency School.[6] In the debate on the regulation of the British financial
system, which began in the 1820s and reached its peak in the 1840s,
members of the Currency School justified their contention that the issue of
bank notes should be controlled on the ground that otherwise the issue
was likely to be excessive in relation to the needs of trade, leading to the
twin evils of inflation and depletion of bullion reserves, and thence to
economic instability. Members of the Banking School, on the other hand,
maintained the 'real bills doctrine', namely the view that bank lending is
always accompanied by matching activity in the real sector of the
economy, qualified by the 'principle of the reflux', which allows for a lag
between the lending and the real activity which enables the loan to be
repaid. This view treats the stock of money supplied as an endogenous

variable, and implicitly assumes that in the short run the velocity of circulation will vary automatically according to the needs of trade.[7]

Endorsement of the view that 'credit' is extended according to the needs of trade left Hobson with the difficulty, which he recognised, that there would appear to be no reason why prices should ever change. He overcame this difficulty partly by making a distinction between consumable and non-consumable goods, and arguing that once non-consumable goods have been produced, those who financed their production possess new financial assets 'unaccompanied by any corresponding expansion of [consumable] goods' (1913, p. 90). Another argument turned on the recent trend towards the formation of joint-stock companies, Hobson asserting that:

> large masses of new credit are due, not to the production of new goods, but to the reorganization of businesses in forms rendering these goods available as securities for credit issues. So long as this change in business structure is proceeding, increased quantities of credit will come into being without any necessarily corresponding increase of goods. (1913, pp. 88–9)

At the same time, there had been 'a great extension and improvement of the banking and financial system', making a further contribution to the expansion of 'credit'. In addition, once prices start to rise, the process becomes cumulative, for 'the healthy condition of the industrial outlook in an era of rising prices will raise the value of the securities which business men can pledge to the banks, and so the latter can expand the volume of credit which they give to business men' (1913, p. 59). All these explanations of the rising price level assume that, while the velocity of circulation varies according to the needs of trade with a given economic and financial structure, it is less than perfectly responsive to structural changes that alter the ratio between financial and real assets.

While Hobson thus concluded that increases in the supply of money taking the form of 'credit' had caused prices to rise after 1895, he attached equal importance (see 1913, p. 114) to a second cause, namely a retardation in the supply of consumable goods. Here, again, Hobson must have found himself faced with a problem, in this case that of how to reconcile the idea of a retardation in the supply of consumable goods with an admitted rapid expansion of investment. Hobson's solution in this case, not surprising in the light of his underconsumption theory, was to distinguish between the ultimate and the immediate effects of profitable investment. While the ultimate effect of a rapid expansion of profitable investment is to increase the supply of consumable goods, and in this lies its justification, the immediate effect is to reallocate resources from the production of consumable goods to the production of investment goods, thereby retarding the supply of the former.

Hobson summarised the remainder of his explanation of the rise of prices as follows:

> If we are passing through an epoch in which an increasing proportion of money is expended (1) upon articles whose production conforms to what is termed the law of decreasing returns, (2) upon luxurious goods and services, (3) upon wars and armaments, (4) upon wasteful processes of competition in the distributive process; and if, further, (5) high tariffs hamper the productivity of large masses of capital and labour, while (6) combinations of capital and labour restrain the output in many large organized trades – the aggregate effect of such changes in the application of productive power may be a considerable retardation in the pace of supply of goods which confront the growing supply of money in the price equation.   (1913, p. 96)

The first two of these factors are not wholly self-explanatory. The first, an example of inflation caused by what have subsequently been termed 'structural characteristics', turns on the fact that a likely consequence of a rapid expansion of investment is a rise in input costs generally, through the effect on the demand for materials such as metals, timber and coal, whose production is subject to decreasing returns.[8] The second refers to the consequences of the recent increase in the richest countries in expenditure on luxury goods and services; 'the net effect of such increases of luxurious consumption, other things equal, will be to restrict the general rate of production by reducing the proportion of wealth which is accumulatively reproductive in the capacity of fixed or circulating capital' (1912, p. 491). Hobson here was in effect explaining the rise in prices in terms of 'overconsumption'. He proceeded to give reasons for believing that each of the factors listed had been operating in the period since 1896.

Those who modify an existing theory may see their modification either as reinforcing the theory, or as replacing it. Whereas Wicksell regarded his theory of the relationship between the price level and the rate of interest as an enhancement of the quantity theory, Hobson took the view that the theory he put forward was a replacement of the quantity theory, which he regarded as disproved.[9] In the last chapter of *Gold, Prices and Wages* Hobson also ridiculed, on the ground that it was contradicted by the facts, Irving Fisher's expanded version of the quantity theory, in which it is assumed both that the ratio of bank deposits to coin and notes is constant, and that the velocity of each is stable, with the result that the quantity of coin and notes, 'M1' in modern parlance, can be said to determine the price level.[10]

Finally, puzzling over the 'apparent' divergence of behaviour between the price level (the purchase price of money) and the rate of interest (the hire price of money), Hobson attempted to resolve the problem by dismissing it, concluding that:

> the so-called purchase-price of money is not a true price at all ... It is only the hire-price of money that really counts on a parity with other prices. Money is in reality always hired and never bought outright. (1913, p. 156)

As Backhouse has pointed out, Hobson was here wrestling with a non-problem. It is not at all unusual in the case of commodities for there to be divergence of behaviour between their purchase price and their hire price; 'if the purchase-price of a car is fixed and the rate of interest rises, the hire price will rise' (Backhouse, 1990, p. 125).

6.2 DOUGLAS'S CREDIT THEORY

The circumstances in which Hobson commented on C. H. Douglas's credit theory were very different from those in which he wrote *Gold, Prices and Wages*. The First World War itself, and the economic and political upheavals that followed it, had called into question the indefinite survival of capitalism. By 1922 the United Kingdom was recording unemployment in excess of 10 per cent of the workforce, while Germany was experiencing hyperinflation; by then, also, the Communist regime seemed to be well established in Russia, and by the end of that year Benito Mussolini had taken power by force in Italy.

Most of these events played a larger part in Douglas being listened to than in the fertilisation of his credit theory, which was first advanced in 1918 in a short article entitled 'The Delusion of Super-Production', in *The English Review*, the theory reappearing in book form in 1920, in *Economic Democracy*. Douglas believed in the virtues of industrial capitalism, and seeking a scapegoat for its current and recent problems, found one in the banks. His argument was that if only the banking system could be reformed, if not revolutionised, capitalism would continue to work as well as it had in the past.

The essence of Douglas's credit theory, which, if it ever became clear, did so only gradually as one work after another by Douglas was published in the 1920s, is as follows. The cost of producing articles is made up of 'A' payments, comprising wages, salaries and dividends paid to individuals, and 'B' payments, comprising payments made to organisations, such as reimbursement for the supply of raw materials or repayment of loans obtained from banks to finance investment. Since organisations are not potential consumers, it follows that if articles are priced at cost, potential consumers can never have sufficient income to pay for them. Douglas believed that the way to overcome this problem was 'by reducing prices below cost [to equality with 'A' payments] to the individual consumer, and then making up this difference between price and cost by a Treasury issue to the producer' (Douglas, 1922a, p. 29). The Treasury would in this case be drawing on the credit created by past and present generations engaged in the production of capital goods, or in other words, on 'social credit'. In some expositions Douglas reinforced this argument with the contention that since, in order to live, receivers of 'A' payments have to spend most of them on goods produced in previous periods, 'the only effective demand of the consumer ... is a few per cent of the price value of commodities' (Douglas, 1920b, pp. 70–1). In the 1920s and 1930s in particular, this theory was to attract a substantial following, not only in the United Kingdom, but also in Canada, Australia and New Zealand.

As economic conditions in the United Kingdom failed to improve in the 1920s, refutation of Douglas's argument became a necessity for those espousing alternative remedies, such as a lowering of the wage rate, a return to the Gold Standard, a lowering of the rate of interest, a redistribution of income in the direction of greater equality, or nationalisation of the means of production. As noted in Chapter 1, the response of the Labour Party to Douglas's ideas was to set up a committee whose members included Hobson – who was thus well-informed when he produced his own response in the same year.[11]

In Part I of an interim Report which bent over backwards to be fair to Douglas's arguments, the committee none the less found these arguments to be illogical and at variance with the facts. In Part II, the committee indicated its own preference for nationalisation of banking, adding, however, that 'to be effective, a policy in regard to banking and credit must be accompanied by an industrial and a fiscal policy' (Webb *et al.*, 1922, p. 11).

When it came to making his own assessment, Hobson wrote, in 'The Douglas Theory', that:

it sometimes seems as if the Douglasites built their case upon a time-lag in the distribution of the money got from the sale of consumable goods.

Most of the costs, in the shape of wages, salaries, and even dividends, incurred for producing any supply of goods, will have been paid before the goods are sold to consumers, and therefore cannot be met strictly out of the prices paid for these.   (1922b, p. 74)

This supposition was confirmed by Douglas's reply (Douglas, 1922b), which, however, did not respond to Hobson's criticism. This criticism was that if 'A' payments in the current period are used to buy goods produced (say) in the previous period, then goods produced in the current period will be bought by 'A' payments received in the next period; as Hobson put it in *The Economics of Unemployment*, 'effective demand for commodities proceeds from the wages, salaries and dividends quite recently paid to the producers of these commodities for making their successors' (1922a, p. 122).

With respect to 'B' payments to suppliers of raw materials, Hobson argued that these ultimately resolve themselves into wages, salaries and dividends, making them indistinguishable from 'A' payments. And with respect to 'B' payments made to banks, Hobson's argument was that the loan component of such payments is typically renewed by banks, and the interest component again resolves itself into wages, salaries and dividends. In short, Hobson rejected outright the proposition that payments to owners of factors of production generate insufficient income to purchase the commodities produced.

7 Hobson as Economist: A Critique[1]

There are two basic ways in which to mount a general critique of a writer's contribution to human thought. On the one hand, the paradigm within which the writer works may be taken for granted, with his or her ideas being assessed within that framework. On the other hand, the writer's very framework may be questioned, in which case descent into detail may be redundant.

Most critiques, being of the orthodox by the orthodox, follow the first path. By contrast, critiques of a heretic, whether by the orthodox or by heretics of a different persuasion, are likely to follow the second path. What we do in this chapter is to use both of these approaches, sometimes singly and sometimes in combination. More specifically, we use the second approach in assessing Hobson's economics from the point of view of heretics not of the Hobsonian persuasion, namely Marxians and members of the Historical and Institutional schools, these being the two leading non-Hobsonian heresies of Hobson's time; some of Hobson's views on these alternative heresies have already been referred to in Chapters 1, 2 and 3. In the case of critiques based on orthodoxy, we introduce an element of dialogue, giving Hobson, so to speak, the right of reply.[2] Modern orthodoxy is, for the purposes of this chapter, given a broad interpretation, neoclassical microeconomics and Keynesian macroeconomics being taken as representative of it.

Marx might have criticised Hobson's economics as follows. Hobson failed to place capitalism in its historical context, as a mode of production that succeeded feudalism and was in turn to be succeeded by socialism and communism; this failure accounts for Hobson's unscientific belief that capitalist societies can survive, with or without resort to imperialist policies. Hobson believed, mistakenly, that class conflict is not a necessary characteristic of capitalism. He adopted a 'social' theory of value instead of the labour theory of value, and was deluded in believing that, by the use of appropriate policies, governments in capitalist societies are able to prevent economic crises.

A critique mounted by a member of the Historical or Institutional schools, which address themselves 'to an explanation of human behaviour in economic systems embedded in actual cultural circumstances' (Gruchy,

1987, p. 4) and subject to evolution over time, might include the following points. The two earliest books written by Hobson as sole author paid due attention to both the historical context and the role of institutions in determining how an economy works. In *The Problem of Poverty*, Hobson described the institutional factors responsible for contemporary poverty in Britain, providing a historical background. And Malcolm Rutherford's summary of the work of the institutionalists W. I. King, J. M. Clark and F. C. Mills as focusing 'on the issue of technological change as it affected (i) the behaviour of firms, particularly their pricing policy, and (ii) the ability of the economic system to maintain high and stable levels of output and employment' (Rutherford, 1994, p. 198), could be applied with almost the same justification to *Evolution of Modern Capitalism*. But *The Problem of the Unemployed* marked the beginning of an unfortunate tendency on Hobson's part to write of economies in the abstract. For example, *Work and Wealth* 'with the exception of a few scattered and inconsequential references to property ... neglects practically the whole of the institution-framework of society' (Hamilton, 1915, p. 571), and 'contains no theory of the appraisal of social classes on the basis of the social functions which they perform, or should be made to perform' (Hamilton, 1915, p. 570). Hobson's lifetime output would have been so much more valuable had he concentrated on building on his early institutional studies.

We turn now to an orthodox critique of Hobson's economics, beginning with general assessments by Marshall and Keynes. Marshall added to the fifth edition of his *Principles* a note, of which the second sentence began 'Mr J. A. Hobson, a critic of Ricardian doctrines who is always vigorous and suggestive, but often hasty, argues ...' (Marshall, 1890–1920, vol. II, p. 409, nt. a). In the sixth edition he modified this to 'Mr J. A. Hobson is a vigorous and suggestive writer on the realistic and social sides of economics: but, as a critic of Ricardian doctrines, he is perhaps apt to underrate the difficulty of the problems which he discusses. He argues ...' (Marshall, 1890–1920, vol. II, p. 409, nt. a). After drawing attention to this change, the editor of the variorum edition of Marshall's *Principles* added the following extract from a letter written by Marshall to the American economist Richard T. Ely, dated 11 July 1901, which 'throws some additional light on Marshall's attitude to J. A. Hobson':

Perhaps Dr. Hobson [*sic*] has communicated to you the fact that the particular passages on which he bases what I regard as misinterpretations of my views, in his 'Distribution' in your series, were mostly expunged from my book; because I had found them to be capable of

being taken – with an adequate disregard of the context – in senses in
which I had not designed them. I sent him my last edition; and he wrote
me a friendly and straightforward answer as to this matter, and similar
comments of mine on his *Social Problem*. He is so very busy with other
things that he may probably not have thought it necessary to write to
you about this. There is an immense deal that is most fascinating about
him; and he is certainly very able. But he is in a hurry; and so he
disappoints me whenever the only good work is slow work.

But perhaps like some other oldish men, I have an 'epidemic' of
supposing that younger men polish off difficulties too hastily.
(Marshall, 1890–1920, vol. II, p. 430)[3]

In short, Marshall saw Hobson's economic writings as lacking in quality
because of the haste in which they were written, a haste perhaps partly
due to the fact that Hobson was 'so very busy with other things'.

Keynes too found Hobson's economic writings lacking in quality. In his
review of *Gold, Prices and Wages*, Keynes wrote that 'one comes to a new
book by Mr. Hobson with mixed feelings, in hope of stimulating new ideas
and some fruitful criticisms of orthodoxy from an independent and individual standpoint, but expectant also of much sophistry, misunderstanding,
and perverse thought' (Keynes, 1913, p. 393). Keynes referred subsequently
to the way in which Hobson's 'cleverness and intermittent reasonableness'
(Keynes, 1913, p. 393) tend to make what is erroneous plausible.

Neither Marshall, nor Keynes in his review of *Gold, Prices and Wages*,
did Hobson justice. The fact that many of Hobson's books were based on
previously-published articles shows that as a writer he was not entirely
'hasty'. It is true that he was always 'busy with other things', notably
journalism; but this is true of many winners of the Nobel Prize for
Economics, some of whom have been regular newspaper columnists. It is
true, also, that Hobson sometimes misunderstood the economic theories he
criticised, but the later Keynes would probably not have accused Hobson
of 'sophistry and perverse thought', an unwarranted accusation that must
have wounded Hobson deeply.

In order to supplement this general critique, we look now in detail at the
contributions to economics made by Hobson in the five areas dealt with in
Chapters 2 to 6.

7.1   ECONOMIC ACTIVITY AND WELFARE

Hobson's contribution to welfare economics can be summarised in three
propositions: social welfare depends on all utilities and all costs accruing

to individuals, whether reflected in the market or not; the resultant 'object-ive' measure must be adjusted first so as to reflect 'real' individual welfare; then this measure in turn must be adjusted so as to reflect social welfare.

A neoclassical critique of this theory might run as follows. The main objection to the first of these propositions is not one of principle but one of application; many utilities and costs not reflected in the market are difficult or impossible to measure, and for that reason cannot be taken into account. Hobson's concept of 'social welfare' is therefore non-operational.

But the objection to the second proposition is one of principle. Ideals have to be treated as exogenous with respect to economic theories. The business of the economist, even when questions of welfare are under dis-cussion, is confined to explaining relationships between given ends and scarce means.[4]

This rules out applying any value judgements to the choices of con-sumers. Even if it did not, contrary to Hobson's view, there is no social consensus as to what is 'wealth' in the Ruskinian sense, and what is 'illth', for the individual consumer; if there is any social consensus at all, it is that 'the consumer is king', however his or her preferences may be formed.

Moreover, Hobson's criticism of contemporary economics for ignoring costs and benefits not reflected in market prices has subsequently been met, in so far as is possible, in the economics of externalities. Indeed, much of what modern theory has to say on external costs and benefits was anticipated by Hobson, in his discussion of the relationship between welfare and production.[5] Hobson was also on the right track in believing that the market undersupplies public goods, though he failed to explain that the reason for this is that the market is in this case unable to reflect consumer preferences because of the impossibility of excluding benefits from those who do not pay.

The objection to the third of Hobson's propositions is also one of princi-ple. Viewing society as an organism carries with it totalitarian overtones impossible to reconcile with liberal democracy; Hegel's organic view of society, for example, led him to the belief that people should be forced to be free.[6] Although Hobson did not go as far as Hegel, he seems at times to have believed, along with Rousseau, that each person should be made to see that if what he/she believes would maximise social welfare differs from 'the general will', he/she must be mistaken. Even if these difficulties did not exist, there is the further problem of discovering 'the general will', which Hobson would no more than Rousseau identify with 'the will of all', determined by majority vote.

J. M. Clark, in the following passage, provided a general reply to these criticisms:

> If Hobson's welfare economics left the scientific economics out, the form of theory which now bears the name can without real unfairness be described as welfare economics with the welfare left out, in a remarkably resolute attempt to meet the real or supposed requirements of economic science. Rejecting 'interpersonal comparisons', this body of theory seems to end in rather complete agnosticism, aside from policies that increase the national dividend without making anyone worse off. But the existence of a single disadvantaged person acts as a veto on scientific approval of any policy – one cannot be scientifically certain that his loss does not outweigh the gains of many. Such a theory cannot recommend that we install tax-supported poor relief or a progressive income tax; but equally it could not recommend that they not be established. It seems clear that this theory has not reached satisfactory final form.   (Clark, 1957, p. 59)

Hobson might add that economists who believe his concept of 'social welfare' to be non-operational should ask themselves if they have ever used the concept of a 'social welfare function', which is no less problematic than that of 'social welfare'; all social welfare functions assume not only that such a thing as 'social welfare' exists, but also that the precise relationship between social welfare on the one hand, and each of the variables contained in the function on the other, is known.

The principal objection to orthodox welfare economics, in the view of J. M. Clark as well as Hobson, is that it provides answers to very few problems. This is why governments often ignore the teachings of orthodox welfare economics. They do so, for example, when they justify high taxes on goods such as tobacco and alcohol on the ground that consumption of them detracts from the 'real' welfare of their individual consumers, and therefore from social welfare.

As orthodox welfare economics is based on the Pareto criterion, it cannot say anything about whether any alternative distribution of income is preferable to the existing one, since any redistribution is unable to meet the Pareto criterion that no one is worse off. Common sense, however, suggests that one distribution of income may generate more social welfare than another. John Rawls (1972), with his 'two principles of justice', has made at least a start in suggesting how one distribution of income may be compared with another. But his ideas have had little impact on welfare economics. In the field of income distribution, too, governments ignore orthodox welfare economics. A progressive income tax is now almost universally in operation, despite the view of orthodox economists that no redistribution of income can be justified by logical argument.

Given the relative impotence of orthodox welfare economics, the time has come for orthodox economists to reconsider the narrow bounds they have placed on welfare economics, and to expand them to the point where ends as well as means are discussed. If they were to take this path, however, they would be well advised to follow Myrdal's advice in the English edition of *The Political Element in The Development of Economic Theory* (1953), by 'working always, from the beginning to the end, with explicit value premises' (Myrdal, 1953, p. vii). They would also find in Hobsonian welfare economics at least a useful point from which to start.

7.2   INCOME DISTRIBUTION AND PRICING

The Hobson/J. B. Clark contention that the concept of rent can be applied to all factors of production is now accepted by orthodox economists. However, while Clark's proof led to the conclusion that distribution of the national product according to marginal product exactly exhausts it, Hobson's proof led to the conclusion that many factors of production receive an economic rent, or surplus, and that some of this surplus is 'unproductive'.

A neoclassical critique of Hobson's conclusions might run along the following lines. There is nothing wrong with Hobson's concept of a 'productive surplus', which simply reflects the idea that the supply price required to induce an increase in the quantity of a factor of production is greater than the supply price required to maintain the existing quantity of it; the problem lies in Hobson's use of the term 'surplus', which is misleading.

There is also nothing wrong with Hobson's concept of an 'unproductive surplus'; this is merely economic rent, taking into account the requirements of a growing economy, under another name. Where Hobson was mistaken was in his belief that economic rent plays a central role in the workings of an economy. In a perfectly competitive economy in which there is also perfect information, and no inputs are in perfectly inelastic supply, no one receives economic rent. In so far as these conditions do not apply in practice, economic rent should be treated as one of John Stuart Mill's 'disturbing causes', explaining why an economy does not always behave as theory predicts.

In addition, Hobson's writings on taxation are not internally consistent.[7] In particular, after stating that taxes should be levied on the surplus, or non-necessary cost, he concludes that they should be levied on the gap between a reservation price and a market price. As Nemmers (1956, p. 113) puts it:

> There is this difference: reservation price because of holding for future markets, can exceed what Hobson would recognise as 'cost'. On the other hand, inclusion within 'cost' of such elements in the case of wages, as 'conventional expenditures and even including some elements of comfort or luxury, not always conducive but perhaps even detrimental to working efficiency' [Hobson, 1919, p. 16], may raise Hobson's 'cost' above reservation price in some cases.

With respect to the theory of prices, Hobson grossly overstated the importance of 'monopoly rent' arising out of bargaining undertaken in the course of exchange. The number of buyers and number of sellers is typically too numerous for any such rent to be substantial.

Hobson might pen the following reply. The supply of many 'specialised' forms of factors of production is in practice perfectly inelastic. This is true of many kinds of skilled labour where, because of the absence of universal access to advanced education, supply is restricted; of many kinds of capital which, *pace* J. B. Clark, cannot realistically be treated as being malleable, where monopoly elements restrict supply; and of unimproved land, of which it is true that all payments made to its owners arise out of the combination of its limited supply in any one place and the alternative uses to which it could be put. Since all but the 'roughest, commonest and most unspecialised' forms of factors of production receive economic rent, economic rent has to be assigned a central role in the theory of income distribution.

The only substantial attempt to develop something akin to this 'surplus' line of thought so far has been that made by Baran and Sweezy, first in Baran's *The Political Economy of Growth* (1957), and then in their joint work, *Monopoly Capital* (1966). It is a substantial defect of the second of these works in particular that the concept of 'economic surplus' is ill-defined. Baran and Sweezy might have been more successful in making converts had they adopted a much more rigorous approach to the question of definition.

7.3 UNDERCONSUMPTION

When Keynes lamented that 'if only Malthus, instead of Ricardo, had been the parent stem from which nineteenth century economics proceeded, what a much wiser and richer place the world would be today!' (Keynes, 1933, p. 144), he lent his weight to the view that an economics based on the underconsumption theory was preferable to one based on Say's Law. The virtue of the underconsumption theory in pre-Keynesian times was that in the explanation of the level of output as a whole it assigned a role to demand, and that until the appearance of over-investment theories of the trade cycle in the 1920s and 1930s it was the only theory to do so; this had the important implication that something can be done to reduce the severity of depressions.

A Keynesian economist might assess Hobson's underconsumption theory as follows. Its main shortcoming is that it fails to recognise investment as an independent determinant of the level of national income. In fact, the level of income is primarily determined by the level of investment, and it is the volatility of investment which is the principal cause of fluctuations in the level of income. While it is true that increasing consumption is one means of increasing the level of income, increasing investment is another. Hobson also failed to recognise the importance for macroeconomics of the monetary sector. Investment depends on the rate of interest, which 'is the reward of not-hoarding' (Keynes, 1936, p. 174), and is determined in the market for financial assets. In his policy recommendations Hobson, at most, hinted at the use of a budget deficit as a remedy for depression.

Hobson might respond in the following way. Given the existence of taxable unproductive surpluses, refraining from increasing taxes when an increase in government expenditure is required to stimulate the economy, thereby causing the budget to be in deficit, is not necessary. More generally, the theory developed by Keynes is a short-run theory in the Marshallian sense; it deals with a period of time too short for there to be a change in the level of output caused by a change in the stock of capital equipment. Sooner or later net investment will add to the capacity of the economy to generate output. When this happens we are confronted with a long-run question that Keynes did not tackle: will there be enough demand to match this additional supply?

Harrod and Domar responded to this question by developing models that showed that, in the long run, aggregate demand will keep pace with supply only if investment grows at a fast enough rate. But their models were less than general in that they assumed a given consumption function. If this assumption is dropped, and replaced by the realistic assumption that investment is a function of the (variable) rate of growth of consumption, in the long run aggregate demand will only keep pace with supply if consumption grows at a fast enough rate.

The underconsumption theory has a practical relevance which, since the late 1970s, has been widely admitted, at least implicitly. As the OECD June 1988 issue of *Economic Outlook* puts it:

> Once thought of as being among the most predictable of macro-economic parameters, household savings ratios climbed steeply in the late 1970s and early 1980s. They subsequently fell back in several OECD countries to historically low levels ... As private consumption spending accounts for well over half of GDP in the average OECD country, movements in savings ratios have had an important influence on GDP growth. Their fall during the 1980s has helped sustain growth in the face of stable or declining real wages and, in Europe at least, declining unemployment also.   (OECD, 1988, p. 2)

In the late 1970s and early 1980s economists as well as politicians and journalists began to talk about the need for a 'consumption-led recovery'. Why? It is hard to find any other reason than the fact that, with the drop in the ratio of consumption to output, the prospects of an increase in invest-ment were poor. In the mid-1980s, as the saving ratio plunged to record low levels, there were calls for an 'investment-led recovery', since further increases in the ratio of consumption to output would probably have led to a level of aggregate demand that the economy did not have the capacity to satisfy.

The conclusion to be drawn from these recent experiences is that Keynes' 'general theory' is in one respect less than general, namely in that it covers only the short run. To be a completely general theory it needs to be supplemented by a long-run analysis, such as that provided by the underconsumption theory.

7.4   TRADE, CAPITAL FLOWS AND IMPERIALISM

Hobson's views on international trade and capital flows are for the most part non-controversial. But his writings on imperialism are open to two basic kinds of criticism. First, as we have seen in Chapter 5, they can be criticised in the light of empirical evidence; and second, their analytical basis can be questioned.

Neoclassical economists regard the phenomenon of imperialism, given its political component, as being outside the bounds of economics. By contrast, Marxian economists see the explanation of imperialism as being very much part of the task of economists. Where the latter disagree with

Hobson is in the conclusions they draw from their explanations. A Marxian critique of Hobson's writings on imperialism might run as follows.

Hobson's explanation of imperialism is 'bourgeois' because it treats an imperialist policy as merely being one of several options open to a capitalist society, rather than as an inescapable stage of capitalist development. There are alternative theories that do not make this mistake. Otto Bauer, for example, argued in *Die Nationalitätenfrage und die Sozialdemokratie* (1907, esp. pp. 400–13) that capitalism's need of outlets for capital and commodities leads to pressure on governments, notably from trusts and cartels, to adopt both protectionist and imperialist policies; subsequently, in 1913, he used Marx's reproduction schema to show that imperialism is a necessary consequence of the coexistence of advanced capitalist countries suffering from overaccumulation and undeveloped or non-capitalist countries suffering from underaccumulation, which results in advanced capitalist countries not only exporting capital but also importing (cheap) labour. Rudolf Hilferding (1910) shows that imperialism is the inevitable consequence of the 'law of the tendency of the rate of profit to fall', the export of capital and consequent imperialist policies being a natural result of the coexistence of high rates of profit in undeveloped countries and low rates of profit in advanced capitalist countries; the monopolies and oligopolies, particularly in the banking sector, characteristic of advanced capitalism provide the pressure on governments to pursue an imperialist policy. Rosa Luxemburg (1913) demonstrates that imperialism is caused by the increasing underconsumption that is an inevitable feature of capitalism, necessitating economic relations with non-capitalist areas.[8] Lenin (1917), acknowledging the important contribution to the explanation of imperialism advanced by the 'bourgeois' Hobson, provides contemporary empirical evidence to illustrate what is in essence an amalgam of Hobson's and Hilferding's theories, adding, however, that what Hilferding had described as the latest stage of capitalism is in fact the 'highest' (that is, last) stage.

All these theories of imperialism share with that of Hobson the premise that 'the taproot of imperialism is economic'. Where they differ is that they recognise a policy of imperialism is inescapable for a capitalist society once it reaches a certain stage of development, and that no reform of the capitalist system can eliminate its imperialistic nature.

The whole basis of Hobson's theory of imperialism might be thought to be questioned not only by Marxian theories, but also by J. Gallagher and R. Robinson's 'The Imperialism of Free Trade' (1953). In this article Gallagher and Robinson argue that Britain's policy of territorial annexation during the last quarter of the nineteenth century had nothing to do with changed domestic economic circumstances, and everything to do with the fact that imperial expansion by other countries from the 1870s blocked off outlets for commodities and capital that had previously been available. But Gallagher and Robinson's thesis is consistent with the existence of chronic underconsumption in the British economy. And Hobson actually anticipated the thesis, stating:

> As this economic imperialism, primarily a British policy, spread to a number of other industrially developed Western powers, the economic conflicts assumed more and more a political shape, each government being induced to use its diplomatic, and in the last resource [*sic*] its armed force for the protection or assertion of the interest of its own traders and investors.   (1931b, p. 18)

In general, Hobson added, 'the early expansion of British capitalism called for no "sabotage" in the interests of owners or financiers' (1936, p. 140), because 'large foreign markets were available for the surplus goods which could not be sold to ill-paid workers in their country of origin' (1936, p. 140).

Nor is there any incompatibility between Hobson's theory and the 'neo-imperialism' argument which emerged after the Second World War, namely, that once world power relationships made territorial expansion difficult if not impossible, economically-developed nations used their economic power to achieve what was previously achieved by political and military means.

All the theories of imperialism considered so far accept Hobson's dictum that 'the taproot of imperialism is economic'. A non-economic explanation of imperialism is to be found in Schumpeter (1919), where imperialism is seen as an atavism, attributable to the survival in otherwise civilised nations of a once-functional warrior instinct and class. This theory is not incompatible with that advanced by Hobson. On the contrary, drawing attention to Hobson's writings on jingoism and related phenomena, Harvey Mitchell (1966, p. 405) shows persuasively that to Hobson 'should go part of the credit traditionally claimed for Schumpeter for having advanced the theory that imperialist drives are motivated by irrational or non-rational motives'. As we saw in Chapter 5, in his later years Hobson came to regard the desire for power, unrelated to economic goals, as an independent cause of imperialism.

7.5 MONEY AND CREDIT

Hobson did not make any important contribution to the theory of money and credit. Like orthodox nineteenth-century economists, he regarded the workings of the financial sector of the economy as being of subsidiary importance; problems in the financial sector were capable of causing temporary upheavals in the real sector, but it was in the real sector of the economy that the lasting sources of change occurred.

Keynes described Hobson's solitary book in the field of money and credit, *Gold, Prices and Wages*, as 'a very bad one' (Keynes, 1913, p. 393). Some of Keynes' specific criticisms are definitional, aimed at Hobson's unusual use of terms. For example, Keynes objected to Hobson's argument that, if all receipts of money were derived from prior acts of sale, prices would remain stable even in an economy experiencing what we now call steady-state growth. But given Hobson's incorporation of velocity as well as stock in his definition of money, price stability under these circumstances is at least theoretically possible. Keynes also objected to Hobson's 'irritation' with the quantity theory of money.

More substantial is Keynes' criticism of Hobson's assumption, made in the process of playing down the importance of gold as a determinant of prices, 'that no new coin can be used more than once' (Keynes, 1913, p. 395). Backhouse (1990) argues that this, and related passages, show that 'Hobson's rejection of the multiplier could hardly be more explicit or more emphatic' (Backhouse, 1990, p. 119).

Hobson might reply to this last criticism by drawing attention to the fact that in *Gold, Prices and Wages* he was exploring the consequences of an increase in money or credit in circumstances where the level of real income/output is constant, which Keynes himself was to do in his *Treatise on Money*, where the Keynesian multiplier is consequently irrelevant.[9] The worst which could be said is that in this context the concept of the 'banking multiplier', which was invented later, might have been discovered.

Hobson's response to the prior criticisms might have been to suggest that he at least deserves credit, not given to him by Keynes, for adapting Marshall's explanation of the fall in prices over the period 1873–96 to explain the rise in prices that took place from 1896. He might continue as follows. In the *Treatise on Money*, Keynes himself found it helpful to use terms in an unconventional way. And in *The General Theory* Keynes himself came to abandon the quantity theory of money; it was in fact *The General Theory* that led to the quantity theory falling out of favour with

orthodox economists. Although the quantity theory was revived by the
monetarists in the 1970s and 1980s, it now appears that this revival was
only temporary.

Keynesians would have no quarrel with Hobson's criticisms of the
social credit theory advanced by Douglas. Keynes himself wrote that:

> the strength of Major Douglas's advocacy has, of course, largely
> depended on orthodoxy having no valid reply to much of his destructive
> criticism. On the other hand, the detail of his diagnosis, in particular the
> so-called A + B theorem, includes much mere mystification.   (Keynes,
> 1936, pp. 370–1)

Hobson, not so much through his own writings as through his major role
in the committee set up by the Labour Party to examine Douglas's theory,
played an important part in exposing this 'mystification'.

8 Conclusion

The importance of Adam Smith in the history of economics derives from his 'imaginative integration of many ideas into a single picture' (Toulmin and Goodfield, 1963, p. 263, referring to the role of Isaac Newton in the history of physics). Hobson, too, painted a picture of the overall functioning of economies which was substantially new. No one has expressed the nature of Hobson's work better than W. H. Hamilton (1915, pp. 565, 567), in his review of *Work and Wealth*:

> it is of a kind with Adam Smith's *Wealth of Nations*. It is, however, unlike the latter in two essentials: first, in the comprehensiveness of the social program which its problem requires it to elaborate; and, secondly, in the extreme complexity of the social ideal, the realization of which is the object at which the program aims ... these two characteristics serve alike to classify the treatise and to indicate its differences in scope and objective from current theory ... His [Hobson's] condemnation of *laissez-faire* and of automatism in all its forms imposes upon him the task of a quite detailed elaboration of a social program. Compared with Smith's quest, his is for a veritable will-of-the-wisp.

In painting such a picture Hobson belongs to a select company that also includes Marx, Jevons/Menger/Walras, and Keynes.[1] But, like Marx, Hobson failed to persuade the majority of economists to adopt the new paradigm he put forward. Indeed, his influence on economic thinking has been much less than that of Marx.

This is not to say that Hobson has had no influence on human thought. Few writers can claim a double achievement comparable with that of Hobson, in being acknowledged as a predecessor both by Lenin in his *Imperialism* and by Keynes in *The General Theory*. And Hobson has had a substantial impact on the discipline of economics, even if we define it in narrow terms, notably in North America. His underconsumption theory 'came across the Atlantic with such impact that at the 1895 meeting of the American Economic Association the subject was brought up' (Dorfman, 1946–59, vol. 3, p. 253). He has had some disciples, notably John A. Ryan of the Catholic University of America, and a succession of economists at the University of Wisconsin.[2] Edwin Nourse stated that Hobson was the 'intellectual daddy of what we did at Brookings on the

Price and Income Books' (Knapp, 1979, pp. 470–1). His was the guiding
light for at least one member of F. D. Roosevelt's New Deal 'brains trust'
during the early 1930s; and Rexford Tugwell (Tugwell, 1968, pp. 42–3)
reported of his 1932 discussion with Roosevelt: 'I explained that what I
had said ... was only an extended version of what economists knew as the
"over-savings theory" ... I explained that it was usually attributed to the
English economist J. A. Hobson'.[3] J. M. Clark went so far as to state, with
reference to Hobson's welfare and underconsumption theories, that
Hobson 'put his finger on the two biggest blind spots in conventional
economics' (Clark, 1957, p. 59). Ryan was thus not grossly exaggerating
when he said, in 1931 in a North American context, that Hobson's 'theory
has not been generally adopted by economists until rather recently, but
now, if you notice, a great many of the economists have adopted it'
(quoted in Dorfman, 1959, vol. v, p. 659).[4] In England, the influential
socialist writer G. D. H. Cole took his economics from Hobson.

Overall, however, Hobson's economic theories have not won wide
acceptance. Many of the criticisms levelled at them reflect the fact that
very few economists are prepared to accept the idiosyncratic framework
within which he was working. What was the paradigm that Hobson proposed? Why has it had relatively little effect on the way people think
about the overall functioning of economies? Do his ideas none the less
have something to offer? These are the three principal questions we
address in the conclusion to this book.

Curiously enough, the definition of economics most widely accepted by
orthodox economists, namely that 'economics is the science which studies
human behaviour as the relationship between ends and scarce means
which have alternative uses' (Robbins, 1932a, p. 16), was acceptable also
to the unorthodox Hobson. In *Free-thought in the Social Sciences* (p. 92)
Hobson quoted Jevons as stating that 'the great problem of Economy,
may, as it seems to me, be stated thus: Given, a certain population, with
various needs and powers of production; required, the mode of employing
their labour so as to maximise the utility of the produce' (Jevons, 1871,
p. 255), and indicated that he approved, provided that 'and so as to
minimise the disutility of producing it' was added. Where Hobson
departed from orthodoxy was in his view of what the 'ends' in this
definition comprise.

Neoclassical economists typically assume the positive 'end' to be the
maximisation of individuals' satisfaction as defined by the individuals
concerned, and the negative 'end' to be the avoidance of changes which
reduce the satisfaction obtained by any individual (this is one way of
expressing the Pareto criterion for maximisation of social welfare). By

contrast, Hobson saw the ultimate 'end' as the preservation of the human species. Given that human beings live in societies, this requires both co-existence between societies, and, following Darwin, the maximum encouragement within each society of diversity as well as efficiency. Hobson believed that coexistence between societies is encouraged by free trade, his support for free trade thus being based not only on economic efficiency grounds, and that such coexistence is threatened by imperialist policies. He also believed both that a market-based economy is the economic structure which most encourages efficiency and diversity, and that a market-based economy often fails to realise these objectives; he thus supported government intervention in the workings of markets wherever this is necessary to ensure that efficiency and diversity are achieved.

Hobson discerned the principal examples of market failure as follows. Markets are inefficient when they fail to reflect all the social costs and benefits of production. They are inefficient when they fail to reflect all the social benefits and costs of consumption. They are inefficient when they allow the owners of factors of production to receive payments which are not required to induce factor supply. They are inefficient when they result in unutilised resources, notably unemployed labour and idle capital. They fail to encourage diversity when they generate a distribution of income which prevents some individuals from fulfilling their potential.

At a more fundamental level, Hobson believed that a principal cause of market failure is lack of competition, often caused by individual competitors being replaced by economic groups or classes. It is true that in *The Physiology of Industry* Mummery and Hobson ascribed underconsumption to *excessive* competition; but in his later writings Hobson saw this as a factor only in the 'early stages' of a depression, whose fundamental cause he now saw as an unequal distribution of income reflecting a lack of competition. Hobson's conclusion was that whenever market failure occurs, for this or any other reason, the government should intervene.

This is a coherent picture of the workings of a whole economy, comparable with that painted by Adam Smith, by Marx, by the founders of neoclassical economics, or by Keynes. In so far as marginalism plays no part in it, it has something in common with the first two. In so far as it envisages an economy based on individuals as opposed to economic classes, it has something in common with the last two.

Why was Hobson's attempt to replace the existing paradigm in economics with a new one unsuccessful? Some have answered this question by following Marshall and Keynes in seeing Hobson's voluminous writings as 'hasty', with his ideas being not fully thought out and poorly expressed. Though widely repeated, this explanation of Hobson's lack of success is

by no means wholly convincing.[5] Those who are developing new ideas
are necessarily involved in such 'a struggle of escape from habitual modes
of thought and expression' (Keynes, 1936, p. viii) that they are rarely able
to express the new ideas with precision; and there are numerous cases of
successful innovators whose writings were voluminous, incompletely
thought out, and inadequately expressed. One example is to be found in
the works of Marx, which though often almost impenetrable, have been
successful in the sense that they have exerted an enormous influence on
the thinking of mankind. Another example is to be found in *The General
Theory*. Menger made converts in spite of the clumsy expression resulting
from his attempt to explain marginal utility without using differential
equations. Léon Walras's limited mathematical training makes the
Elements of Pure Economics (1874) almost unreadable, but this did not
prevent Schumpeter from claiming that 'it would be hard to find a
theorist who does not acknowledge Walras' influence' (Schumpeter, 1954,
p. 829). While incomplete argument and inadequate expression no doubt
played some part in Hobson's failure to make converts, there were more
important factors at work.

Thomas Kuhn's description of revolutionaries in the physical sciences,
which shows them as facing unwillingness among the practitioners of the
discipline concerned, for reaons of personal pride and 'sunk capital', to
relinquish the existing paradigm, has not been conclusively rebutted. If his
thesis is applicable to the physical sciences, where the possibility of controlled experiment ensures at least a certain amount of objectivity, it is so
much the more likely to be applicable to the social sciences, including
economics, where the objective element resulting from the possibility of
controlled experiment does not exist. The inability of economists to accept
a fundamental challenge to their discipline is widely recognised. Hamilton
(1915, p. 564) puts it in the case of Hobson as follows:

> Unfortunately, when the field of economics was marked out, no
> supreme pre-wisdom made provision for so extraneous a product as
> Hobson's *Work and Wealth*. In fact, to assign so cosmic a contribution
> to a particular place in an orderly economic universe is to do violence
> either to an excellent treatise or to a modest science. This is not because
> the book lacks unity, relevancy, or economic purpose, but because it
> ramifies into fields economically uncharted and because its lines of
> argument run athwart the conventional grooves of economic discussion.

Given the fundamental conservatism of economists, it is not surprising
that, in the eyes of some historians of economic thought, there has never

been a 'Kuhnian revolution' in the discipline; or that others, who point to the emergence of the neoclassical paradigm in the 1870s as an example of such a revolution, are unable to agree on what it was that allowed this unique paradigm shift to occur (see, for example, Black *et al.*, 1973).

In addition, it would be unrealistic to expect that many of those economists predisposed towards the preservation of the existing economic system would be easily converted to a theory challenging the current distribution of income and wealth, such as that advanced by Hobson, particularly given that the existing paradigm supported it. In any case, 'orthodoxy usually has a reasoned justification of its position which it does not feel called upon to mobilize afresh in response to every attack' (Clark, 1940, p. 357). And those economists predisposed towards a change in the existing economic system may well have found Hobson's theory less attractive than the more radical ideas already in the field, emanating from Marx. So Hobson, in attempting to develop a theory that he saw as being in the best interests of society as a whole, did not attract much support from either conservatives or radicals.

As we saw in Chapter 2, it was, in fact, the view of Hobson himself that, in the social sciences, choice between theories reflects more the relative power of vested interests than the current state of knowledge. In expressing this view, Hobson predicted implicitly the failure of his own theories to gain support. Almost ever the optimist, however, he none the less held out hope that education would in time lead mankind to less selfish and more enlightened views.

Another factor that has told against acceptance of Hobson's paradigm is his rejection of 'marginalism', which has led some economists to conclude that his ideas are simply out of date, failing to incorporate the technical improvements in economics that began in the 1870s. The element of truth in this judgement lies in the fact that Hobson did not fully understand the concept of infinitesimal changes at the margin. But if he had, he would still have argued that incorporation of this concept in economic theory is not necessary if one's object is to understand the larger issues of economics, just as Marx would have argued that the workings of a capitalist economy can be understood without reference to the (resource-allocation) concept of 'prices-of-production'.

In the case of the attempt to overthrow Say's Law, why did Hobson fail and Keynes succeed?[6] The answer lies not only in the deficiencies of Hobson's underconsumption theory, but also in the fact that Hobson's attempt to overthrow Say's Law lacked several forms of support that Keynes' theory was to receive in the 1930s, namely unemployment on an unprecedented scale, a theory which did not challenge orthodox microeconomics, and a challenger whom the orthodox regarded as having academic status and prestige. In fact, Hobson's failure ever to obtain an academic post was a great handicap to him in his attempt to have not only his underconsumption theory but also his other unorthodox theories taken seriously by the economics profession.

What does Hobson's paradigm offer which may be useful to economists in the late twentieth century? First, while incorporating a short-run analysis of unemployment that is less general than that to be found in Keynes' *General Theory*, Hobson's paradigm is in another respect *more* general in that it offers as well a long-run analysis. But given Keynes' success in introducing a demand-side explanation of fluctuations in the level of economic activity, the more important lesson to be learnt from Hobson's paradigm follows from its exposition in detail of where and why an economy based on private property and markets fails to serve mankind. Hobson's paradigm thereby provides a guide to governments as to where intervention in the workings of markets is required. It is true that it runs counter to the desire of economists to align themselves with physical scientists rather than social scientists, by limiting themselves to what can be measured without having to make value judgements. But as a result, governments have to make many economic decisions without the benefit of advice from economists, advice which Hobson's paradigm is capable of providing.

Notes and References

1 Hobson's Life and Times

1. Since Hobson's family tree has been traced back only as far as Robert Hobson (1752–1821) of Bonsall, near Derby, one cannot rule out the possibility that Hobson was related to the mid-seventeenth-century carrier Thomas Hobson of Cambridge who offered his customers 'Hobson's choice', though the difference of locality makes it unlikely.

2. Hobson's dry wit, for which he was well known among his colleagues, was unfortunately rarely translated into his books. An exception is to be found in his autobiography, in which he recalled the Derby School speech day of 1873, attended by the Prince of Wales, the future Edward VII, who was no saint. 'My memory of that event,' he wrote, 'is registered in a prize for "Divinity" bestowed by the royal hand. It was long before the full humour of this proceeding came home to me' (1938b, p. 22).

3. In his autobiography, Hobson stated that he attended these lectures in 1875. But while the Cambridge Board of Extra-Mural Studies offered Political Economy in Derby in both 1873 and 1874, the subject was never offered thereafter (see BEMS 26/1, University of Cambridge Library); this is no doubt the basis of Kadish's assertion that it was in 1874 that Hobson attended the lectures.

4. Though the young Hobson sometimes saw Spencer in the streets of Derby, and though Spencer wrote a complimentary letter to Hobson in 1901 following the publication of *The Psychology of Jingoism*, and Hobson replied, the two never had occasion to speak with one another.

5. Some commentators notwithstanding, Hobson did not take Modern Greats, the first students in which graduated in 1906. While his B.A. degree was entitled *In Literis Humanioribus*, the course in which he enrolled was called *Literae Humaniores*. The obituary of Hobson in *The Derbyshire Advertiser and Journal* says of his failure to obtain a first in *Literae Humaniores* that 'so many men who in later years became distinguished, shared his fate about the same time, that one is tempted to wonder whether the examiners in the most trickly examination in the world were not working for some years on wrong lines' (5 April 1940, p. 8). No examples are provided of other such 'men who in later years became distinguished'.

6. Although Hobson's outline of the underconsumptionist position in his letter from America on 8 June 1888 appeared to be inspired by what he saw in the United States, it almost certainly followed his conversion to the underconsumption theory by Mummery. Hobson wrote of Mummery and his 'heretical notions about spending and saving' (Mummery, 1913, p. 9) that after a year or two,

> by persistent force and ingenuity of argument, he overbore all my preliminary objections. We then went together into the close work of

135

developing what seemed to us a new and necessary statement of the relations between Production and Consumption in the modern industrial system, involving a diagnosis of under-consumption or over-saving, as the main cause of trade depressions with their accompanying unemployment.   (Mummery, 1913, pp. 9–10)

The Physiology of Industry was published within a year or so of Hobson's American letter of 8 June 1888. It was to be the only book on which he and Mummery collaborated. Mummery died in 1895, in an unsuccessful attempt to climb Nanga Parbat in the Himalayas.

7.   Hewins was subsequently to become the first Director of the London School of Economics and Political Science.

8.   Sismondi referred to 'an orthodoxy' in political economy in the Preface to the second edition of his *Nouveaux principes d'économie politique*, first published in the *Revue Encyclopédique* in 1826.

9.   In his obituary of Hobson, G. D. H. Cole wrote:

I myself can well remember, from my undergraduate days, the vindictiveness with which I heard Hobson's subversive notions assailed – with the natural consequence that I began reading his books with a strong predisposition in their favour.   (Cole, 1940, p. 354)

10.   See also Kadish, 1990, pp. 150–1.

11.   However, in 1897 Hobson gave lectures to students at the London School of Economics and Political Science on the economics of distribution (Hobson, 1900b, p. vi). Much of the material in these lectures was incorporated in *The Economics of Distribution*.

12.   The original of the latter part (pp. 10–16) of this sixteen-page address is in the Hobson archives, Hull University Library, where it is stated that pages 1–9 are to be found in the Keynes Papers. However, all that has been found of this address in the Keynes Papers is typescript consisting of one and a half pages, probably the section preceding that quoted by Keynes in the *General Theory*, containing material which reappeared in revised form in ch. I of Hobson's *Confessions of an Economic Heretic*.

13.   This is presumably what is to be found on pages 365–6 in *The General Theory*.

14.   Compare, however, the following excerpt from a letter written by Keynes to Kahn the previous day:

Thanks very much for taking so much trouble about the Mummery. Hobson never fully understood him and went off on a side-track after his death. But the book Hobson helped him to write, *The Physiology of Industry*, is a wonderful work. I am giving a full account of it but old Hobson has had so much injustice done to him that I shan't say what I think about M's contribution to it being, probably, outstanding. (Keynes, 1973, vol. XIII, p. 634)

15.   J. B. Clark deserves equal credit for this discovery; his relevant article was published in the same issue of the *Quarterly Journal of Economics* as that by Hobson.

16. Allett comments that the fact 'that the Rainbow Circle took its name from the Rainbow Tavern in Fleet Street, where it held its first monthly meetings, is ... a fair indication that its program was going to differ somewhat from [T. H.] Green's emphasis on temperance as a key instrument of social reform' (1981, p. 23). However, the Circle moved its meeting-place because 'a dispute arose with the Tavern, which some remembered as over the inadequate consumption of alcohol' (Clarke, 1978, p. 56).

17. The earliest use of the term 'the new liberalism' in this sense seems to have been in Atherley-Jones (1889).

18. Hobson's recognition of the importance of Ruskin's ideas took time; while a student at Oxford he attended only one of Ruskins lectures (Hobson, 1921, p. 672). But while Hobson conveyed the impression in 1938 that Ruskin's influence on him dated only from the late 1890s (1938b, p. 38), he had, in fact, stated as early as 1888 that *Sesame and Lilies* was the best of Ruskin's books (*The Derbyshire Advertiser*, 2 March, p. 8), implying that by then he had already read many, if not all, of Ruskin's works.

19. In Hobson (1938b) the year of publication of the article is wrongly stated as 1899.

20. One of those leaders Hobson 'saw much of' was the Boer general, Jan Smuts subsequently to become South African prime minister, to whom Hobson carried personal introductions 'from two relations who knew him at Cambridge' (Hobson, 1938b, p. 117). Of these relations, one was undoubtedly his elder brother, Ernest William, who was a Fellow of Christ's College, where Smuts was a student. E. W. Hobson, who was Professor of Mathematics at Cambridge, subsequently became mathematics supervisor of the young John Maynard Keynes.

21. This book had its origin in lectures given to the London branch of the Christian Social Union, which were published initially in a series of articles in *The Ethical World*, though it also incorporated material from articles published in other journals.

22. Hobson struck his contemporaries as being frail, and there were numerous occasions in his life when ill-health prevented him from carrying out commitments.

23. The *Nation* had always depended on financial support from the Rowntree family, which in the early 1920s declared itself no longer willing to cover the increasing losses. Massingham, having become a bitter opponent of Lloyd George, and veering towards the Labour Party, was in no position to raise funds from members of the Liberal Party, while Keynes and Ramsay Muir *were*, through their association with the Liberal Summer School movement. Hence Massingham's resignation in December 1922 was accepted, and Keynes persuaded his colleague Hubert Henderson to become the new editor. Initially, at least, Hobson, like most of his colleagues, thought Massingham to have been badly treated. See Clarke, 1978, pp. 215–16.

24. Note, however, the critical private remarks made by Lenin, quoted in footnote 12 to Chapter 7.

25. The *New Age*, edited by Douglas' supporter A. R. Orage, was a periodical providing *inter alia* a mouthpiece for Douglas and his followers. In the early months of 1922 there was an exchange of views between Hobson and Douglas in the *Socialist Review*; this suggests that Hobson may have played

a leading part in the writing of the Labour Party committee's report. Unfortunately the month of publication of the report is not known.

26. The 1926 letters are included in the Keynes Papers.

27. One of those by Hobson has not survived.

28. Clarke (1990, pp. 113–14) points out that Hobson presumably used the term 'heretic' because of Keynes' application of it to him in a broadcast in 1934, Keynes having ten years earlier referred to a 'heresy' of his own when delivering his lecture entitled 'The End of *Laissez-Faire*'.

29. Further assessments of Hobson the man by writers who, with the exception of Clark, knew him personally, are to be found in Burns (1940), Brailsford (1948), Clark (1940), Joad (1940) and Tawney (1949). The most comprehensive published factual biography is that by Lee (1972), which is based on the account of some one hundred pages to be found in Lee (1970), to which in turn the 'life' in this book is considerably indebted. A substantial biographical account is also to be found in Allett (1981, ch. 1), Clarke (1974), Freeden (1988, introduction) and King (1992).

30. The Deane and Cole estimates show the annual *per capita* rate of growth to have fallen within this range for the whole of the nineteenth century, but their estimates for the period 1801–31 are criticised in Crafts (1980); Crafts (1985, pp. 45 and 103) estimates the annual *per capita* rate of growth for the period 1801–31 to have been only 0.52, but for the period 1821–51 to have been 1.19. There is continuing debate over Crafts' criticism of the Deane and Cole estimates for the period 1801–31 (see especially Crafts and Harley, 1992; and Jackson, 1994).

31. The Corn Laws restricted the import of corn; the Navigation Act prohibited the use of foreign merchant ships.

32. For further discussion of 'the Great Depression', see in particular Beales (1934), and Rostow (1948), chs 3 and 7.

33. Some support for this perception is to be found in Rostow's estimation that, for the period 1790–1914, the 'years 1884–7 were probably the worst continuous sequence, from the point of view of unemployment' (1948, p. 49).

34. These estimates of unemployment are 'according to the official figures, which for various reasons understated it' (Hobsbawm, 1968, p. 175).

35. See Porter (1968), pp. 5–18. Liberals had been, and remained, divided on the question of Empire.

36. In so far as it can be defined at all, the term 'Radical' in nineteenth-century Britain described those who opposed the aims, methods and principles of the Establishment. See Taylor (1957), ch. 1.

37. The Independent Labour Party was 'independent' in the sense that it was not controlled by the trade unions. Consequently, it was able to put forward relatively more radical policies.

38. In 1903, at a by-election, a seat in Parliament had for the first time been won by a man labelling himself as a member of the Labour Party, namely Will Crooks.

39. Clause (d) of the 'Party Objects' in the new constitution adopted in 1918 reads:

> To secure for the producers by hand or by brain the full fruits of their industry, and the most equitable distribution thereof that may be possible,

upon the basis of the common ownership of the means of production and
the best obtainable system of popular administration and control of each
industry and service. (quoted in Cole, 1949, p. 72)

This clause was subsequently replaced (in 1995).

2   Economic Activity and Welfare

1. In arguing for the principle of minimum sacrifice in 'The Pure Theory of
    Taxation' (*Economic Journal*, 1897), however, Edgeworth settled for a less
    rigorous approach, and glossed over the problems associated with making
    interpersonal comparisons. See, for example, the conclusions he drew from
    the diagram in n. 3, p. 560.
2. In the text of the second edition of Jevons' *Theory of Political Economy*
    (1879), the term 'political economy' was replaced by the term 'economics',
    a reflection of the fact that during the 1870s an increasing number of econ-
    omists were attempting to divorce their discipline from the discussion of
    ends.
3. A variant of this states that the criterion for an increase in welfare is that
    those who are better off are capable of compensating those who are worse
    off. This is less defensible, since if the compensation is not paid, inter-
    personal comparisons are implicitly being made. The Pareto criterion was
    first enunciated in *Manuale di Economia Politica* (1906).
4. *History of Economic Analysis* was published posthumously, Schumpeter
    having died in 1950.
5. Hobson's 'large speculative idea' has much in common with Karl Popper's
    'conjecture' (see Popper's *Conjectures and Refutations*). Both emphasise
    the crucial dependence of advances in knowledge on imaginative insights.
6. In attaching importance to the time available to enjoy consumption, Patten
    anticipated a theme to be taken up in Linder (1970).
7. Adam Smith clearly believed such an adjustment could be made when he
    described diamonds as 'useless', though he thereby incurred the subsequent
    wrath of neoclassical economists.
8. Rousseau's concept of the 'general will' had been revived by Bernard
    Bosanquet, to whose *The Philosophical Theory of the State* (1899) Hobson
    referred readers of *The Social Problem*.
9. For incisive discussions of this contribution by Hobson to political theory
    see in particular Clarke (1974) and Freeden (1978). Hamilton (1915,
    p. 570), reviewing *Work and Wealth*, testified to the difficulty Hobson faced
    by expressing 'surprise that one finds the concept of social welfare, as
    elaborated in the treatise, saturated with individualistic notions'. See also
    Allett (1981) and Townshend (1990).
10. This statement occurs in the first three editions of Marshall's *Principles*, but
    was dropped thereafter (Marshall, 1890–1920, vol. II, p. 131).
11. This statement dates from the second edition of Marshall's *Principles*
    (1891).
12. In *Work and Wealth* (p. 320), Hobson admitted that there may, however, be
    a positive correlation between individual wealth and satisfaction.

13. Hobson stated that race is also a relevant factor in this context, although he gave no examples.
14. Little of Marx's writings along similar lines was known in 1901, when Hobson named those whom he supported.
15. The common attribution to Bentham of the statement that 'push-pin is as good as poetry' is apparently due to John Stuart Mill (1969, vol. x, p. 113). Mill's omission of the reference by Bentham to music as well as poetry is unfortunate, as Bentham personally believed poetry to be a misuse of words.
16. It is not clear whether Hobson was referring, among others, to the 'vulgar plutocrat' when he asserted that some people 'are inherently and eternally incapable of wealth' (1901b, p. 50).
17. Whenever the term 'needs' is used in the special Hobsonian sense, it will appear henceforth in this book, as 'needs'.
18. Modern efficiency wage theories imply that profit-maximising firms will raise the wage rate to the level at which labour cost per unit of 'efficiency' is minimised. To this extent, but to this extent only, they imply that firms meet the 'needs' of their employees.
19. This procedure for calculating 'social' or 'co-operative' value was first suggested by Friedrich von Wieser, in *Der Natürliche Werth* (1889). Hobson made no reference to von Wieser's priority, even though he was familiar with *Der Natütrliche Werth*, the English translation of which he referred to in *The Economics of Distribution* (p. 247).
20. An example of a raft economy is to be found in Slawomir Mrozek's play, *Out At Sea*, where three men attempt to establish by a democratic process who is to be the first to be eaten, though Hobson no doubt did not have in mind such an extreme case of a raft economy. With respect to a war economy, Hobson acknowledged subsequently that, in time of war, not all act as if they are part of an organic society, as is evidenced by 'war-profiteering' (1919b, p. 41).

3 Income Distribution and Prices

1. This chapter draws substantially on Schneider (1994a).
2. Caselli and Pastrello build on this 'Hobsonian suggestion' in arguing that over the period 1960–83, the United States was relatively more successful than European countries in maintaining employment growth because employment in its 'dealers' sector did not fall during cyclical downturns.
3. By 'marginal net product' Marshall meant marginal product minus incidental expenses associated with the employment of an additional unit of a factor, plus incidental savings.
4. An unsigned editorial note separating the article by Hobson from that by Clark, which contained the first exposition of the marginal productivity theory of distribution, refers to 'the different methods of treatment followed by them with substantial identity of conclusion' (*Quarterly Journal of Economics*, 1891, p. 288). It is curious that this note makes no reference to an article by Sidney Webb, published in the same journal in 1888, which went some way to anticipating the argument of the later articles.
5. The idea that the concept of rent can be applied to returns to capital and labour as well as land was not, however, originated by Hobson; it dates back

to an appendix to Richard Whately's *Elements of Logic* (1826), written by Nassau Senior, as Whately acknowledges in the Preface, pp. viii–ix.

6.   Hobson could have drawn on no less an authority than Adam Smith to support this view, as in *The Wealth of Nations* Adam Smith argued that the 'difference between the most dissimilar characters, between a philosopher and a common street porter, for example, seems to arise not so much from nature, as from habit, custom, and education' (1976, pp. 28–9). However, in a lecture delivered in 1933, Hobson objected to this pronouncement by Adam Smith, on the ground that it takes the doctrine of equality between men much too far (1933b, p. 2).

7.   The figures are Hobson's.

8.   It did not occur to Hobson to question the very concept of 'capital', as participants on one side of 'the Cambridge controversies' were later to do (see Harcourt, 1972).

9.   In *The Economics of Distribution* (p. 165) Hobson acknowledged Cairnes' authorship of the idea that factors of production belong to non-competing 'layers'. He made no reference, however, to the fact that Cairnes had also anticipated his main line of argument, stating in *Some Leading Principles of Political Economy Newly Expounded* that commodities sell at a price in excess of their cost of production 'where skilled labour represents a monopoly' (1874, p. 77).

10. Heterogeneity of employers with respect to efficiency is a sufficient condition for the demand schedule to slope downwards to the right.

11. See Ricardo, 1951–73, vol. I, pp. 70–2.

12. See 1891b, pp. 269–71.

13. Hobson in fact refers to a 'diminishing return', but it is clear from the text that he means by this a fall in the net return to the factor as a whole.

14. This line of argument was foreshadowed in *The Physiology of Industry*, where (p. 172) it was labelled 'the law of the Limiting Requisite in Production'. For a formal treatment of this 'law', see Backhouse, 1994, pp. 89–92.

15. For these reasons, Hobson concluded that 'the attempt here to apply the law of rent so as to yield a basis for a sound theory of distribution has certainly brought to light no easy "rule of thumb", but it has perhaps served to make more clear the character and the origin of some of the difficulties which must be met with in this branch of the science' (1891b, p. 288).

16. See 1891b, p. 276, figs I and II, from which Figures 3.3 and 3.4 have been derived by rotating Hobson's origin (point *B*) 180° from the surface and relabelling it O, so as to bring the diagrams into line with modern practice; some other points in Hobson's fig. II have been relabelled so as to make for consistency with the labelling in his fig. I. Hobson's diagrammatic treatment suffers from the deficiency that he uses his *BC* axis (*OQ* in our diagram) to rank factor grades by quality without making any reference to factor quantities, mistakenly believing that he could at the same time attach a quantitative significance to the areas in his diagrams.

17. Hobson first developed this argument in 'The Economics of Bargaining' (1899), which provided the basis for ch. I of *The Economics of Distribution*.

18. In *The Economics of Distribution* Hobson acknowledges the influence of Böhm-Bawerk, whose *Positive Theorie des Kapitals* (1889) appeared in

English translation in 1891. But Böhm-Bawerk's analysis of price determination where bargaining plays a part is based on Menger's *Grundsätze der Volkswirthschaftslehre* (1871).

19. Hobson implicitly assumes that bargaining itself involves no effort or sacrifice.

20. In *Democracy after the War* (1917) Hobson was to substitute for 'surplus' his own neologism, 'improperty', later defined as comprising rents, profits, monopoly fees and so on, which 'involve no labour in their origin and no appreciable sacrifice' (1937, p. 40).

21. The single tax system recommended by Hobson differs from that advocated by Henry George, in which taxes are levied solely on rent received from land and other natural resources.

22. Hobson stated that he did 'not believe that well-to-do people would accumulate and leave behind them less than they do now, if the State were to take one-half or more of their estates instead of the tenth which it now takes on average' (1919b, p. 116).

23. Hobson was not always so optimistic about the prospects of harmony in business, even when 'well-ordered'.

24. Use of the concepts of 'absorption of the surplus' and 'social utilisation of the surplus' and the idea that the surplus is responsible for unemployment, are just some of several respects in which Hobson anticipated arguments subsequently to be put forward by Paul Baran and Paul Sweezy, best known for their analysis of 'monopoly capital'; others include the description of price and output policies followed by oligopolies and the notion of advertising as waste. The fact that Hobson himself often did not acknowledge his sources does not excuse Baran and Sweezy from failing to acknowledge their debt to Hobson. While Sweezy wrote a mildly appreciative article on Hobson in 1938, Hobson's name is not even mentioned in either Sweezy's *The Theory of Capitalist Development* or Baran and Sweezy's *Monopoly Capital*; it occurs just twice in Baran's *The Political Economy of Growth*, and then only in connection with the theory of imperialism.

25. Subsequently, however, Hobson was to write that 'profits, not wages, as some economists pretend, have been the "residuary legatee" in the economic system, taking what remains of the product of industry, after the other factors have been paid their necessary hire' (1919b, p. 21).

26. Hobson, however, provided no proof that the total product would be exactly exhausted. Nor was proof of product exhaustion provided in Clark (1891), in the case of the marginal productivity theory of distribution; the proof was developed in stages, in Wicksteed (1894), Flux (1894) and Wicksell (1902), and acknowledged by Wicksell to be applicable only under extremely stringent conditions. These conditions are spelt out later in the text.

27. Robinson (1934) makes this point, but then goes on to defend Hobson's conclusion that, under the circumstances assumed, the wage rate will equal the average product; 'Marshall and Mr Hobson are each right in what they assert, and wrong in what they deny' (Robinson, 1934, p. 404).

28. The total product is the integral of $(20 - 4x)$ over the range 0 to 4.

29. Note that 48 is also the integral of $(16 - 2x)$ over the range 0 to 4.

30. An appropriate example can be derived from Cassel's statement that 'if a pit has to be dug, the addition of one more man will make *little* difference to

the day's output unless you give the man a spade' (1923, vol. I, p. 172; emphasis added); withdrawal of one man or one spade might reduce output by 8 and 10 units respectively, while withdrawal of both reduces it by only 12. When a spade is withdrawn, one man could, following Robertson (1931, p. 47), be supplied with a bucket and sent to fetch beer for the others; when a man is withdrawn, one of the remaining men could conceivably become a little more productive with two spades rather than one, for example, by regularly putting one in a stream to be washed while using the other.

31.   This example has been constructed to produce results similar to figures plucked out of the air, so to speak, by Hobson, in a case involving three factors where withdrawal of 1 unit of each of three factors individually results in a reduction of product of 8, 10 and 10 units respectively, but where the withdrawal of the 3 units simultaneously reduces the total product by not 28 units but only 18 (1900b, pp. 145–7). Hobson followed up this example with another, involving a commodity produced with 1 unit of each of three factors, the individual withdrawal of any of these factors resulting in total loss of the product. He was, however, mistaken in believing that his second example provides a general refutation of the marginal productivity theory; the example is a special case, in that it does not involve diminishing returns.

32.   Hobson was anticipated with respect to this argument by Friedrich von Wieser, who in *Der Natürliche Werth* (1889) criticised Menger's theory of distribution for failing to allow for the role of 'co-operation' between what he called 'the productive elements'. As already noted, Hobson made no reference to von Wieser's priority, even though he was familiar with *Der Natürliche Werth*, the English translation of which he referred to in *The Economics of Distribution* (p. 247).

33.   Clark (1899, p. 3) stated that 'free competition tends to give to labour what labour creates'. Wicksteed (1910, pp. 344–5) said of 'the most miserable earners of starvation wages' that 'we may assume that they are already getting as much as their work is worth'; although he added that, in consequence 'our problem is partly perhaps to see that they get (not from their employers and consumers but from communal funds) something more than they are worth, but very certainly to see whether they cannot be made worth more'.

34.   See, in particular, *Free-thought in the Social Sciences*, pp. 108–111.

35.   Hobson's insistence on factor supply as an important determinant of the distribution of income is reinforced in Preiser (1952), where an extensive argument is developed to show that '*behind the elasticity of supply lies the power embodied in property*' (Preiser, 1952, p. 213, emphasis in original).

36.   Note, however, that Wicksell (1902) demonstrates that product exhaustion can be proved in a case other than that of constant returns to scale. The case Wicksell considers, believed by him to be a common one faced by firms because of the existence of indivisibilities, was that of fixed factor proportions, characterised by returns increasing at a diminishing rate before they in fact begin to diminish. Profit maximisation in long-run equilibrium entails operating at that scale where returns cease to increase, that is to say, where the average and marginal products resulting from the jointly-demanded factors are equal. Given the existence of variable proportions elsewhere in

the economy, competition will ensure that each of the factors receives that share of the average product resulting from the jointly-demanded factors which equals its marginal product.

37. Marshall's copy of *Wealth and Welfare* 'was withdrawn by Mrs Marshall when the Librarian of the Marshall Library, Mr P. Sraffa (incautiously, as he realised too late) drew her attention to the notes. After her death the volume was returned to the Library, but was kept in reserve during Pigou's lifetime' (Bharadwaj, 1972, p. 32, n. 5).

4 Underconsumption

1. This chapter draws substantially on Schneider (1994b).
2. A leading feature of 'advance economics' was the wages fund doctrine, which in the 1860s was criticised by Francis Longe, Fleeming Jenkin and W. T. Thornton. After John Stuart Mill recanted in his 1869 review of Thornton's *On Labour*, and Walker attacked it in the 1870s, the wages fund doctrine rapidly disappeared from orthodox economics. See Blyth (1987).
3. See, for example, Mummery's and Hobson's assertion that 'labourers are paid out of the value they assist in producing ... their wages are no more advanced from any special fund than the landlord's rent or the capitalist's profit' (1889, p. 76). Marx's *Capital* is cited in support of this assertion; the idea goes back to Hodgskin (1825).
4. Thus the classical 'consumption' is identical with the modern 'absorption' (see Alexander, 1952). In an open economy this exceeds aggregate demand to the extent that imports are greater than exports.
5. de Tocqueville comments that 'most of the words coined or adopted' for the use of a democratic people 'will mainly serve to express *the wants of business*, the passions of party, or the details of public administration' (1840, vol. III, p. 134, emphasis added).
6. Marx's treatment of underconsumption as involving disproportionality between the means of production and articles of consumption departments lends itself to this interpretation. See also Sweezy (1942), where no clear line is drawn between disproportionality and underconsumption as causing realisation crises.
7. Thinking along similar lines, Backhouse (1994, p. 82) describes underconsumption as a case of 'intertemporal disequilibrium'.
8. Malthus was expounding the essence of his underconsumption theory in correspondence with Ricardo as early as September 1814. The importance of the Ricardo–Malthus correspondence was probably never appreciated by Hobson, at least not before the publication of *The General Theory*. In his very first 'London Letter' for *The Derbyshire Advertiser*, Hobson noted the large number of new books being published, stating that it was now possible to read Ricardo's letters to Malthus, 'if anyone cares' (7 October 1887, p. 8).
9. For a detailed history and analysis of 'the Treasury View', see Clarke (1988).
10. For a brief account of the 'Ricardian equivalence theorem', see Abel (1987).
11. For details, see Haberler, 1937, pp. 68–79.

12. Clarke (1990) argues that the concept of the 'individualist fallacy' may have been Hobson's most important influence on Keynes. But when Keynes stated in his obituary of Edgeworth that 'the whole is not equal to the sum of its parts' (Keynes, 1926, p. 150) he was almost certainly drawing on his flirtation with organicism in the *Treatise on Probability* (see pp. 277, 343).

13. The tendency of the distributive trades to suffer relatively little unemployment during a depression had already been noted in *The Physiology of Industry*.

14. The substance of both these articles was incorporated in *The Problem of the Unemployed* (1896a).

15. In 1677, Yarranton wrote, in *England Improved*, 'admit' there be in England and Wales a hundred thousand poor people unimployed [*sic*]' (quoted in *The Oxford English Dictionary*, 2nd edn, vol. XXIX, p. 1). In 1888, the journal *Science* carried the statement: 'The chief purpose of the inquiry was to ascertain ... the extent of unemployment generally' (quoted in *The Oxford English Dictionary*, 2nd edn, vol. XXIX, p. 1). The word 'unemployment' is not used in *The Physiology of Industry*.

16. This was also Sismondi's view, but there is no direct evidence that Hobson was influenced by Sismondi. However, Sismondi's ideas are summarised briefly in J. M. Robertson's *The Fallacy of Saving* (1892), which is quoted in Hobson's *The Evolution of Modern Capitalism*, and singled out for special mention in his *Confessions of an Economic Heretic*.

17. An implicitly approving reference to Malthus (and his follower, Thomas Chalmers) is also to be found in *The Physiology of Industry* (p. 101). But there Mummery and Hobson follow Malthus further, including luxurious expenditure among the recommended remedies for trade depression.

18. Thus Haberler's contention that 'the under-consumption theory is a theory of the crisis and depression rather than a theory of the cycle' (Haberler, 1937, p. 112) is not entirely applicable to Hobson's version of the theory.

19. The existence of 'target saving' had been noted by Marshall (Marshall, 1890–1920, vol. I, pp. 234–5), and *à la* Hobson was to be used by Keynes in *The General Theory* (pp. 93–4) to justify the assumption that one should be agnostic as to whether saving increases or decreases with (say) a rise in the interest rate.

20. Allett (1981, pp. 109–11) states that Hobson dropped this argument in works published from 1929 onwards. But the argument was not deleted from the second (1931) edition of *The Economics of Unemployment*, and it is cited as a possible explanation of underconsumption in point 7 of the 'Notes on Oversaving' sent by Hobson to Keynes in August, 1931.

21. The Bank of England was, in fact, nationalised in 1946, and has not to date been subjected to the threat of privatisation.

22. Hobson had always regarded it as necessary to impose guidelines on public works, so as to avoid resources being withdrawn from areas where they were currently efficiently employed. In *The Problem of the Unemployed*, for example, he argued that 'the product of the labour employed on public relief works should not be brought into competition with the products of outside labour' (p. 157), and that 'the wages paid should be somewhat lower than those paid for similar work in the outside market' (p. 157).

23.   On balance, it seems that Malthus intended his statement to be taken literally, although Eltis (1980, pp. 52–5) and Hollander (1987, pp. 253–5) argue to the contrary.

24.   Mummery and Hobson quoted Alfred [and Mary Paley] Marshall as stating in the *Economics of Industry* that 'though men have the power to purchase, they may not choose to use it' (1879, p. 154), commenting that Marshall 'fails to grasp the critical importance of this fact' (1889, p. 102, n. 1). Schumpeter (1954, p. 1088, text and n. 5), citing the approving reference to this comment in Keynes (1936, p. 19, n. 1), concluded that Mummery and Hobson were referring to hoarding, but the context makes it clear that they had in mind saving-and-investing, not hoarding, as the alternative to consuming.

25.   Of course, another difference is that, unlike Keynes, Hobson never developed an analysis of the monetary sector.

26.   In the 'Banana Parable' the success of a campaign to increase saving in a community producing (perishable) bananas leads to a downward spiral in the level of income, halted according to one supposition when the 'campaign peters out as a result of the growing poverty' (Keynes, 1930, p. 160).

27.   The reproduction of this passage in Keynes (1979, p. 210) lacks Hobson's capitals.

28.   Where financial assets consist solely of money, Keynes arrived at this conclusion by an alternative route. Assuming that the stock of money is determined by those who supply it, he concluded that it is not within the power of those who demand money to alter in aggregate the amount which they hoard (Keynes, 1936, p. 174). If 'hoarding' is confined to idle balances, this argument implicitly assumes a given transactions demand for money function.

29.   Keynes would no doubt have preferred his theory to be described as stating that the difficulty arises when planned investment falls short of full employment saving.

30.   The only ground for omitting income distribution from the following model is the complexity that would follow. For examples of underconsumption models incorporating income distribution, see Bauer (1936), a version of whose model is set out in English in Sweezy (1942), pp. 186–9, Eltis (1980), and Costabile and Rowthorn (1985).

31.   Expressing the underconsumption theory in this way makes it clear why Keynes could never have accepted it. While Keynes made many references to the stimulating effect of an increase in consumption on investment, his view that investment depends above all on entrepreneurs' expectations, as well as on innumerable other factors, would have precluded him from accepting the idea that investment is simply a function of the rate of growth of consumption.

32.   Suppose an initial capital stock K_0 grows at the rate g. In period 1, capital stock will be $K_0 + gK_0$. In period 2, capital stock will be $(K_0 + gK_0) + g(K_0 + gK_0)$. Net investment thus increases from gK_0 in period 1 to $gK_0 (1 + g)$ in period 2; that is to say, it grows at the rate g.

33.   This diagram is an adaptation of one to be found in Pilvin (1952).

34.   But Hobson did not go the whole way to anticipating the 'Banana Parable'. As already noted, in his letter to Hobson of 24 July 1931, Keynes pointed

out that in his Banana Parable 'there is no real saving corresponding to the surplus savings' (Keynes, 1973, vol. XIII, p. 330); that is to say, because income falls, the planned additional saving is not realised.

35. Whereas Keynes referred to the thrift campaign petering out as a result of growing poverty, Robinson anticipated the language of *The General Theory*; following the introduction of the thrift campaign, 'output will consequently decline until the real income of the population is reduced to such a low level that savings are perforce reduced to equality with investment' (Robinson, 1933, p. 25).

36. To assume a growth rate of 25 per cent per period of one or two years is unrealistic, but it simplifies the arithmetic.

37. This diagram is an adaptation of one to be found in Dubey (1962).

38. Clark may have avoided expressing the acceleration principle in terms of net output so as not to show investment as in part depending on itself.

5 Trade, Capital Flows and Imperialism

1. As Porter (1968, p. 110) points out, some elements of an explanation of imperialism in economic terms are to be found in two articles by Ernest Belfort Bax, published in the journal *Justice* on 16 June 1894 and 1 May 1896. In particular, Bax referred to the exhaustion of home markets and the advantages of cheap native labour as factors leading capitalists to draw on public revenue for territorial annexation, this being 'the true meaning of modern foreign policy' (Bax, 1896, p. 7). Contrary to Hobson, however, he believed that a capitalist country pursuing a policy of territorial annexation would receive support from all other capitalist countries; this led him to urge workers in capitalist countries to unite with the oppressed 'barbarians' against the capitalists.

2. Emmanuel (1972, pp. ix–x) argues that the theory of comparative advantage is applicable to situations in which there is international immobility of labour, even if there is no barrier to the international movement of capital. This is true in the absence of Ricardo's assumption that in the long run the supply of labour will adjust to the demand for it through population changes. as in this case capital will not move if it is not accompanied by the labour required to work with it.

3. Cain (1978) cites 'Can England Keep her Trade?' as one primary source for his contention that before 1898 Hobson 'advocated imperialism and protection' (Cain, 1978, p. 568). But Hobson makes no reference in this article to territorial annexation. He also asserts that keeping out foreign goods would only 'encourage the alienation of capital' (1891d, p. 10); the only forms of 'protection' he advocates are protection from labour inflow and capital outflow. Some support for Cain's contention is, however, to be found in Hobson's *Derbyshire Advertiser* column of 7 April 1888, where Hobson wrote approvingly that 'those who look to the future are more and more coming to regard an Imperial Federation between England's sons all over the earth as the only sure protection against the otherwise inevitable decay, which history teaches us is the lot of nations which have reached the proud position England now occupies' (*Derbyshire Advertiser*, 7 April 1888, p. 8).

4. Some of Cobden's views, as reflected in his writings, together with Hobson's opinions on them, are to be found in *Richard Cobden: The International Man.*

5. Ultimately, Hobson argued, protection would redistribute income in a more unequal direction, thus exacerbating unemployment, as he had already stated in *International Trade.*

6. By 'discount rate' is meant the rate of interest at which a central bank is prepared to make a short-term loan to a private-sector financial institution. The importance of the discount rate lies in the fact that it significantly influences short-term interest rates in general, and consequently also long-term interest rates.

7. As noted later, in Chapter 6, this 'indirect mechanism' was discovered by Thornton (1802), and endorsed by Marshall in 1887 in his evidence to the Gold and Silver Commission. For Hobson's exposition of it, see in particular ch. VII of his *International Trade.*

8. Porter (1968, p. 194, n. 3) states:

> Many writers have neglected Hobson's *C. R.* article of Aug 1898 and assumed that ch. vi of *Imperalism* was the first statement of the economic theory of imperialism ... Three writers, M. P. Schneider ('Underconsumption and Imperialism'), and Koebner and Schmidt (*Imperialism*), have correctly attributed its origins to the year 1898, although without explaining the political events which stimulated it.

Porter cites Langer (1935–6) as one of the 'many writers'. Sweezy (1938) and Nemmers (1956) are others.

9. Brewer (1990) points out, with respect to a similar statement in *Imperialism: A Study,* that if human needs are illimitable, then underconsumption is impossible, whatever the distribution of income. Brewer adds, however, that Hobson's 'message is clear enough; excess saving may occur when some have high incomes and save a lot, while others would like to spend more but do not have any income to spend' (Brewer, 1990, p. 78).

10. Hobson may have drawn here on Disraeli's statement, made in 1852 in his pre-imperialist days, that 'these wretched colonies will all be independent ... in a few years, and are a millstone around our necks' (Monypenny and Buckle, 1929, vol. 1, p. 1201).

11. See Giffen (1899).

12. Magnusson (1994) stresses that Hobson's recognition of the political and ideological aspects of imperialism distinguishes his theory of imperialism from that of Lenin, who 'in making notes from Hobson's book for his own pamphlet – besides mocking Hobson's political views with scribbles in the margin such as "Ha ha!!", "ethical socialist", "quaint", "ha-ha!! the essence of philistine criticisms of imperialism" ... characterises, for example, the chapter in which Hobson treats the "scientific defence of imperialism" as "twaddle"' (Magnusson, 1994, p. 151).

13. Mary Kingsley was another. For a fascinating account of her ideas see Porter, 1968, ch. 8.

14. Fieldhouse (1961) makes these facts the central feature of his criticism of Hobson's theory of imperialism. His article also rejects the idea of any monocausal explanation of imperialism.

15. Cain (1978, p. 582) suggests that Paish's revelation that capital did not follow the flag may also have contributed to Hobson's more benevolent attitude towards the export of capital in *An Economic Interpretation of Investment*.

16. Hobson went on to make a partial exception in the case of Rhodes, stating that 'the subtle bonds between property and personal power must be held to have exercised a powerful influence on his policy' (1917, p. 85).

17. For a more detailed account of changes in Hobson's views on imperialism over this period, see Cain (1990).

18. A second edition of *Imperialism: A Study* had appeared in 1905, with only relatively minor changes from the first.

19. For an early, ambitious attempt to test Hobson's theory of imperialism in the light of empirical evidence, see Schneider (1959), pp. 63–91.

20. Kennedy (1987), in an attempt to explain the combination of higher risk and higher returns on foreign compared with domestic investments, suggests that 'in the eyes of many savers … foreign and colonial railroad bonds must have been better substitutes for the safest domestic bonds than were domestic industrial equities' (Kennedy, 1987, p. 153).

21. For more detailed figures, see Imlah, 1958, ch. 3.

22. Cairncross argues that 1900 is an exception to this rule; in that year it was not exports but a domestic boom that pulled the economy out of a slump.

23. As already noted, however, Cecil Rhodes was not regarded by Hobson himself as a clear example.

6 Money and Credit

1. This chapter was omitted from the revised edition of the book, published in 1931.

2. Henceforth, whenever the term 'quantity of money' is used in the Hobsonian sense it will be enclosed in quotation marks.

3. Henceforth whenever the word 'credit' is used in the Hobsonian sense it will be enclosed in quotation marks; Hobson's own procedure, by contrast, was to enclose the word 'money' in quotation marks.

4. One of the many criticisms made by Keynes in his review of Hobson's book (Keynes, 1913) was that Hobson seemed unaware that adherents to the quantity theory knew of, and accepted, this argument. It is doubtful whether Keynes could have cited any published writings, apart from Marshall's evidence to the Gold and Silver Commission, in support of his assertion. Given that, during Wicksell's visit to Cambridge in 1916, 'Keynes did not in fact have much time to spare for this foreign colleague whose name meant little to him' (Gårdlund, 1958, p. 295), it is most unlikely that Keynes at that time was aware of the arguments in Wicksell's *Geldzins und Güterpreisen*.

5. This is the mirror image of Wicksell's explanation of falling prices in the late nineteenth century, namely that investment opportunities had dwindled so fast as to force the rate of discount down, notwithstanding the increase in the quantity of money. There is no direct evidence that Hobson was familiar with Wicksell's analysis, but the probability is that he was not, as none of Wicksell's books was translated into English until the 1930s, though among

the books Hobson reviewed is at least one that had not been translated from the German.

6. *The Physiology of Industry* explicitly rejects 'the arguments of the currency school' (1889, p. 196).

7. For a succinct account of the Currency School and Banking School ideas, see Schwartz (1987).

8. For an account of 'structural characteristics' which lead to inflation see Maynard (1962), chs 3–5.

9. Hobson's '"irritation" with the quantity theory so annoyed Keynes that he refused to review any more of his books' (Skidelsky, 1983, p. 218).

10. Fisher, in fact, went on to relax these assumptions. This does not entirely negate Hobson's criticism, however, as it is often theories in their unqualified form that exert the most influence on subsequent thinking.

11. The other members of the committee were Sidney Webb, R. J. Davies, MP, Frank Hodges and F. B. Varley of the Labour Party National Executive, and G. D. H. Cole, Hugh Dalton, C. M. Lloyd, Sir Leo Chiozza Money, R. H. Tawney and Arthur Greenwood (secretary).

7   Hobson as Economist: A Critique

1. The subject-matter of this chapter is primarily a general critique of Hobson as economist. Criticisms of specific economic arguments put forward by Hobson have been incorporated in chs 2–6.

2. This approach is also used in the discussion of Marxian critiques of Hobson's theory of imperialism.

3. The edition from which the passages referred to by Marshall were expunged was the third (1895); the edition of which Marshall sent Hobson a copy was the fourth (1898). The letter has no bearing on the change cited in the text between the fifth and sixth editions of Marshall's *Principles*, as the fifth edition did not appear until 1907.

4. Robbins (1932a, p. 16) summarises this neatly in the statement that 'economics is the science which studies human behaviour as the relationship between ends and scarce means which have alternative uses'.

5. Pigou, whose writings are the principal source of this element of modern welfare economics, may well have been influenced by Hobson, whose writings are cited five times in Pigou's *Wealth and Welfare*.

6. These totalitarian overtones can be traced back as far as Plato's *Republic*. See, for example, Popper (1945).

7. For a detailed critique of Hobson on this count see Nemmers, 1956, pp. 111–28.

8. Of course, any particular Marxian writer would not endorse all these theories.

9. For the same reason, Hobson might object to being described, *a là* Backhouse (1990), as working along the same lines as Cantillon and Hume, both of whom ascribed real consequences to an increase in a country's stock of gold.

8   Conclusion

1. Hamilton (1915, p. 562) has a different list, arguing that economists of different persuasions 'are agreed that the thrilling crises in the history of

theory center about the names of such protestants as Quesnay and Smith and Bentham, of George and Marx, of Hobson and Veblen'.

2. For more details on Ryan, see Nemmers, 1956, p. 2, n. 3, where reference is made also to Hobsonians at the University of Wisconsin; on the latter, see also Rutherford (1994, p. 208, n. 21, quoting Bronfenbrenner).

3. Lee (1972) refers to Hobson's views penetrating the Roosevelt 'brains trust'.

4. For details of Hobson's influence on North American economists, see the references to Hobson in Dorfman (1946–59), vols III, IV and V.

5. An extreme example of this explanation is to be found in Nemmers (1956, p. viii), where Martin Bronfenbrenner says of Hobson's innumerable books and periodical articles that 'most were pot-boilers'.

6. Unlike Keynes, Hobson never once referred explicitly to Say's Law. This is not surprising, as despite the term being invented by F. M. Taylor in 1911, it only came into common use through Keynes's reference to it in *The General Theory*. See Kates (1994).

Bibliography

This bibliography only includes works that are cited in the text; superscript [1] and [2] indicate articles by Hobson reprinted respectively in Backhouse (1992) and Cain (1992). The most extensive Hobson bibliography published is that in *J .A. Hobson after Fifty Years: Freethinker of the Social Sciences*, which is based on J. E. King, 'J. A. Hobson: A Preliminary Biography', Discussion Paper 7/90, School of Economics and Commerce, La Trobe University. That bibliography sets out Hobson's publications chronologically in so far as information permits, within as well as between years, a practice which is followed here, with the exception that for each year books are listed alphabetically and before articles. A. J. K. Lee's unpublished Ph.D. thesis, *A Study of the Social and Economic Thought of J .A. Hobson*, University of London, includes a bibliography which runs to 139 pages.

Where not otherwise indicated, the first edition of a work is placed in brackets following the title in the case of books, and the journal volume in the case of articles.

Abel, A. B. (1987) 'Ricardian Equivalence Theorem', in J. Eatwell, M. Milgate and P. Newman (eds), *The New Palgrave: A Dictionary of Economics*, vol. 4, pp. 174–8.

Aldcroft, D. H. and P. Fearon (1972) *British Economic Fluctuations 1750–1939* (London: Macmillan).

Alexander, S. S. (1952) 'Effects of a Devaluation on a Trade Balance', *IMF Staff Papers*, vol. 2, pp. 263–78.

Allett, J. (1981) *New Liberalism: The Political Economy of J. A. Hobson* (Toronto: University of Toronto Press).

Atherley-Jones, L. A. (1889) 'The New Liberalism', *Nineteenth Century*, vol. 26, pp. 186–93.

Backhouse, R. E. (1990) 'J. A. Hobson as a Macroeconomic Theorist', in M. Freeden (ed.), *Reappraising J. A. Hobson: Humanism and Welfare* (London: Unwin Hyman), pp. 116–36.

Backhouse, R. E. (ed.) (1992) *Writings on Distribution and Welfare*, in *J .A. Hobson: A Collection of Economic Works*, 6 vols (London: Routledge/ Thoemmes Press).

Backhouse, R. E. (1994) 'Mummery and Hobson's *The Physiology of Industry*', in J. Pheby (ed.), *J . A. Hobson after Fifty Years: Freethinker of the Social Sciences* (London: Macmillan) pp. 78–99.

Baran, P. (1957) *The Political Economy of Growth* (New York: Monthly Review Press).

Baran, P. and P. M. Sweezy (1966) *Monopoly Capital: An Essay on The American Economic and Social Order* (New York: Monthly Review Press).

Bauer, O. (1907) *Die Nationalitätenfrage und die Sozialdemokratie* (Vienna: Ignaz Brand).

Bauer, O. (1986) 'Die Akkumulation des Kapitals', *Die Neue Zeit*, vol. 31 (1913) pp. 831–8 and 862–74, trans. J. E. King included in 'Otto Bauer's "Accumulation of Capital" (1913)' *History of Political Economy*, vol. 18, pp. 87–110.

Bauer, O. (1936) *Zwischen zwei Weltkriegen? Die Krise der Weltwirtschaft, der Demokratie und des Sozialismus* (Bratislava: Eugen Prager).

Bax, E. B. (1894) 'Missionary and Mercantile Enterprise', *Justice*, 16 June, p. 4.

Bax, E. B. (1896) 'The True Aims of "Imperial Extension" and "Colonial Enterprise"', *Justice*, 1 May, pp. 7–8.

Beales, H. L. (1934) 'The "Great Depression" in Industry and Trade', *Economic History Review*, vol. v, pp. 65–75.

Bentham, J. (1825) *The Rationale of Reward* (London: John and H. L. Lunt).

Bharadwaj, K. (1972) 'Marshall on Pigou's *Wealth and Welfare*', *Economica*, vol. 52, pp. 32–46.

Black, R. D. C. *et al.* (eds) (1973) *The Marginal Revolution in Economics: Interpretation and Evaluation* (Durham, N. Carolina: Duke University Press).

Blyth, C. A. (1987) 'Wage Fund Doctrine', in J. Eatwell, M. Milgate and P. Newman (eds), *The New Palgrave: A Dictionary of Economics*, vol. 4, pp. 835–7.

Board of Extra Mural Studies (BEMS), University of Cambridge, 26/1, University of Cambridge Library.

von Böhm-Bawerk, E. (1981) *The Positive Theory of Capital* (London: Macmillan), trans. W. Smart from *Kapital und Kapitalzins. Zweiter Abtheilung: Positive Theorie des Kapitals* (Innsbruck: Wagner, 1889).

Booth, C. (1892–7) *Life and Labour of the People in London*, 9 vols (London: Macmillan).

Booth, W. (1890) *In Darkest England, and the Way Out* (London: International Headquarters of the Salvation Army).

Bosanquet, B. (1899) *The Philosophical Theory of the State* (London: Macmillan).

Brailsford, H. N., A. Creech Jones, J. A. Hobson and E. F. Wise (1926) *The Living Wage* (London: Independent Labour Party).

Brailsford, H. N. (1948) *The Life Work of J. A. Hobson* (London: Oxford University Press).

Brewer, A. (1990) *Marxist Theories of Imperialism* (1980), 2nd edn (London: Routledge).

Burns, C. D. (1940) 'John A. Hobson', *New Statesman and Nation*, vol. 6, p. 459.

Burrows, J. H. (1978) 'The Teaching of Economics in the Early Days of the University Extension Movement in London 1876–1902', *History of Economic Thought Newsletter*, vol. 20, pp. 8–14.

Cain, P. J. (1978) 'J. A. Hobson, Cobdenism, and the Radical Theory of Economic Imperialism', *Economic History Review*, 2nd series, vol. xxxi, pp. 565–84.

Cain, P. J. (1979) 'International Trade and Economic Development in the Work of J. A. Hobson before 1914' *History of Political Economy*, vol. 11, pp. 406–24.

Cain, P. J. (1990) 'Variations on a Famous Theme: Hobson, International Trade and Imperialism, 1902–1938', in M. Freeden (ed.), *Reappraising J. A. Hobson: Humanism and Welfare* (London: Unwin Hyman) pp. 31–53.

Cain, P. J. (ed.) (1992) *Writings on Imperialism and Internationalism*, in *J. A. Hobson: A Collection of Economic Works*, 6 vols (London: Routledge/Thoemmes Press).

Cairncross, A. K. (1953) *Home and Foreign Investment 1870–1913* (Cambridge University Press).

Cairnes, J. E. (1874) *Some Leading Principles of Political Economy Newly Expounded* (London: Macmillan).

Cassel, G. (1923) *The Theory of Social Economy*, 2 vols (London: T. Fisher Unwin), trans. B. McCabe from *Theoretische Sozialökonomie* (Leipzig: C. F. Wintersche 1918).

Caselli, G. P. and G. Pastrello (1987) 'Un suggerimento Hobsoniano su terziario e occupazione: U.S.A. 1960–1983. La specificità Americana e la debolezza Europea', *Politica Economia*, vol. 3, pp. 105–23.

Clark, J. B. (1891) 'Distribution as Determined by a Law of Rent', *Quarterly Journal of Economics*, vol. 5, pp. 289–318.

Clark, J. B. (1899) *The Distribution of Wealth: A Theory of Wages, Interest and Profits* (New York: Macmillan).

Clark, J. M. (1917) 'Business Acceleration and the Law of Demand: A Technical Factor in Economic Cycles', *Journal of Political Economy*, vol. xxv, pp. 217–35.

Clark, J. M. (1940) 'John A. Hobson, Heretic and Reformer', *Journal of Social Philosophy*, vol. 5, pp. 356–9.

Clark, J. M. (1957) *Economic Institutions and Human Welfare* (New York: Alfred A.Knopf).

Clarke, P. F. (1974) Introduction, in J. A. Hobson, *The Crisis of Liberalism* (1909) (Hassocks: Harvester) pp. ix–xxxviii.

Clarke, P. F. (1978) *Liberals and Social Democrats* (Cambridge University Press).

Clarke, P. F. (1981) 'Hobson, Free Trade and Imperialism', *Economic History Review*, 2nd series, vol. xxxiv, pp. 308–12.

Clarke, P. (1988) *The Keynesian Revolution in the Making, 1924–1936* (Oxford University Press).

Clarke, P. (1990) 'Hobson and Keynes as Economic Heretics', in M. Freeden (ed.), *Reappraising J. A. Hobson: Humanism and Welfare* (London: Unwin Hyman) pp. 100–15.

Cohen, G. A. (1994) 'Back to Socialist Basics', *New Left Review*, no. 207, pp. 3–16.

Cole, G. D. H. (1940) 'John A. Hobson, 1858–1940', *Economic Journal*, vol. L, pp. 351–60.

Cole, G. D. H. (1948) *A History of the Labour Party from 1914* (London: Routledge & Kegan Paul).

Cole, G. D. H. (1958) 'J. A. Hobson', *New Statesman*, vol. 56, 5 July, p. 12.

Coppock, D. J. (1953) 'A Reconsideration of Hobson's Theory of Unemployment', *Manchester School*, vol. 21, pp. 1–21.

Corry, B. A. (1992) 'Involuntary Unemployment – A Historical Note', Paper 262, Department of Economics, Queen Mary and Westfield College, University of London.

Costabile, L. and R. E. Rowthorn (1985) 'Malthus's Theory of Wages and Growth', *Economic Journal*, vol. LXXXXV, pp. 418–37.

Court, W. B. H. (1965) *British Economic History 1870–1914: Commentary and Documents* (Cambridge University Press).

Crafts, N. F. R. (1980) 'National Income Estimates and the British Standard of Living Debate: A Reappraisal of 1801–1831', *Explorations in Economic History*, vol. 17, pp. 176–88.

Crafts, N. F. R. (1985) *British Economic Growth during the Industrial Revolution* (Oxford University Press).

Crafts, N. F. R. and C. K. Harley (1992) 'Output Growth and the British Industrial Revolution: A Restatement of the Crafts-Harley View', *Economic History Review*, new series, vol. XLV, pp. 703–30.

Deane, P. (1968) 'New Estimates of Gross National Product for the United Kingdom, 1830–1914', *Review of Income and Wealth*, vol. 14, pp. 95–112.

Deane, P. and W. A. Cole (1967) *British Economic Growth* (1962), 2nd edn (Cambridge University Press).

Derbyshire Advertiser and Journal, (1940) Obituary of J. A. Hobson, 5 April, p. 8.

Domar, E. D. (1946) 'Capital Expansion, Rate of Growth and Employment', *Econometrica*, vol. 14, pp. 137-47.

Domar, E. D. (1947) 'Expansion and Employment', *American Economic Review*, vol. 37, pp. 34–55.

Dorfman, J. (1946–59) *The Economic Mind in American Civilisation*, 5 vols (New York: Viking Press).

Douglas, C. H. (1918) 'The Delusion of Super-Production', *English Review*, vol. XXVII, pp. 428–32.

Douglas, C. H. (1920a) *Economic Democracy* (London: Cecil Palmer).

Douglas, C. H. (1920b) *Credit-power and Democracy* (London: Cecil Palmer).

Douglas, C. H. (1922a) *The Control and Distribution of Production* (London: Cecil Palmer).

Douglas, C. H. (1922b) 'The Douglas Theory: A Reply to Mr. J. A. Hobson', *Socialist Review*, vol. 19, pp. 139–45.

Dubey, V. (1962) 'The Dangers of Accumulation: A Second Look at Malthus' Critique of Ricardo', *Indian Economic Review*, vol. 6, pp. 30–40.

Edelstein, M. (1977) 'Realized Rates of Return on U.K. Home and Overseas Protfolio Investment in the Age of High Imperialism', *Explorations in Economic History*, vol. 13, pp. 283–329.

Edelstein, M. (1982) *Overseas Investment in the Age of High Imperialism: The United Kingdom, 1850–1914* (New York: Columbia University Press).

Edgeworth, F. Y. (1881) *Mathematical Psychics: An Essay on the Application of Mathematics to the Moral Sciences* (London: Kegan Paul).

Edgeworth, F. Y. (1890) 'Review of *The Physiology of Industry*', in *Journal of Education*, new series, vol. XII, p. 194. For Edgeworth's authorship, see J. Bonar, (1926) 'Memories of F. Y. Edgeworth', *Economic Journal*, vol. XXXVI, p. 651.

Edgeworth, F. Y. (1897) 'The Pure Theory of Taxation', *Economic Journal*, vol. VII, pp. 46–70, 226–38 and 550–71.

Eltis, W. A. (1980) 'Malthus's Theory of Effective Demand and Growth', *Oxford Economic Papers*, new series, vol. 32, pp. 19–56.

Emmanuel, A. (1972) *Unequal Exchange: A Study of the Imperialism of Trade* (New York: Monthly Review Press), trans. B. Pearce from L'échange inégal (Paris: François Maspero, 1969).

Ensor, R. C. K. (1936) *England: 1870–1914* (Oxford University Press).

Feinstein, C. H. (1972) *National Income, Expenditure and Output of the United Kingdom, 1855–1965* (Cambridge University Press).

Flux, W. A. (1894) 'Review of *Essay on the Co-ordination of Laws of Distribution*', *Economic Journal*, vol. IV, pp. 308–13.

Fieldhouse, D. K. (1961) 'Imperialism: An Historiographical Revision', *Economic History Review*, 2nd series, vol. XIV, pp. 187–209.

Fisher, I. (1911) *The Purchasing Power of Money* (New York: Macmillan).

Freeden, M. (1978) *The New Liberalism: An Ideology of Social Reform* (Oxford: Clarendon Press).

Freeden, M. (1988) Introduction, in M. Freeden (ed.), *J. A. Hobson: A Reader* (London: Unwin Hyman).

Gallagher, J. and R. Robinson (1953) 'The Imperialism of Free Trade', *Economic History Review*, 2nd series, vol. VI, pp. 1–15.

Gårdlund, T. (1958) *The Life of Knut Wicksell* (Stockholm: Almqvist & Wiksell) trans. N. Adler from *Rebell i det nya riket* (Stockholm: Bonniers, 1956).

George, H. (1879) *Progress and Poverty; An Inquiry into the Causes of Industrial Depressions and of Increase of Want with Increase of Wealth: The Remedy* (San Francisco: W. M. Hinton).

Giffen, G. (1899) 'The Excess of Imports', *Statistical Journal*, vol. 62, pp. 1–69.

Gruchy, A. G. (1987) *The Reconstruction of Economics: An Analysis of the Fundamentals of Institutional Economics* (New York: Greenwood Press).

Haberler, G. (1937) *Prosperity and Depression: A Theoretical Analysis of Cyclical Movements* (Geneva: League of Nations).

Halèvy, E. (1951) *A History of the English People in the Nineteenth Century – IV: Victorian Years 1841–1895*, 2nd edn (London: Ernest Benn), trans. E. I. Watkin from *Histoire du peuple anglais au dix-neuviéme siécle* (Paris: Hachette, 1913–47).

Halèvy, E. (1952) *A History of the English People in the Nineteenth Century – VI: The Rule of Democracy 1905–1914*, 2nd edn, Book i (London: Ernest Benn), trans. E. I. Watkin from *Histoire du peuple anglais au dix-neuvième siècle* (Paris: Hachette, 1913–47).

Hamilton, W. H. (1915) 'Economic Theory and "Social Reform"', *Journal of Political Economy*, vol. 23, pp. 562–84.

Harcourt, G. C. (1972) *Some Cambridge Controversies in the Theory of Capital* (Cambridge University Press).

Harrod, R. F. (1948) *Towards a Dynamic Economics* (London: Macmillan).

Hewins, W. A. S. (1891) 'Review of *The Physiology of Industry*', *Economic Review*, vol. I, pp. 133–4.

Hilferding, R. (1981) *Finance Capital: A Study of the Latest Phase of Capitalist Development* (London: Routledge & Kegan Paul), trans. M. Watnick and S. Gordon, from *Das Finanzkapital: eine Studie die jüngste Entwicklung des Kapitalismus* (Vienna: I. Brand, 1910).

Hobsbawm, E. (1968) *Industry and Empire: An Economic History of Britain since 1750* (London: Weidenfeld & Nicolson).

Hobson, J. A. (1887–97) 'London Letter', in *The Derbyshire Advertiser and North Staffordshire Journal* (Derby).

Hobson, J. A. (1888) 'First Impressions of America', in *The Derbyshire Advertiser and North Staffordshire Journal* (Derby).

Hobson, J. A. (1891a) *Problems of Poverty: An Inquiry into the Industrial Condition of the Poor* (London: Methuen), 5th edn 1905.

Hobson, J. A. (1891b) 'The Law of the Three Rents', *Quarterly Journal of Economics*, vol. 5, pp. 263–88.[1]

Hobson, J. A. (1891c) 'The Element of Monopoly in Prices', *Quarterly Journal of Economics*, vol. 6, pp. 1–24.[1]

Hobson, J. A. (1891d) 'Can England Keep her Trade?', *National Review*, vol. LXXXXVII, pp. 1–11.[2]

Hobson, J. A. (1893) 'The Subjective and the Objective View of Distribution', *Annals of the American Academy of Political and Economic Science*, vol. IV, pp. 378–403.[1]

Hobson, J. A. (1894) *Evolution of Modern Capitalism: A Study of Machine Capitalism* (London: W. Scott), revd edn 1906a.

Hobson, J. A. (1895a) 'The Meaning and Measurement of "Unemployment"', *Contemporary Review*, vol. LXVII, pp. 415–32.

Hobson, J. A. (1895b) 'The Economic Cause of Unemployment', *Contemporary Review*, vol. LXVII, pp. 744–60.

Hobson, J. A. (1896a) *The Problem of the Unemployed* (London: Methuen).

Hobson, J. A. (1896b) 'Human Cost and Utility', *Economic Review*, vol. VI, pp. 10–20.[1]

Hobson, J. A. (1898a) *John Ruskin: Social Reformer* (London: Nisbet).

Hobson, J. A. (1898b) 'Free Trade and Foreign Policy', *Contemporary Review*, vol. LXIV, pp. 167–80.[2]

Hobson, J. A. (1899) 'The Economics of Bargaining', *Economic Review*, vol. XX, pp. 20–41.[1]

Hobson, J. A. (1900a) *The Economics of Distribution* (New York: Macmillan).

Hobson, J. A. (1900b) *The War in South Africa: Its Causes and Effects* (London: Nisbet).

Hobson, J. A. (1901a) *The Psychology of Jingoism* (London: G. Richards).

Hobson, J. A. (1901b) *The Social Problem: Life and Work* (London: J. Nisbet).

Hobson, J. A. (1902) *Imperialism: A Study* (London: Constable), 3rd edn 1938a (London: Allen & Unwin).

Hobson, J. A. (1903) 'The Inner Meaning of Protection', *Contemporary Review*, vol. LXXIV, pp. 365–74.[2]

Hobson, J. A. (1904) *International Trade: An Application of Economic Theory* (London: Methuen).

Hobson, J. A. (1906b) *Canada To-day* (London: T. Fisher Unwin).

Hobson, J. A. (1906c) *The Fruits of American Protection: The Effects of the Dingley Tariff on the Industries of the Country, especially upon the Well-being of the People* (New York: New York Reform Club Committee on Tariff Reform).

Hobson, J. A. (1909a) *The Crisis of Liberalism: New Issues of Democracy* (London: P. S. King), new edn with introduction by P. F. Clarke (London Hassocks: Harvester, 1974).

Hobson, J. A. (1909b) *The Industrial System: An Inquiry into Earned and Unearned Income* (London: Longmans, Green).

Hobson, J. A. (1909c) 'Can Protection Cure Unemployment?', *National Review*, vol. LIII, pp. 1015–24.

Hobson, J. A. (1911a) *The Science of Wealth* (London: Williams and Norgate).

Hobson, J. A. (1911b) *An Economic Interpretation of Investment* (London: The Financial Review of Reviews).

Hobson, J. A. (1912) 'The Causes of the Rise of Prices', *Contemporary Review*, vol. 102, pp. 483–92.

Hobson, J. A. (1913) *Gold, Prices and Wages, with an Examination of the Quantity Theory* (London: Methuen).

Hobson, J. A. (1914) *Work and Wealth: A Human Valuation* (New York: Macmillan).

Hobson, J. A. (1915) *Towards International Government* (London: Allen & Unwin).

Hobson, J. A. (1916) *The New Protectionism* (London: T. Fisher Unwin).

Hobson, J. A. (1917) *Democracy after the War* (London: Allen & Unwin).

Hobson, J. A. (1919a) *Richard Cobden: The International Man* (London: T. Fisher Unwin).

Hobson, J. A. (1919b) *Taxation in the New State* (London: Methuen).

Hobson, J. A. (1921) 'The Ethical Movement and the Natural War', *Hibbert Journal*, vol. xx, pp. 667–79.

Hobson, J. A. (1922a) *The Economics of Unemployment* (London: Allen & Unwin) revd edn 1931a.

Hobson, J. A. (1922b) 'The Douglas Theory', *Socialist Review*, vol. 19, pp. 70–7.

Hobson, J. A. (1922c) 'A Rejoinder to Major Douglas', *Socialist Review*, vol. 19, pp. 194–9.

Hobson, J. A. (1925) 'Neo-Classical Economics in Britain', *Political Science Quarterly*, vol. 40, pp. 337–83.[1]

Hobson, J. A. (1926a) *Free-thought in the Social Sciences* (London: Allen & Unwin).

Hobson, J. A. (1926b) 'Economic Art and Human Welfare', *Journal of Philosophical Studies*, vol. 1, pp. 467–80.[1]

Hobson, J. A. (1929a) *Wealth and Life: A Study in Values* (London: Macmillan).

Hobson, J. A. (1929b) 'Government Loans and Unemployment', *The Nation* (London), vol. 44, pp. 903–4.

Hobson, J. A. (1930) *Rationalisation and Unemployment: An Economic Dilemma* (London: Allen & Unwin).

Hobson, J. A. (1931b) *Poverty in Plenty: The Ethics of Income* (London: George Allen & Unwin).

Hobson, J. A. (1931c) *Towards Social Equality* (London: Oxford University Press).

Hobson, J. A. (1932a) *From Capitalism to Socialism* (London: Hogarth Press).

Hobson, J. A. (1932b) 'The World's Economic Crisis', *The Nation* (New York), vol. 135, pp. 53–4.

Hobson, J. A. (1933a) 'Underconsumption: An Exposition and a Reply', *Economica*, vol. 13, pp. 402–17.

Hobson, J. A. (1933b) 'Our Selves' (Hull University Library: Paper Relating to J. A. Hobson 24f).

Hobson, J. A. (1936) *Veblen* (London: Chapman and Hall).

Hobson, J. A. (1937) *Property and Improperty* (London: Gollancz).

Hobson, J. A. (1938b) *Confessions of an Economic Heretic* (London: Allen & Unwin).

Hodgskin, T. (1825) *Labour Defended Against the Claims of Capital* (London: Knight & Lacey).

Hollander, S. (1987) *Classical Economics* (Oxford: Basil Blackwell).

Imlah, A. H. (1969) *Economic Elements in the Pax Britannica: Studies in British Foreign Trade in the Nineteenth Century* (1958) (New York: Russell & Russell).

Ireson, F. (1910) *The People's Progress: A Study of the Facts of National Wealth, with some Answers to Socialists* (London: John Murray).

Jackson, R. V. (1994) 'Old and New Views of the Rate of Economic Growth during the Industrial Revolution', in G. D. Snooks (ed.), *Was the Industrial Revolution Necessary?* (London: Routledge).

Jenks, L. H. (1927) *The Migration of British Capital to 1875* (New York: Alfred A. Knopf).

Jevons, W. S. (1871) *Theory of Political Economy* (London: Macmillan).

Joad, C. E. M. (1940) 'On J. A. Hobson', *Monthly Record* (of the South Place Ethical Society), May, pp. 5–6.

Kadish, A. (1990) 'Rewriting the *Confessions*: Hobson and the Extension Movement', in M. Freeden (ed.), *Reappraising J. A. Hobson: Humanism and Welfare* (London: Unwin Hyman) pp. 137–66.

Kates, S. (1994) 'The Malthusian Origins of the *General Theory* or How Keynes Came to Write a Book About Say's Law and Effective Demand', *History of Economics Review*, vol. 21, pp. 10–20.

Kennedy, W. P. (1987) *Industrial Structure, Capital Markets and the Origins of British Economic Decline* (Cambridge University Press).

Keynes, J. M. (1913) 'Review of *Gold, Prices and Wages*', *Economic Journal*, vol. XXIII, pp. 393–8.

Keynes, J. M. (1921) *Treatise on Probability* (London: Macmillan).

Keynes, J. M. (1926) 'Obituary of F. Y. Edgeworth', *Economic Journal*, vol. XXXVI, pp. 140–53.

Keynes, J. M. (1930) *Treatise on Money* (London: Macmillan).

Keynes, J. M. (1933) 'Robert Malthus: The First of the Cambridge Economists', in *Essays in Biography* (London: Macmillan) pp. 95–149.

Keynes, J. M. (1936) *The General Theory of Employment Interest and Money* (London: Macmillan).

Keynes, J. M. (1973) *The Collected Writings of John Maynard Keynes*, D. Moggridge (ed.), vol. XIII (London: Macmillan).

Keynes, J. M. (1979) *The Collected Writings of John Maynard Keynes*, D. Moggridge (ed.), vol. XXIX (London: Macmillan).

Keynes, J. N. (1891) *The Scope and Method of Political Economy* (London: Macmillan).

Keynes Papers, Modern Archives, King's College, Cambridge.

King, J. E. (1988) 'J. A. Hobson', in *Economic Exiles* (London: Macmillan) pp. 109–35.

King, J. E. (1992) 'J. A. Hobson, 1858–1940', in P. Arestis and M. C. Sawyer (eds), *A Biographical Dictionary of Dissenting Economists* (Cheltenham: Elgar) pp. 262–8.

King, J. (1994) 'J. A. Hobson's Macroeconomics: The Last Ten Years (1930–40)', in J. Pheby (ed.) *J. A. Hobson After Fifty Years: Freethinker of the Social Sciences* (London: Macmillan) pp. 124–42.

King, J. E. (forthcoming) 'Underconsumption', in G. C. Harcourt and P. Riach (eds), *The Second Edition of the General Theory*.

Knapp, J. G. (1979) *Edwin G. Nourse: Economist for the People* (Danville, Ill.: Interstate).

Knowles, L. C. A. (1924) *The Economic Development of the British Overseas Empire* (London: George Routledge).

Koebner, R. (1949) 'The Concept of Economic Imperialism', *Economic History Review*, 2nd series, vol. II, pp. 1–29.

Koebner, R. and H. D. Schmidt (1964) *Imperialism: The Story and Significance of a Political Word, 1840–1960* (Cambridge University Press).

Kohn, H. (1951) Entry on 'Imperialism' in *Encyclopaedia Britannica*, vol. 12, pp. 122.

Kuhn, T. S. (1962) *The Structure of Scientific Revolutions* (Chicago: Chicago University Press).

Lange, O. (1942) 'Say's Law: A Criticism and Restatement', in O. Lange, F. McIntyre and T. O. Yntema (eds), *Studies in Mathematical Economics and Econometrics* (Chicago: University of Chicago Press) pp. 49–68.

Langer, W. L. (1935–6) 'A Critique of Imperialism', *Foreign Affairs*, vol. 14, pp. 102–19.

Layton, W. T. (1912) *An Introduction to the Study of Prices with Special Reference to the History of the Nineteenth Century* (London: Macmillan).

Lee, A. J. K. (1970) 'A Study of the Social and Political Thought of J. A. Hobson', unpublished Ph.D. thesis, University of London, .

Lee, A. (1972) 'Hobson, John Atkinson (1858–1940)', in J. M. Bellamy and J. Saville (eds), *Dictionary of Labour Biography*, vol. I (London: Macmillan) pp. 176–81.

Leijonhufvud, A. (1968) *On Keynesian Economics and the Economics of Keynes* (New York: Oxford University Press).

Lenin, V. I. (1933) *Imperialism: The Highest Stage of Capitalism* (1917) (London: Martin Lawrence) trans. collectively from the Russian.

Linder, S, B. (1970) *The Harriëd Leisure Class* (New York: Columbia University Press).

Liv, W. T.-C. (1934) *A Study of Hobson's Welfare Economics* (New York: Stechert).

Lowe, R. (1878) 'Imperialism', *Fortnightly Review*, new series, vol. XXIV, pp. 453–65.

Luxemburg, R. (1951) *The Accumulation of Capital* (London: Routledge & Kegan Paul), trans. A. Schwarzchild from *Die Akkumulation des Kapitals* (Leipzig: Frankes, 1913).

Magnusson, L. (1994) 'Hobson and Imperialism: An Appraisal', in J. Pheby (ed.), *J. A. Hobson after Fifty Years: Freethinker of the Social Sciences* (London: Macmillan) pp. 143–62.

Malthus, T. R. (1820) *Principles of Political Economy Considered with a View to their Practical Application* (London: John Murray).

Marshall, A. (1888) 'Minutes of Evidence given before the Gold and Silver Commission', in *Appendix to Final Report of the Royal Commission appointed to inquire into the Recent Changes in the Relative Values of the Precious Metals* (London: HMSO) Vol. II, pp. 1–33 and 38–53.

Marshall, A. (1961) *Principles of Economics* (1890–1920), variorum edn, C. W. Guillebaud, (ed.), 2 vols (London: Macmillan).

Marshall, A. and Mary P. Marshall, (1879) *The Economics of Industry* (London: Macmillan).

Marx, K. (1887) *Capital: A Critical Analysis of Capitalist Production*, 2 vols (1867) (London: Swan Sonnenschein), trans. S. Moore and E. Aveling from *Das Kapital: Kritik der politischen Oekonomie*, 3rd edn (Hamburg: O. Meissner, 1883).

Marx, K. (1933) *Critique of the Gotha Programme* (1875) (New York: International Publishers), trans. from the first, Engels edn of 1891, with passages cut out by Engels restored.

Maynard, G. (1962) *Economic Development and the Price Level* (London: Macmillan).

Menger, C. (1951) *Principles of Economics* (Glencoe, Ill.: The Free Press), trans. J. Dingwall and B. F. Hoselitz from *Grundsätze der Volkswirtschaftslehre* (Vienna and Leipzig: Hölder-Pichler-Temsky, 1871).

Middlemas, F. (1969) *Whitehall Diary, vol. II, 1926–1930* (London: Oxford University Press).

Mill, J. S. (1969) 'Bentham' (1834), in *Collected Works of John Stuart Mill*, vol. x, J. M. Robson (ed.), (Toronto: University of Toronto Press).

Mill, J. S. (1843) *A System of Logic, Ratiocinative and Inductive, Being a Connected View of the Principles of Evidence and the Methods of Scientific Investigation*, 2 vols (London: John W. Parker).

Mill, J. S. (1848) *Principles of Political Economy with Some of their Applications to Social Philosophy*, 2 vols (London: John W. Parker).

Mill, J. S. (1859) *On Liberty* (London: John W. Parker).

Mill, J. S. (1863) *Utilitarianism* (London: John W. Parker).

Mirowski, P. (1989) *More Heat than Light. Economics as Social Physics: Physics as Nature's Economics* (Cambridge University Press).

Mitchell, H. (1966) 'Hobson Revisited', *Journal of the History of Ideas*, vol. 26, pp. 397–416.

Monypenny, W. F. and G. E. Buckle, (1929) *The Life of Benjamin Disraeli, Earl of Beaconsfield* (London: Murray).

Mrozek, S. (1967) 'Out at Sea', in *Six Plays by Slawomir Mrozek*, trans. N. Bethell (New York: Grove Press).

Mummery, A. F. and J. A. Hobson (1889) *The Physiology of Industry: Being an Exposure of Certain Fallacies in Existing Theories in Economics* (London: J. Murray).

Mummery, A. F. (1895) *My Climbs in the Alps and the Caucasus* (London: Nelson, 1913 edn, which includes an appreciation by J. A. Hobson).

Myrdal, G. (1953) *The Political Element in the Development of Economic Theory* (1929) (London: Routledge & Kegan Paul), trans. P. Streeten from *Das Politische Element in der Nationalökonomischen Doktrinbildung* (Junker und Dünnhaupt, 1932); 1st edn, in Swedish, 1929.

Nell, E. (1992) *Transformational Growth and Effective Demand* (London: Macmillan).

Nemmers, E. E. (1956) *Hobson and Underconsumption* (Amsterdam: North Holland).

OECD (1988) *Economic Outlook*, no. 43, pp. 1–13.

Oxford English Dictionary (1989) J. A. H. Murray, H. Bradley, W. A. Craigie and C. T. Onions (eds), 2nd edn (prepared by J. A. Simpson and E. S. C. Weiner) (Oxford University Press).

Paish, G. (1911) 'Great Britain's Capital Investments in Individual Colonial and Foreign Countries', *Statistical Journal*, vol. 74, pp. 167–87.

Paish, G. (1914) 'The Export of Capital and the Cost of Living', Supplement to *Statist*, vol. 79, pp. i–viii.

Pareto, W. (1971) *Manual of Political Economy* (1906) (New York: Augustus M. Kelley), trans. A. S. Schwier from *Manuel d'économie politique* (Geneva: Librairie Droz, 1927), 1st edn in Italian.

Patten, S. M. (1893) 'Cost and Utility', *Annals of the American Academy of Economic and Political Science*, vol. III, pp. 409–28.

Pigou, A. C. (1912) *Wealth and Welfare* (London: Macmillan).

Pigou, A. C. (1920) *Economics of Welfare* (London: Macmillan).

Pilvin, H. (1952) 'A Geometric Analysis of Recent Growth Models', *American Economic Review*, vol. 62, pp. 594–9.

Popper, K. R. (1945) *The Open Society and its Enemies* (London: Routledge & Kegan Paul).

Popper, K. R. (1963) *Conjectures and Refutations: The Growth of Scientific Knowledge* (London: Routledge & Kegan Paul).

Porter, B. (1968) *Critics of Empire: British Radical Attitudes to Colonialism in Africa 1895–1914* (London: Macmillan).

Preiser, E. (1952) 'Property and Power in the Theory of Distribution', *International Economic Papers*, vol. 2, pp. 206–20, trans. J. Kahane from 'Besitz und Macht in der Distributionstheorie', in *Synopsis, Festgabe für Alfred Weber* (Heidelberg, 1949).

Rawls, J. (1972) *A Theory of Justice* (London: Oxford University Press).

Ricardo, D. (1951–73) *The Works and Correspondence of David Ricardo*, P. Sraffa (ed.), 11 vols (Cambridge University Press).

Robertson, D. H. (1931) 'Wage-Grumbles', in *Economic Fragments* (London: P. S. King).

Robertson, J. M. (1892) *The Fallacy of Saving: A Study in Economics* (London: Swan Sonnenschein).

Robbins, L. (1932a) *An Essay on the Nature and Significance of Economic Science* (London: Macmillan).

Robbins, L. (1932b) 'Consumption and the Trade Cycle', *Economica*, vol. 12, pp. 413–30.

Robinson, J. (1933) 'The Theory of Money and the Analysis of Output', *Review of Economic Studies*, vol. 1, pp. 22–6.

Robinson, J. (1934) 'Euler's Theorem and the Problem of Distribution', *Economic Journal*, vol. XLIV, pp. 398–414.

Robinson, J. (1949) 'Review of R. F. Harrod, *Towards a Dynamic Economics*', in *Economic Journal*, vol. LIX, pp. 68–85.

Rostow, W. W. (1948) *British Economy of the Nineteenth Century* (London: Oxford University Press).

Rowntree, B. S. (1901) *Poverty: A Study of Town Life* (London: Macmillan).

Ruskin, J. (1862) *Unto This Last* (London: Smith, Elder).

Ruskin, J. (1872) *Munera Pulveris* (London: Smith, Elder).

Rutherford, M. (1994) 'J. A. Hobson and American Institutionalism: Underconsumption and Technological Change', in J. Pheby (ed.), *J. A. Hobson after Fifty Years: Freethinker of the Social Sciences* (London: Macmillan), pp. 188–210.

Schneider, M. P. (1959) 'Underconsumption and Imperialism: A Study in the Work of J. A. Hobson', unpublished M.Sc. thesis, University of Cambridge.

Schneider, M. (1987) 'Underconsumption', in J. Eatwell, M. Milgate and P. Newman (eds) *The New Palgrave: A Dictionary of Economics*, vol. 4, pp. 741–5.

Schneider, M. (1994a) 'The Role of Hobson in the Emergence of the Marginal Productivity Theory of Distribution', *Discussion Paper A.94.05*, School of Economics, La Trobe University.

Schneider, M. (1994b) 'Modelling Hobson's Underconsumption Theory', in J. Pheby (ed.) *J. A. Hobson after Fifty Years: Freethinker of the Social Sciences* (London: Macmillan) pp. 100–23.

Schumpeter, J. A. (1951) 'Imperialism', in *Imperialism and Social Classes* (Oxford: Basil Blackwell), trans. H. Norden from 'Zur Sociologie der Imperialismen', *Archiv für Sozialwissenschaft und Sozialpolitik*, vol. XLVI (1918–9), pp. 1–39 and 275–310.

Schumpeter, J. A. (1954) *History of Economic Analysis* (London: Allen & Unwin).

Schwartz, A. J. (1987) 'Banking School, Currency School, Free Banking School', in J. Eatwell, M. Milgate and P. Newman, (eds), *The New Palgrave: A Dictionary of Economics*, vol. 1, pp. 182–5.

Senior, N. (1826) 'On Certain Terms which are Peculiarly Liable to be Used Ambiguously', in R. Whately, *Elements of Logic* (London: Mawman).

Shaw, G. B. (ed.) (1889) *Fabian Essays* (London: The Fabian Society).

Sismondi, J.-C.-L. Simonde de (1847) 'Preface to New Principles of Political Economy, and the Light which They May Cast on the Crisis which England is at this Time Experiencing' (1826), in M. Mignet (ed.) *Political Economy and the Philosophy of Government* (London: John Chapman). Trans. from 'Nouveaux principes d'économie politique, jour qu'ils peuvent jeter sur la crise qu' éprouve aujourd'hui l'Angleterre', *Revue Encyclopédique*, vol. XXXI (1826).

Skidelsky, R. (1983) *John Maynard Keynes: Hopes Betrayed 1883–1920* (London: Macmillan).

Smith, A. (1976) *An Inquiry into the Nature and Causes of the Wealth of Nations* (1776), 2 vols, R. H. Campbell and A. S. Skinner (eds), W. B. Todd (textual ed.) (London: Oxford University Press).

Spencer, H. (1874) *The Study of Sociology* (London: Henry S. King).

Sweezy, P. M. (1938) 'J. A. Hobson's Economic Heresies', *The Nation* (New York) vol. 147, pp. 209–10.

Sweezy, P. M. (1942) *The Theory of Capitalist Development* (New York: Oxford University Press).

Taylor, A. J. P. (1957) *The Trouble Makers: Dissent over Foreign Policy 1792–1939* (London: Hamish Hamilton).

Taylor, A. J. P. (1965) *English History 1914–1945* (London: Oxford University Press).

Taylor, F. M. (1911) *Principles of Economics* (New York: The Ronald Press Company).

Tawney, R. H. (1949) 'Hobson, John Atkinson (1858–1940)', in *Dictionary of National Biography 1931–1940* (London: Oxford University Press) pp. 435–6.

Thornton, A. P. (1959) *The Imperial Idea and its Enemies* (London: Macmillan).

Thornton, H. (1802) *An Enquiry into the Nature and Effects of the Paper Credit of Great Britain* (London: J. Hatchard and F. and C. Rivington).

Toqueville, A. de (1835 and 1840) *Democracy in America*, and *Democracy in America: Part the Second* (London: Saunders and Otley) 4 vols., trans. H. Reeve from *De la démocratie en Amérique*, and *De la démocratie en Amérique: Seconde partie* (Brussels: Hauman, 1835 and 1840).

Toulmin, S. and J. Goodfield (1963) *The Fabric of the Heavens* (Harmondsworth: Penguin).

Townshend, J. (1990) *J. A. Hobson* (Manchester University Press).

Toynbee, A. (1884) *Lectures on the Industrial Revolution in England* (London: Rivingtons).

Tugwell, R. G. (1968) *The Brains Trust* (New York: Viking).

Walker, F. A. (1879) *Money in its Relation to Trade and Industry* (New York: Henry Holt).

Walras, L. (1954) *Elements of Pure Economics* (1874) (London: Allen & Unwin), trans. W. Jaffé from *Éléments d'économie politique, ou Théorie de la Richesse Sociale* (Paris: R. Pichon et R. Durand-Auzias, 1926).

Webb, S. (1888) 'The Rate of Interest and the Laws of Distribution', *Quarterly Journal of Economics*, vol. 2, pp. 188–208.

Webb, S. *et al.* (1922) *Labour and Social Credit: A Report on the Proposals of Major Douglas & The 'New Age'* (London: Labour Party).

Wicksell, K. (1936) *Interest and Prices* (London: Macmillan), trans. R. Kahn from *Geldzins and Güterpreisen* (Jena: Gustav Fischer, 1898).

Wicksell, K. (1902) 'On the Problem of Distribution', in E. Lindahl (ed.), *Selected Papers on Economic Theory* (London: Allen & Unwin), trans. R. S. Stedman from 'Till fördelningsproblemet', *Ekonomisk Tidskrift*, vol. 4 (1902) pp. 424–33.

Wicksteed, P. H. (1894) *An Essay on the Co-ordination of the Laws of Distribution* (London: Macmillan).

Wicksteed, P. H. (1910) *The Common Sense of Political Economy: Including a Sutdy of the Human Basis of Economic Law* (London: Macmillan).

von Wieser, F. (1893) *Natural Value* (London: Macmillan). trans. C. A. Malloch from *Der natürliche Werth* (Vienna: Alfred Holder, 1889).

Yellen, J. L. (1984) 'Efficiency-Wage Models of Unemployment', *American Economic Review*, vol. 74, pp. 200–5.

Index of Names

165

Index of Subjects